Gladstone Mills

GRIST FOR THE MILLS

Reflections on a life

Gladstone Mills

GRIST FOR THE MILLS

Reflections on a life

Ian Randle Publishers
Kingston, Jamaica

Published in Jamaica 1994 by

Ian Randle Publishers
206 Old Hope Road, Box 686
Kingston 6

©1994 Gladstone Mills

All rights reserved. No part of this publication may be reproduced, stored in a retrieval system, or transmitted in any form, or by any means electronic, photocopying, recording or otherwise, without the prior permission of the author or publisher.

ISBN 976-8100-22-2

A catalogue record for this book is available from the National Library of Jamaica.

Book and Cover Design by Michael Gordon
Printed in Jamaica by Stephensons Litho Press Ltd.

To my wife Winnifred, who has provided strong support for more than four decades

CONTENTS

Preface   vii

Acknowledgements   ix

Introduction   xi

1 Jamaica: The Turn of the 1920s - 1930s   1

2 A Rural Upbringing   12

3 A Mid-Victorian Public School   30

4 In the Service of the Crown   52

5 Student Days in Britain   78

6 Liaison Officer in London: Taking Care of Future Leaders   93

7 Escape to Cloistered Academia?   110

8 In the Service of the Nation   131

9 Cricket, Cricket, Cricket   162

10 Postscript: Election 1993 and its Aftermath   184

   Index   196

PREFACE

This story is an attempt to portray a perspective on a period spanning approximately sixty years, from the end of the 1920s to the present. It is set primarily in Jamaica but its dimensions are wider. They extend to the entire English-speaking Caribbean from first-hand knowledge and experience of all the Caribbean Community (CARICOM) member states during the past three decades. This experience stems mainly from my responsibilities at the University of the West Indies (UWI) and from opportunities provided as leader of a number of regional teams assigned to study and report on various regional issues.

The scope extends even further: beyond the boundaries of this region to the United Kingdom (UK), as a student during the closing stages of the Second World War and the immediate post-war years; and also, as Liaison Officer for West Indian Students in the British Isles; to Continental Europe, the USA and Latin America, and beyond, to Africa, Asia and Australia — the last three continents for seminars and meetings.

The period covered, and particularly the past five years, has witnessed dramatic changes both world-wide and internally. Indeed, the pace of change has been more rapid than at any other time in history. Beginning with the props which were put in place by Gorbachev's mid-1980s initiatives of *perestroika* and *glasnost*, the stage was set for the dramatic events of the end of that decade and of the early 1990s. Occurring in cataclysmic succession were the disintegration of the economic and political systems of the USSR, and of other Eastern European powers, the symbolism of the collapse of the Berlin Wall, and of Soviet-type communism culminating in the end of the Cold War, leaving the USA as the sole super-power. Since mid-century, revolutionary changes have been set in train with the decolonization process, the beginning of the Cold War, the economic boom in industrial countries, and phenomenal advances in technology notably in the field of communications. All these developments, following the end of World War II, were to have fundamental consequences for Jamaica and the entire Caribbean.

This is not, however, a chronological history of the period, nor is it an autobiography. It represents reflections on my times, on the context in which I have lived, in particular from the perspective of two careers in public service which have spanned a period of more than 50 years.

To attempt to take a retrospective view of a context, conditions and events of more than fifty years ago, in which one was a participant or an observer, is fraught with pitfalls. As we grow older, recent events and incidents seem to recede from the memory, while some from the distant past remain almost intact. In explanation, we are told that the mental tape was fresher then; hence, a better quality and a more durable recording.

But problems of recollecting such observations obviously arise, with the probability of giving expression to a record exaggerated at one extreme or the other. The dark moments tend to overshadow the entire picture or, alternatively, be buried in deep recesses of the mind. Moreover, advancing years take their toll, blurring the boundaries of the memory.

Yet, the exercise also has possibilities and advantages not normally available to the historian or the social scientist acting solely in a professional capacity. Such a study would no doubt be founded on objective indicators. More, however, is needed to put flesh on this bare skeletal frame. Fortunately this flesh can be filled in by those of us who were participants or observers at the time.

Kingston
August 1994

ACKNOWLEDGEMENTS

The seeds which led to the completion of this book were planted with the publication of an article in the *Sunday Gleaner* (August 1985) on the late President of Guyana, Forbes Burnham, as I knew him as a student in London during the 1940s. That piece was followed over the next five years by a series of reminiscences which included recollections of life as a youngster growing up in the sleepy country town of Chapelton during the 1920s and 1930s.

I owe a special debt of gratitude to Paget deFreitas, editor of the *Observer*, Rupert Lewis, Trevor Munroe and Edwin Jones, colleagues in the department of government, and Christopher Roberts of the *Gleaner*, all of whom urged and encouraged me to use these articles as the nucleus of a book of reflections. I cannot fully express my appreciation of the interest and time devoted by Jimmy Carnegie and Louis Lindsay who not only provided encouragement, but read all the chapters very carefully and made numerous suggestions; and also to Brian Meeks. My sister Sybil Wood was a mine of information and of documents and other printed materials left by our mother. She came to my rescue on several occasions to refresh my memory about certain events of the distant past.

Appreciation is also due to Oliver Clarke, chairman and managing director of the *Gleaner* Company Ltd., who graciously gave me permission to reprint those parts of the manuscript which had appeared in *Gleaner* publications.

Last but by no means least, I must express appreciation to Ruby Simmonds of the student affairs department and Denise Brown of the department of government at the University of the West Indies who performed the unenviable task of deciphering my handwriting and producing drafts of the manuscript.

The task and the processes involved in preparing this manuscript for publication coincided with the serious illness of my wife Winnifred, during the past five years. The project could not have been completed without the considerable support generously provided by family members, especially my cousins Hilda Lawrence and Enid Douglas, brother Don and his wife Sonia, and by Winnifred's niece, Frances Lawrey-Bravo, and her former student-nurse colleague and close friends, Ruby Welds-Jeffers and Norma Lawson-Weller, respectively.

The publishers wish to the thank Jack Tyndale Biscoe for the photo of Chapelton.

INTRODUCTION

It is difficult to explain the significant dimensions of the intellectual and administrative movement in the post World War 2 society without reflecting on the contributions of Gladstone Mills. *Grist for the Mills* embodies a wider universe, offering important insights and lessons for anyone interested in the interaction of people, movements and ideas in Jamaica and beyond.

This book is more than an autobiography of a brilliant administrator, distinguished scholar, and a moral exemplar. It is an historical essay without losing its autobiographical momentum. It is a refreshing symposium of memoirs, ideas and analyses resulting in an authoritative portrait of his time. He gives us fresh insights into the nature of political organization and practice in Jamaica, and captures the fluctuating relationships and tensions between impulses to change and to preserve a society still searching for itself.

Grist for the Mills is a study in character. There are sharp, shrewd and clear characterizations of family members, friends, colleagues and public figures. Constructed unconsciously is a fine portrait of the author. He emerges as a gentleman of unruffled calm, caring much for good government and little for partisan engagement. He is exceptionally intelligent, witty and a good listener. A man of robust integrity, he would flatter no one, great or small, always speaking his thoughts.

It is out of this crucible that *Grist for the Mills* has been constructed. It is an immensely readable and compelling book. Its triumph is that it enlightens the Jamaican society about the main concepts of the national political sociology of over sixty years.

Skillfully integrated into this are the beliefs and ideals, feelings and actions of a patriot who has himself helped to positively shape that profile.

Grist for the Mills is a model of what reflections should be: factual, vivid and contemporary.

Gladstone Mills has had two outstanding careers spanning over 50 years of public service. Strong scholarly orientations and a brilliant career in the Jamaica Civil Service (1938-1960) facilitated easy transition to the University of the West Indies as Director of Training in Public Administration, and shortly thereafter, to a chair in that discipline.

In both career streams, he offered consistently purposeful professional leadership. In the civil service he managed several strategic desks at home and overseas. Thus, he has been instrumental in shaping path-breaking policies and institutions in the public domain via chairmanship of over a dozen official Commissions/Committees. At the UWI he offered high quality academic and administrative leadership, functioning as teacher, departmental head, Dean of the Faculty of Social Sciences and respected representative of academic colleagues, University and country.

All his professional work within those two career streams won the international reputation that assured him seats on the editorial advisory boards of major disciplinary academic journals; membership in the premier professional organizations, and the status of an expert on numerous international missions, studying and advising on academic and civic development matters.

Prof. Mills is also among the most sensitive students of West Indies cricket, chronicling its movement, and assisting its administration.

For his enormous contributions, a grateful nation has conferred on him several high honours, including the Order of Jamaica and the UWI has retained his services as an Emeritus Professor.

Edwin Jones
October 1994

1

JAMAICA: THE TURN OF THE 1920s-1930s

A profile of Jamaica at the turn of the 1930s reveals an island of approximately one million people, less than half of its present population. The Kingston and St. Andrew (KSAC) conurbation was not as dominant in population proportions as it was to become by mid-century. The majority of residents of that area, including the middle and upper classes, lived below Half-Way-Tree — the upper income strata not yet having migrated to the upper reaches of St. Andrew, nor taken to the hills. Cargill and Seymour Lands, bearing the names of prominent earlier proprietor families, and Mona were extensive estates accommodating a mere few residents. The less isolated 'Pens', formerly cattle-grazing areas, such as Jones, Rollington, Vineyard and Admiral would not be elevated to the euphemistic status of towns until the early 1940s.

Jamaica would suffer from the social and economic consequences of the Great Depression which hit the great industrial countries between 1929 and 1933; and later from the impact of the emergence of Hitler and nascent Nazism in Germany and the election of Franklin D. Roosevelt to the Presidency of the USA.

It was a time when agriculture and agricultural products still formed the bedrock of the Jamaican economy. Sugar and bananas were the primary assets, followed by citrus and coffee. The manufacturing industry was confined to the centuries-old agro-industry of sugar processing.

Tourism was in its infancy, centered on Port Antonio, in association with the United Fruit Company's Boston banana trade and Montego Bay, on the basis of the reportedly curative powers of the water of Doctor's Cave. Kingston boasted a quintet of famous hotels: Constant Spring, Mona Great House, Manor House, Myrtle Bank, South Camp Road, none alas, still in existence. Ocho Rios was still a charming, quiet and unspoilt village with a profusion of murmuring, soporific streams and less silent cataracts.

A few miles away, even then a focus of outings for the few natives who could afford the trip, were the picturesque Dunn's River and more dramatic Roaring River Falls, the latter taken out of service since 1946 as a venue for visitors and transformed into a source of hydro-electric power. Negril was primarily swamp land and would not become an objective of government activity for another quarter of a century when Chief Minister and Minister of Development Norman Manley challenged the two-year old Central Planning Unit to initiate ideas for a framework for the development of this far western outpost.

Bauxite was already being mined and processed at MacKenzie in British Guiana, and a geological survey, undertaken by J.G. Sawkins 60 years before, had indicated the presence of large deposits of that mineral in Jamaica. It was not until the early 1940s when Sir Alfred D'Costa rediscovered the cause that Jamaicans acknowledged that the red dirt in which children played games and the red mud which encased the wheels and mudguards of cars in the parishes of Manchester, St. Elizabeth, and St. Ann was an important potential resource. No one imagined at that time that bauxite would replace sugar and bananas as the country's leading revenue and foreign exchange earner within two decades.

In the depression years at the turn of the thirties the sugar industry was in a state of crisis, suffering from a disastrous slump in world prices. Demand fell short of supply; the latter stimulated by European, including the British government's policy of providing subsidies for their beet-based production. At that time 40 sugar factories were in operation compared to the 9 which are in operation today. Other agricultural products such as citrus and coffee also faced adverse international market conditions. These factors and the attendant social conditions, rising unemployment and atrociously low wages were setting the stage for the riots of 1938, the emergence of Alexander Bustamante and Norman Manley, and the Moyne Commission.

Despite falling prices, the banana industry had come to the rescue of the economy, especially in St. Mary and Portland, where *green gold* formed the foundation of fortunes. In 1929 banana growers led by Charlie Johnson created their cooperatively owned marketing and shipping company, the Jamaica Banana Producers Association Ltd. By 1931 the company's ships, with passengers as second class 'cargo' had begun to ply between Jamaica and London in competition with the United Fruit Company Ltd.

During the 1930s, banana exports were to represent almost 60% of the total value of Jamaica's export trade. By 1937 more than 360,000 tons were exported, representing 87% of the United Kingdom's total imports of bananas. These figures contrast dramatically and depressingly with 1993 exports of 76,770 tons or about 16% of UK imports. The considerable decline is a consequence of the disappearance of shipping and markets during World War II, the impact of Panama disease on production, and more recently, competition from Central America and the Windward Islands.

At the turn of the thirties social, economic and political life was dominated by landed proprietors and managers of the sugar and banana plantations, and merchant-businessmen of downtown Kingston whose shops engaged in a thriving trade on the still prosperous and busy King, Harbour and Port Royal Streets. Incoming ships unloaded their cargo on the *finger* piers jutting out on the waterfront at King, East and Hanover Streets and George's Lane. Even then, the cargo traffic on drays and trucks had begun to clutter and congest the rectangular grid of narrow streets and lanes behind the piers. Thirty years later, the port would be moved westward to Newport West and the piers replaced by alongside quays. In those days King Street was the mecca of business activity as it was to remain until the 1960s, dying gradually with the development of New Kingston and the proliferation of uptown shopping plazas.

Looking down towards the harbour from the Kingston Parish Church and Parade, one saw a scene of shops on both sides of the street: L.A. Henriques, of jewellery and delicate chinaware, established on the same spot in 1918, and lower down, Nathan's at the corner of Barry Street, Hanna's, and members of the various Issa family enterprises. Interspersed among the dry goods and hardware emporia, were government buildings: the Treasury, Supreme Court and Post Office headquarters. The banks too were well represented:

Nova Scotia, Barclays, Canadian Imperial and the local Government Savings Bank. At a time when racial and 'shade' discrimination was at its zenith, the banks and other commercial houses, even at the lowest clerical levels, were staffed exclusively by persons of a white or high colour/complexion.

The late Hon. Amy Bailey observed that when other commercial houses began to hire black girls, they were not to be seen by customers at the counter, but were 'hidden away' upstairs doing the books. Another two decades would pass before Miss Bailey and 'Fighting Barrister' Ethelred Erasmus Adolphus Campbell, and later, Mayor Walker (father of insuranceman 'Molo'), would break down these barriers and open the way ultimately for the recruitment and rise to the top of bright black natives of ability such as Douglas Folkes, Don Banks and Delroy Lindsay in the banking world.

At Christmas, King Street presented a spectacular sight of brilliantly sparkling *starlight*, and of shops lit up and decorated in a kaleidoscope of colours, competing with countless balloons clutched by children. The crowded street reverberated with cries of merriment from children, sounds from horns, tin whistles and the chirping of toy birds. The air was disturbed intermittently by the rifle-like *rat-a-tat* of the inevitable firecrackers, and the occasional thunderbolt.

Throughout the years, in parts of Kingston *Bag-an-pan* would roam the streets and higglers, not yet dignified with the euphemistic designation 'Informal Commercial Importers' (ICIs), walked up and down from early morning, warbling their wares: 'Buy yuh coconut oil! Fresh Feesh! Grater cake!'

Commercial air travel did not reach Jamaica until December 1930 with PANAM sea-planes conveying their cargo of passengers and mail. The few who could afford to go overseas to the USA and the UK on holiday, students and businessmen, and those migrants in search of work in the USA, Cuba and Central America, travelled by steamer or cargo boat, sharing their voyage with export bananas.

There were no airports. The Palisadoes peninsula was a deserted swamp, known only for the pirates of Port Royal and for Lewis Galdy's miraculous survival during the 1692 earthquake and tidal wave.

Outside of Kingston, the ports such as Port Antonio, Lucea and Montego Bay were actively involved in transporting incoming and outgoing freight, while the 90-year old railway was still managed as a government department and not yet converted into a statutory corporation. Its steam engines transported passengers and freight through the pock-marked Cockpits and lush hinterland to the west and northeast coasts and to inland Frankfield. The new dimensions of dominance by overland lorries and bustling buses remained a distant dream of a rare few.

This was a time when motor cars, owned by a very few, were mainly American Buicks, Fords and Chevrolets. Continental European cars were rare. The Volkswagen *Beetle*, Hitler's *People's Car*, was not yet invented, and the Japanese Toyota and Honda were non-existent. Without self-starting mechanisms, cars posed an ever-present risk of broken arms to drivers or their helpers as they operated the crank below the radiator and hurriedly attempted to avoid the handle's strong recoil reaction.

There was no Queen's or Nelson Mandela highway to facilitate comfort and encourage speed. Instead there were narrow, winding, unasphalted roads, whose contours threatened terror to drivers motoring over Mount Diablo, the Junction, Spur Tree and Melrose Hills. Indeed, a fairly common sight was presented by Model T Fords, *Tin Lizzies*, making a temporary stop in the struggle over the mountains and belching steam from their radiators. In the city, no Jamaica Omnibus Services nor minibuses yet, but open-sided electricity-powered tramcars, rocking and rolling *en route* to Rockfort or Papine.

By the beginning of the 1930s, the island had experienced more than four decades of partial restoration of representative government . In this limited form of representative government, the Governor exercised executive and virtually autocratic powers, with advice from a Privy Council consisting entirely of officials and the Governor's nominees.

Colonial rule was characterized by government by bureaucracy in which decision-making positions were held exclusively by the Governor, his deputy the Colonial Secretary, and other senior officials. At the time, the Governor and Colonial Secretary were Sir Edward Stubbs and Mr. Arthur Jelf, respectively. In essence, political and administrative roles were fused in the persons of officials who were generally expatriate, transient personnel with one eye fixed on career advancement elsewhere in the colonial service, particularly in Africa and Asia. In the undemocratic Legislative Council, comprising a mix of nominated, *ex-officio*, and elected members, the last group was elected on a franchise and eligibility for candidature which were based on income and property qualifications. Even greater restrictions were imposed on women, who had to be 25 years old and literate. Thus, the electorate represented about ten per cent of the population. Although on his return from serving a prison sentence in the USA, Marcus Garvey had founded the People's Progressive Party and fought the general election of 1930, generally, such organizations were in their infancy and unsystematized. Hence, the elected component of the Legislative Council entered the chamber as individuals unbound by party cohesion.

Yet, excluded from sharing in executive authority and responsibility, and often denied opportunities for playing a positive and creative role in government, they acted in concert, venting their resentment and frustration in vitriolic attacks on civil service departmental heads, some of whom were Legislative and Privy Council members. Younger generations of Jamaicans, born after those turbulent years, do not realize that it was not until the mid-1940s that elected members of the legislature became associated with the administration of departments. It was not until the 1950s that they would have direct responsibility as political heads, that is, ministers.

During the 1920s and 1930s, when government's functions were directed primarily towards the preservation of law and order and tax collection, expenditure on economic development and the social services was minimal. Public works, mainly in the form of road construction and maintenance served as a pseudo-social service; a palliative for the significant incidence of unemployment. Hence, the Director of Public Works who controlled the largest share of the budget was, along with the Governor, the most frequent butt of the attacks, notably by the distinguished barrister and long-time Member of the Legislative Council (M.L.C.) for Clarendon, J.A.G. ('JAGS') Smith (SNR). Other council members whose names gained common currency included teacher D.T. Wint of St. Ann, H.A.L. Simpson of Kingston, George Seymour-Seymour of St. Andrew, A.B. Lowe of St. James, Ken Abendana and Harold Allan of Portland, R.H. Ehrenstein of St. Thomas and T.J. Cawley and E.A. McNeil of St. Catherine.

Public opinion was ill-informed, apathetic and inarticulate. Only limited channels were open to the majority of citizens for communicating their grievances, needs and aspirations to the decision-making centres of the political and administrative system with any real hope of effective responses in ameliorating their living conditions.

In a situation of a restricted franchise, unsystematized political parties and an inchoate labour movement the working class and peasantry had no really effective representative voice, JAGS and Garvey, notwithstanding. By contrast, the dominant economic interests — sugar plantation and other landed proprietors, and the mercantile community (commodity importers and distributors) — wielded considerable influence. They were represented as the governor's nominees on the Privy and Legislative Councils and additionally, through election to the latter, on the basis of restrictive qualifications. Moreover, absentee sugar barons exercised a lobbying voice at Whitehall and Westminster, in London. The influence of growers and merchants would be strengthened locally later, through collective representation in chambers of commerce and specialized commodity associations.

Simmering discontent with social and economic conditions and the lack of effective representational machinery for resolving the problems and needs of the mass of the population would ultimately erupt into civil disturbances not only in Jamaica, but throughout the Caribbean, during the period 1934 to 1938. The way was being paved for the momentous Moyne Commission; but this historic event will form part of a later stage in the story.

The 1929-1930 cricket season saw the emergence of Jamaica's, and perhaps the West Indies', greatest batsman, George Headley who would later be dubbed *the Black Bradman*. In that series against England, the West Indies' first home series, he became the youngest 'immortal', scoring a century in his first Test match at Kensington, Barbados in January 1930. The following month he scored a century in each innings at Bourda, British Guiana in a match recording the West Indies' first Test victory. Six weeks later, he saved the West Indies by scoring a double century when his side was set a massive target of 836. Twenty years later, Denzil Batchelor would write of Headley:

> Black Bradman indeed! There are times when I think the Don at his very best was fit to be called 'the White Headley'.

This last match of the 1929-30 series was also significant for Andy Sandham's triple century, the first in Test cricket, and the calling off of the game as a draw after nine days' play, when the boat arrived as scheduled, to take the England team home. Unless my memory is playing tricks, this was my first view of a Test, taken as a ten year old to Sabina Park by my father. O.C. ('Tommy') Scott, our leading spinbowler, trundled to the wicket ceaselessly; the records revealing figures of 80+ overs and 5 wickets for 266!

That 1930 Test was Sabina's maiden venture. Melbourne Park shared as hosts of first class matches for many years and would continue to do so until 1958.

Football was a popular sport, with outstanding Jamaica players Clarence Passailaigue, DeLeon, and the inimitable Arthur McKenzie. Passailaigue, (261 Not Out), a member of the team in that remarkable first Test played at Sabina, also shared with Headley in a sixth wicket partnership of 487 for Jamaica against Lord Tennyson's team, which remains the oldest first class record after more than 60 years. Decades later, the terms *forwards* and *halves* would be replaced by the modern *strikers* and *linkmen*. In 1930, Jamaica was represented at the Central American Games in Cuba in football and athletics: Joe McKenzie winning our first medal, a silver in high jump and the track and field team including Sir Herbert McDonald, Archdeacon E.L. Maxwell, with G.C. Foster as coach. In 1920 B.M. Clark, who had monopolized the tennis singles championship for five consecutive years and would win again on two subsequent occasions, teamed with Donald Leahong as Jamaica's representatives to Wimbledon.

At the even more popular high school level, St. George's College, winners of the Manning Cup in 1929, boasted in their lineup goalkeeper and cricketer Johnny Groves; and flying forwards DeLeon and Huntley Munroe, later Director of Public Prosecutions and Trevor's father. Wolmer's, the 1930 champions, included Donald Leahong, who would become more famous as many times island tennis champion; and J.T. Burrowes, destined to become a Rhodes Scholar and gynaecologist. Cornwall College, along with Munro the only two country schools competing at the time for the privilege of playing the Manning champions for the coveted Olivier Shield, triumphed in both years, with teams which included John ('Bull') Sinclair later on the Treasury staff, and Sidney O.Martin, the latter also a track champion, who would serve as long-time Senior Medical Officer of Annotto Bay's hospital.

At the inter-schools athletic championships sports, a number of performers were destined to distinguish themselves in public life. In the 1929 winning Wolmer's team, captain and class I champion Sidney Chambers would become Jamaica's and Nigeria's Director of Statistics and later, President of the Jamaica Employers Federation; and long-jumper Jimmy Lloyd, Permanent Secretary to Chief Minister Bustamante, Prime Ministers Sangster and Shearer and Administrator of Grenada. In the midst of preoccupations with his run up and with guarding his goal in the Manning Cup competition, Lloyd could never have imagined that a little more than 30 years later, he would be embroiled in a bruising public battle with Grenada's Chief Minister Eric Gairy, culminating in the latter's removal from office by the Colonial Office. And there were two future ambassadors at those 1929 games: Sir Egerton Richardson, winner of the class I long jump for Calabar High School; and Sir Laurence Lindo of Jamaica College (J.C.), champion of the 100 and 440 yards, would, like his distinguished sports predecessors at that school, Norman Manley and N.N. (Crab) Nethersole, win the Rhodes Scholarship. Richardson, would become perhaps our most distinguished civil servant, as Financial Secretary and afterwards, as Permanent Representative to the UN and ambassador to the U.S. Lindo, following stints as Chief Secretary at home and Administrator of Dominica, would break ground for Jamaica at the Court of St. James's at independence, and remain as our top diplomat there, until his retirement.

A future Minister of Finance and later, tragically, short-term Prime Minister Sir Donald Sangster of Munro College, secured second place at hurdles; while A.F. Brown, who 14 years later, would win one of the first set of Colonial Development and Welfare (CD&W) medical scholarships in 1943, accumulated 14 of the four year old Kingston College's (K.C.) 14 1/2 points — their maiden points. The year 1930, was Calabar's and this would continue for four successive years. With Melbourne Park again acting as hosts — sharing this privilege with Sabina and Kensington over the years until the birth of the National Stadium — Herman McMorris of Chapelton and Calabar dominated the meet, as he would in the following year. And his team included the younger Harvey DaCosta, a future Rhodes Scholar and Attorney General of the West Indies Federation.

For indoor recreation and entertainment, city folk were blessed with the almost 20 year old theatre generously given to the city by Colonel Ward, the nephew of Wray and Nephew Ltd.; and there were other centres of cultural activities, such as the recently opened Ormsby Memorial Hall on Victoria Avenue, and Garvey's Edelweiss Park. And the literary aficionados were no doubt thrilled by the visit, in February 1930, of Rudyard Kipling, the prolific author, creator of *Kim*, composer of *Gunga Din*, the *Recessional* and of the well-worn *If*.

For many years drama groups had been visiting Jamaica, of which the most popular and frequent were the players led by Florence Glossop-Harris who also performed in Montego Bay. The music-loving public was regaled with regular opera seasons and concert performances by baritone, William Spooner and tenor,

Granville Campbell and enjoyed the annual musical festival. Other forms of entertainment were provided by multi-talented Gerardo Leon (one of the talented uncles of current music teacher, Mrs. Fay Lindo) and by teams of comedians: Ernest Cupidon and Tony Ableton, and Racca and Sandy.

At the end of the 1920s and during the early 1930s, Kingston had many music teachers especially pianists and violinists, including Mrs. Barbara Cover, Misses Burrough, Sybil Foster-Davis and Violet Mills, Mrs. Vermont, Miss Edith Armstrong the great-grand-aunt of current concert pianist David Johns, and Mrs. Ruby Delgado, who would journey regularly to J.C. in a vain attempt to make a violinist of me!

Two decades before the international commercialization of television and visions of the video cassete recorder, the cinema remained the most popular form of entertainment. Within a few years, the elegant Carib cinema would emerge to dominate the Cross Roads scene, and the Tivoli cinema would provide entertainment primarily for residents of Kingston's west end. The so-called 'theatres' — consisted of the enclosed movie houses at Cross Roads and the open-air Gaiety and Palace, on East Queen Street and Victoria Avenue, respectively.

We were still in the age of the silent film, dominated by Charlie Chaplin, Harold Lloyd and Rudolph 'The Sheik' Valentino. But soon the first *talkie* reached us: Al Jolson's *Singing Fool*, with his unforgettable tear-jerking *Climb upon my knee, sonny boy*.

To Jamaicans, looking northward to the USA as an outlet for those seeking jobs and higher education, and north-eastward to the Mother Country from whom all blessings and sorrows flowed, the British West Indies or the Caribbean as a region remained remote. A few had had the experience of serving overseas with fellow West Indians in the regional regiment during World War I. Despite the activities of Grenada's Albert Marryshow, the 'Father of Federation', and of Trinidad's Captain Cipriani, like JAGS a scourge of the Governor and of department heads, other territories were scarcely spoken of, save in the context of the fledgling cricket team which had entered the test arena in England in 1928 and had recently returned from Australia; and distant Jamaica was prevented by transportation constraints from participating in the inter-colonial tournament until 1947.

As for the wider Caribbean basin, knowledge, even awareness, of the French and Dutch territories, was non-existent. The Spanish countries fared better because of the trek by Jamaicans and other

West Indians between the end of the 19th and the early 20th centuries to work on construction of the Panama Canal, of railways and in the sugar or banana plantations of Cuba, Costa Rica, and Nicaragua. Although some perished in the Panama project, others settled in these countries and founded bilingual families which represent significant proportions of the populations of Camaguey and Santiago (Cuba) and on the Atlantic coast in Colon Panama, Limon Costa Rica, and Bluefields Nicaragua. Moreover, on the same coast, in Spanish Honduras and Nicaragua, are to be found the Garifunas, descendants of runaway slaves from the West Indies.

As Chairman of the Electoral Committee, I have visited all these countries except Cuba, to observe elections or take part in conferences between 1988 and 1991 and have had discussions with some of our distant cousins. They have a strong interest in establishing contact and developing links with Caribbean peoples. Jamaica is situated only 90 miles from Cuba at the nearest point. My uncle Johnnie used to tell of hearing, as a boy growing up in St. Ann, the guns of the Spanish-American War. Yet, psychologically and ideologically, Jamaica lies a great distance away today, despite the closer relations between the Castro and Manley governments during the period of Democratic Socialism of the latter part of the 1970s.

This wider socio-economic, political and cultural context provides the setting for the portrait of life in a small rural town in which a youngster was growing up during the closing years of the 1920s and the early 1930s.

2

A RURAL UPBRINGING

My father 'Papa' Gilbert Maxwell Mills was a policeman.

Born in the small St. Ann hill village of Sturge Town, eight miles from Brown's Town, he was the eldest of three children. He had a sister, Rhoda, and brother, John James 'J.J.', born six months after Marcus Garvey. Their father combined small farming with working on a large estate and their maternal grandfather, Rev. Maxwell was a Baptist parson. Indeed, this was the source of Papa's middle name which has also been handed down to me and to one of my own sons. All three children were born on 'Triumph' property, where former PNP minister Arnold 'Scree' Bertram's grandmother Ada Mills also lived. The family later moved to neighbouring Shawbury and Penshurst. Shawbury was the home of David Mills, father of Mrs Hyacinth Lindsay, Chief Parliamentary Counsel, and Mrs Marie Slyfield, Executive Director of the government's Administrative Reform Programme.

Following emancipation in 1838, it was the policy of the majority of planters to drive their ex-slaves from the estates, and in some cases they were directly ejected. The same result was achieved by subjecting them to high rents. Gradually, spurred by the initiative and considerable support given by Baptist missionaries led by William Knibb and James Philippo, and determined to purchase their own land, the population settled themselves on a social basis in district villages and on their own scattered individual households.

Sturge, who emerged as the leading abolitionist in Great Britain after Wilberforce and Clarkson, lent £400 for the purchase of land, its division into village lots and the settlement of 100 families in a village. Thus was Sturge Town born. It was among the first of a set of 'Free Villages' established under Baptist church sponsorship and which retained a strong religious influence for a long time. A church and a day school were established in Sturge Town in 1840.

This was the school attended by the three Mills children with fellow pupils, their first cousin Laura, later to marry their headmaster Dawes — parents of Neville the novelist; and Rhoda Palmer, who would become the wife of famous legislator D. T. Wint. Mother ('Mama') Josephine Isilda, the only child of Joseph Payton, a small farmer of August Town in St. Andrew, was an elementary school teacher, musician, soprano concert singer and chorister. Among the memorabilia which she retained was a clipping dated June 27, 1917 from the *Daily Chronicle*, of a news item on a ceremony held at St. Cyprian's Church and citing in full, the address presented to her by Canon R.J. Ripley when she retired at the age of 26, after ten years as organist, to marry my father.

Situated on the west bank of the Hope river, about one mile from the western boundary of the old Mona estate (now the site of the University of the West Indies), August Town's claim to fame rests primarily on the reputation of the 'prophet' Alexander Bedward. It was in this very small village that 100 years ago, this religious leader of the masses in his church and on the banks of the August Town river, preached against British colonialism. Impelled by land deprivation and a sense of oppression by the plantocracy and the colonial government, the Bedwardites were inspired to follow a leader whose preaching was a commingling of strains of religion and politics. Bedward was a forerunner of Garvey and out of Bedwardism, Rastafarianism later came.

Grandpa Joe was the only grandparent we knew, the others having died earlier. In the Providence Church in Liguanea is a prominently displayed tablet dedicated to the memory of my maternal great grandparents, Thomas and Rose Payton, and grand uncle, Thomas Alexander Payton, all of whom died between 1887 and 1907. Grandpa Joe's house was on the flat, a short distance from Bedward's church. My mother was born in 1891 a few months before his first arrest and imprisonment and during the year of the Great Exhibition at Kingston Race Course. She grew up in August Town during the early part of this century at the height of the preacher's activities. As children, we were regaled with tales about his attempts at flying from the trees. Grandpa Joe would provide fascinating, first-hand accounts, and take us down to the section of the river within easy walking distance of his house, where Bedward *'Dip dem in the healing stream, Dip dem to cure bad feeling.'*

No longer a quiet, peaceful village despite Bedwardite activities, August Town is now a relatively large bustling community which serves partly as a dormitory for UWI staff and students. My abiding memory is of waking to the warbling, the soothing sound of barble doves and the scent of plants, particularly of mint and other tea bushes. No *Angola*, notorious for violence, existed then to rent the relatively peaceful air with gunfire.

Entering the police force in 1908 at the lowest recruiting level, Papa had risen rapidly through the ranks. He had reached the informally set summit as sergeant major after ten years, which was a record at the time. Non-white natives of ability were condemned to indefinite frustration because of their inability to rise to officer posts. Positions of inspector and above were reserved for 'white' Jamaicans and British imports, many of them of inferior ability. The young seem to assume that institutions which they currently take for granted have always existed in the same form in which they found them. In fact, highly significant developments have occurred during the past half century with an impact on the civil service and the police force.

The pace of upward occupational mobility has been phenomenal and opportunities for career advancement and for further training undreamt of in my father's day have been opened. Today, an ambitious and able constable recruit to the police service can realistically set his sights on the possibility of rising to the exalted ranks of the high command. In reflecting on the recent history and current position of commissioner, we cannot but marvel at the significant fact that Messers Robinson, Campbell, Bowes, Williams, Ricketts, and Thompson, six Jamaicans, all rose from the ranks to the highest rung of the ladder. Papa vented his career frustrations through poetical compositions which were regularly published in the *Daily Mail*.

Having attained the zenith of his career at age 35 and with the prospect of remaining for another quarter of a century at the same level, Papa was released in 1935 at age 52. I recall vividly his funeral service at St. Andrew's Parish Church, Half-Way-Tree: the trumpet sounds of the 'Last Post' and the volley of gunfire over his grave. His death occurred shortly before I sat the Senior Cambridge exams and affected me deeply.

He had served at Lawrence Tavern, Matilda's Corner, Stony Hill, Half-Way-Tree and Old Harbour and had then moved to Mandeville as sergeant major in charge of the parish of Manchester. There, were born three children, almost evenly spaced between July 1918 and July 1921: a girl, Sybil, myself, and the last, Don.

In 1925 the family moved to Black River for a relatively brief stint, then to Chapelton in 1926, where Mama would remain as a widow, until her retirement in 1956.

Chapelton was a small, sleepy but charming country town of about 900 souls, situated in the hills and hinterland of Clarendon, 48 miles from Kingston. Chapelton was the parish capital, but during my youth May Pen began to challenge it for this position; and as the latter developed into a bustling centre of activity, bolstered partly by the nearby American base at Vernamfield, the ambiguity was brought to an end and Chapelton surrendered its prestigious place in 1944.

All entry to, and egress from the town by road required hill climbing. Approaching from May Pen, twelve miles away, the road meandered via Soursop Turn, by-passing Sevens sugar estate, then winding its way over the wooden bridge at the Ivy Store railway siding at Cross Roads; and we could hear the rumbling as cars crossed the bridge a little more than a mile away. Climbing from Cross Roads up Green's Hill, the road stretched past our houses on the flat, entered the town, and departed by another, Trafalgar Hill via Summerfield and Danks through cane fields and citrus groves, past Crooked River *en route* to Trout Hall and Frankfield. A tributary of this road, branching behind the cenotaph and between the Parish Church and elementary school, flowed down the third hill, Salem, by the Congregational church of that name (now the United Church of Jamaica and Grand Cayman), to Bottom Chapel and by way of Suttons, to Rock River.

The centrepiece of the town was a small village green dominated by the Cenotaph commemorating the town's dead in World War I, topped by the inevitable but attractive clock tower — all surrounded by the police station, the elementary school, and St Paul's Anglican Parish Church which dates from King Charles II and celebrated its 325th anniversary in 1991. Built originally as a *Chapel of Ease*, the church gave its name to the town, as *Chapel Town*. In the school cottage, located within the school's environs and abutting on the police station, head teacher Robinson lived with his family including daughter Helen, later Lusan, and sons Philip, who would become Deputy Collector General, and Ancel. In the same vicinity as the station, were the market, Dr Fraser's Drug Store, and a few shops including the Abrahams' and Khouri stores.

A few chains down from St. Paul's, was a dry goods store owned by the Sullivans, Keith's parents and grandparents of Kay, the artist. On the other side of the road, the tax office, where Joe Smith, a collector general tobe served, and the courts office, with Ken Brandon, the Resident Magistrate (RM), renowned as a dispenser of rough justice. And within five years, this office would be graced by the presence of prospective barristers Ivan Eccleston and Huntley Munroe, future high court judge and director of public prosecutions, respectively. And later, resident magistrates, Herbert Duffus, who would become Chief Justice, Alfred B. Rennie, crown solicitor and high court judge in the making, and John Verity, uncle of the Junior Institute's Bob, all subsequently knighted.

Joe Smith and Eccleston married local ladies of the Abrahams clan, Carmen and Deborah, elder sisters of Andrew and George, who were both babies at the time. Next door to the courts office, Donald Sangster would arrive later, to establish a law office and also to practice politics, while Ivan Tomlinson, before his long stint as citrus specialist and more recently as President of the Jamaica Agricultural Society (JAS), would rove the environs as agriculture department plant disease inspector.

At the brow of Trafalgar Hill lay the 120 acre Tavanore property of Manley Lopez, Chapelton merchant, one of whose daughters would marry engineer R.D.C 'Dossie' Henriques of the Henriques brothers family and firm, owners of Kingston Industrial Works and Garage and of Beacon match factory. A few years before, the other daughter was killed by a shark while swimming in Kingston harbour. A decade later, Clarendon College, which celebrated its silver anniversary in 1992, would be founded by Rev. Lester Davy and would shortly after, move to Tavanore where C.L. Stuart would preside as Head for a quarter of a century. (In Pops Stuart's house was born Bruce Golding, today Chairman of the Jamaica Labour Party (JLP), though he was taken as a baby to Ginger Hill in St. Catherine). A short distance below on Trafalgar Hill, was the home of the Paisleys', father and son Dwight in the public works department, and Dwight's son, Brian now a public relations executive; and collector of taxes, J.C. Whyte, with daughters Marion Skinner, and Monica of the Jamaica Information Service. Not far away in Summerfield, was Sam Chen's grocery where economist and financial expert Dr. Paul Chen-Young would live with his grand-uncle and leave for Clarendon College each morning.

Moving back through the town one could see Brenton Lopez's bakery and on the opposite side, the post office where, among others, Muriel Munroe neé Ford, Trevor's mother, served. Further up, at the corner of the hospital hill, was the McMorris store and *en route* to the hospital in the able charge of Dr. Vincent Rob a famous surgeon, were the Snaiths and Frasers. Dr. Rob would be succeeded by Dr. Pershadsingh, whose brother, attorney Ram was a fellow Nutford House resident, and father occasionally visited our home on a Saturday. Above the post office, side by side, each with an up-hill driveway, were the residences of the resident magistrate and the inspector of police; next, Sidney Abrahams of the income tax department and cricket board, whose sister Phyllis would marry Carlton Alexander, in the house where future permanent secretary O. St. C. Risden would grow up later, and the Oswins, one sister Jennie, who became Mrs. Rudolph Irvine. Opposite them, were the Mellads with one family member, Dr. E.V. Mellad, MLC for Portland. The Mills family lived about 200 yards from the Oswins in a three-bedroom wooden house rented from nearby Rock River's head teacher Felix Robotham of Colonel's Ridge, father of JC alumnus and former M.P. Dr. Upton Robotham. (Coincidentally, Upton's sister, Myrtle would work with me in the Ministry of Finance later). Next to us was Cyril Atkinson, then the J.A.S. agricultural instructor before his elevation to the positions of JAS Secretary and Parliamentary Secretary in the Ministry of Agriculture. Moving further down, another set of Lopez sisters: Melba and Charlotte ('Lulu') and also Frank Smith, working with Major Moxsy, planter and JBPA agent, and destined to become a RAF veteran of World War II; Brenton Lopez and sons Vernie and Ken, future judge and engineer; and Dr. Thompson, Mrs. McCrea, widow of a deputy inspector general of police and Sir Herbert MacDonald's aunt, and her daughter, Mrs. Lena Harvey. On the other side of the road, were the Farquharsons with Jean, later Mrs. G. Arthur Brown and of JBC; and returning in our direction, Busha Tom Abrahams's family of sons and daughters on the hill. Next, the McMorrises, relatives of cricketer Easton, UWI's Physics Department's Dr. Neville and Victoria Mutual Society's chairman, Vayden (who as a youngster often spent vacations with his uncle). Opposite to us and adjacent to the McMorris family, were the Whites: R.O.C. High Court judge to be, and his elder sister Ivy, a future deputy principal of Shortwood training college; and the Campbells, whose son Selvin would graduate to enter the entrepreneurial scene in the fish processing business.

On the outskirts of the town lived a number of prominent individuals who left indelible impressions on the psyche of a boy; none more so than JAGS Smith. Residing at *The Ark* some four or so miles from Chapelton, by the end of the 1920s he had already established a reputation, firmly founded as long-time MLC for Clarendon, politician and advocate *par excellence*. The younger Norman Washington Manley had only recently arrived at the Bar to challenge his pre-eminence. Even as youngsters we were intrigued by the battle between the two in the famous Alexander murder case of 1931, in which Manley appeared as defence counsel for Mrs. Alexander, accused of murdering her husband.

Recollections are clear of JAGS Smith, dignified, solemn and serious-looking, being chauffeur-driven past our house into and out of town. Vague memories remain of his election campaign of 1930 when he was challenged by W. Hyde McCaulay, Spaldings businessman, and of his inevitable triumph, acclaimed with banners bearing the message 'Smith Hide McCaulay!' This was the first election of which I was conscious: a quiet, violence-free contest, a far cry from today's elections. But party politics had not yet appeared on the scene; we were friends of Busha Tom's children and played games with his sons, especially Clare and Tom, but at the time we were unaware that their father was JAGS's political agent. At home, our parents discussed JAGS's deeds in the courts and in the Legislative Council in what seemed to us as faraway Kingston. An old elementary schoolmate of mine, Gladstone Taylor O.D., currently Secretary of the local cane farmers' association branch, now owns and resides at *The Ark*.

Another frequent visitor to the town was U. Theo ('U.T.') McKay of James Hill, elder brother of internationally famed poet and novelist Claude, author of *My Green Hills of Jamaica*.

U.T. was a member of the Clarendon Parochial Board, and also prominent in the J.A.S.; he seemed larger than life when he entered Chapelton, usually on Saturdays for JAS branch meetings, and had strongly supported McCaulay against JAGS in the 1930 election.

Living near Cross Roads, about two miles from town were the Lamparts: Ewart, Lawrie and Ronald, future Assistant Chief Electoral Officer, Education Officer and Senior Medical Officer, respectively. Ewart was among the second batch of students entering the new Kingston College, while Ronald would develop a reputation as Senior Medical Officer in charge of the Princess Margaret Hospital,

Morant Bay, and for his consistent advocacy of legalizing ganja. And farming at Four Paths, (not the better known Four Paths close to May Pen,) was Gaston Girvan, brother of Jamaica Welfare's D. Thom and uncle of Norman, now Professor and Director of UWI's Consortium Graduate School of the Social Sciences.

Seen in town occasionally from nearby Morgans Valley was Dr. Abrahams, whose sister Miss Lou operated a shop on the other side of the village green. From Chapelton we often looked across the valley towards the Bull Head Mountain to see the mix of smoke, steam and mist as the train meandered through Morgan's pass, part of properties originally owned by Sir Henry Morgan.

Among other regular visitors was Rev. R.E. Phillips of Colonel's Ridge, eight miles away to the north, who would be elected Member of the House of Representatives in 1944 under the new constitution, and was the father of Ambassador Reg. Phillips and Dr. Heloise Lewis of UWI's Faculty of Education. Then there was Archdeacon Lennon of Mocho, that giant of a man, my godfather, on holiday from Calabar, Eastern Nigeria who often brought me gifts. A missionary teacher there, like a number of other Jamaicans, he was also a member of Nigeria's Federal Legislative Council and, on returning home later, would be elected a member of the Federal West Indies Parliament. At the other end of the economic and social spectrum were members of the squirearchy, represented by the McWhinnies and their close relative, Major Moxsy, large-scale cattle and vegetable farmer of nearby Suttons and chairman of Clarendon's parochial board, who would contest the Legislative Council seat unsuccessfully against JAGS in 1935, and later, would establish Jamaica Vegetables Limited of Bull Savannah.

At the end of the 1920s and during the early 1930s, Chapelton, like other small rural towns boasted few public utilities. There was no electricity nor telephones and the number of homes with indoor running water or sewers could be counted on the fingers of one hand. Generally, the facilities enjoyed by a lower middle class family, such as ours, consisted of goblet, basin, wash pan, and chamber pot — normally kept under the bed or in a closet — an outside pit latrine and shower in an outroom. Cooking was carried out on a stove fed by wood and an oven, both located in a kitchen separated from the main sections of the house and supplemented by a coal stove within the house.

As there were no refrigerators we bought ice from a passing truck, usually for Sunday use. This was mainly used for making ice-cream and calf's feet jelly. In a corner of our small dining room or in the pantry stood a large clay Spanish jar and on a table, a smaller vessel, a pitcher, also of clay, both keeping our drinking water cool. The jar, which I inherited, now stands in a corner of my patio serving not utilitarian, but aesthetic, decorative purposes. For our daily bread, we waylaid Brenton Lopez's bread cart as it passed the house. Adorning the living-room walls were large framed photographs of Grandpa Joe displaying winged collar, and Grandma Fanny wearing the Queen Alexandra hair and dress styles; also, of persons presumably admired by our parents: former four times 19th Century British Prime Minister William Ewart Gladstone and hero of the Boer and First World Wars, Earl Kitchener of Khartoum.

We woke to the sensuous scent of coffee being drawn in a bag after being ground in a small hand mill. We children had to be content with bush tea: fever grass, john charles, the thick leaf of life, cerasee whose taste still lingers, but pressed on us with the admonition 'it's good for you'. Fortunately, to compensate, there was sometimes the more pleasant ramgoat dashalong. Periodically, and particularly in preparation for returning to school after holidays, we were subjected to a washing out by Glauber or Epsom salts and by the more dreaded castor oil. Discipline was stern, but kindly, emphasized occasionally by the strap, and the dictum 'children must be seen, but not heard'. And we were continuously indoctrinated with the tenets of the 'Golden Rule': *'Do unto others as you would that they should do unto you'.* I often ask myself if this precept should not preferably be expressed in a different form so as to reflect the behaviour of those who tend to impute the worst to others, expecting them to behave as they themselves would. In my study and teaching of Caribbean Public Administration during the past three decades, I have often wondered whether the authoritarian and non-participative syndrome which expresses itself in excessive centralization does not have its genesis in this dictum. Perhaps it is this cultural conditioning which determines the relations between teacher and pupils in the educational system and culminates at the work place in the reluctance to delegate.

Mama's Aunt Ada, the maternal grandmother of Enid Douglas, professional in public health and Daphne, UWI's professor of library studies, lived with the family for several years, helping to look after us children during our growing up period. My most vivid memory of her is of her repeated response to our complaints that the porridge was hot or cold:

> When it is cold, you want it hot,
> When it is hot, you want it cold,
> Never wanting what is got,
> Always wanting what is not.

Indoors, in between the playing of dominoes to the accompaniment of banging and breaking the pieces, there were other games, such as tee-(tic)-tac-toe and cards, a variety of the latter taught us by uncle, J. J. As long as I can remember, Uncle Johnnie unfailingly spent a portion of every vacation from Mico with our family in the country. As children we looked forward to his impending arrival in the earlier years like the coming of Santa Claus, even on non-Christmas occasions. He taught us whist, donkey, sevens, strip-me-naked and others; and we enjoyed home concerts and occasional parties to the music of the hand-cranked Victrola gramophone (symbolized by dog and horn) especially when Uncle Johnnie was down. He was a music lover; this was among the variety of subjects he taught at Mico, and he enjoyed dancing. I was especially fascinated by the dancing of Carmen Abrahams and Joe Smith. Records which I recall we had in those early days were *Sonny Boy; Ramona; I hear the mission bells above; Chiquita; 12 O'clock: Oh, How different tonight; The Desert Song; A Room with a View;* and sacred music such as *The Old Rugged Cross.*

Occasionally Mama sang at a concert in the church hall and there were red letter days with visiting performers from Kingston including the famous Granville Campbell, William Spooner and Gerardo Leon. Our cinema entertainment was restricted to religious lantern slides shown in Church and the rare silent film, the mechanism driven by Delco plant. The film which left an indelible impression was *Uncle Tom's Cabin* with its hanging horrors disturbing the imagination and sleep. Even more rare were the visits to the real cinema in May Pen, already threatening to supplant Chapelton as the parish capital.

Usually only our sister was taken on these trips, and to Milk River Bath. Don and I were left at home and I certainly resented this for a long time. The only consolation being our inclusion in the annual trip to Kingston to spend a few days. From this jumble of memories one stands out clearly: the impression made on a country boy by the glamorous lights of the Gaiety and Palace cinemas on East Queen Street and Victoria Avenue. At Palace we saw our first talkie film: *Love Parade*, starring Jeanette McDonald and Maurice Chevalier, the dashing French musical artist.

We were regaled with Anancy stories, and played 'guess me this riddle and p'raps not'. Another popular game was 'pitcha or no pitcha' (picture or no picture), opening a book randomly and challenging a contestant to guess correctly whether there was a picture on one of the pages where it was open. But we also had other uses for books: some of us were voracious readers, spending hours poring over and devouring novels and textbooks, by sunlight, and at night, by 'Home Sweet Home' kerosene lamp in the absence of electricity. In the aftermath of Hurricane Gilbert of September 1988, I recalled those times, including the problem of obtaining ice. Some of the books in my parents' small collection were *The Sweet Silvery Sayings of Shakespeare*, *Men with Backbone*, and *The Story of a West Indian Policeman* by a former inspector, Herbert Thomas.

But apart from these and the other school books, such as Blackie's *Tropical Reader* and Nelson's, I seem to have consumed countless fictional works, primarily novels of romance and adventure, often completing one each day. Among my favourites were Anthony Hope's *Prisoner of Zenda*, Jeffery Farnol's *Beltane the Smith*, Dumas' *Three Musketeers* and *The Man in the Iron Mask*, *Lorna Doone*, the *Tarzan* Series, H. Rider Haggard's *She* and *King Solomon's Mines* and Baroness Orczy's *Scarlet Pimpernel* series.

Even at the advanced age of eleven or twelve, I still found fascination in the tales of Hans Christian Andersen and the Grimm Brothers. We collected cigarette cards, some adorned by photographs and pen pictures of movie stars of the day: Valentino, Norma Shearer, Mary Pickford, Pola Negri; others of famous sports figures and record breakers such as Sir Malcolm Campbell with speedboat and automobile.

In such a community, blessed with a collection of youngsters, on recollection life never seemed dull. We played cricket at school, the outfield almost entirely devoid of grass, with the appearance of clay all around, it was like the Sabina wicket at its worst. We played in our back and front yards, sometimes six and out where the space was restricted, posing a test of discipline for the impetuous who could not exercise restraint when batting. Beginning with rustic and rudimentary equipment, balls of bamboo root and bats of coconut bough or of roughly hewn wood, we graduated to cork and composition balls, especially when Sidney Abrahams, a future Jamaican player, was home on holidays from Wolmer's. As we grew older, we travelled occasionally to the other Four Paths, 15 miles away. This was the centre of Clarendon cricket, led by Dickie Vassell, Alvin and Gifford Lawson and Martin Waddell. It is gratifying to see the revival of this parish as a cricket force currently, in reaching the finals of the new All-Island League competition in 1990 and '91.

Other activities included hop-scotch and hide and seek, especially taking advantage of the cellars underneath our houses but trying to avoid jiggers/chigoes from attacking the soles of our feet. These cellars provided a mine for the excavation of small nanny goats, disclosing their identity by the concave impression left in the earth. And we played rounders, starving (throwing a ball from teammate to teammate and preventing opponents from getting hold of it) and chevy chase with two teams, each lined up at their base, and members of each attempting to capture their opponents by touching them while running, lining up the captured prisoners while their teammates tried to rescue them.

We spun gigs, played games of marbles, throwing the metal *taah* as close to the line as possible to decide who gets first pitch at the marbles in the ring, with the winner reaping the victory spoils of marbles or cashew nuts. There were ring games played in the school yard and our back-yards. We roamed the open spaces: the bushes and woods, the streams, climbing trees, catapulting birds with slingshots or snaring them with springes. I clearly recall knocking down a woodpecker from a tree trunk merely by throwing a stone. Some older boys, especially the Abrahams and McMorrises, engaged in bird shooting on Pennant's property and travelling as far as the May Pen woods.

We climbed trees in the backyard and voraciously consumed oranges and mangoes. Once, I won a competition against Tom Abrahams and Don for eating the largest number of purple star apples. This was at considerable physical expense: what a bind! Since then, in an ongoing aversion to this fruit lasting for 60 years, I have not eaten one.

During the cooler months between December and February Mama took us for early morning walks and at times we were scared by what seemed to be duppies among the banana plants and then greatly relieved that they were merely shadows reflected from the leaves by the moonlight. Yet, we remained ever mindful of the stories of the dreaded rolling calf, chains clanging and clanking as it moved down the road at midnight. And in the evenings there were the ritual trips on foot to the post office to enquire for letters; a social pastime made necessary by the absence of a mail delivery system in a rural town.

Among our most enjoyable and memorable experiences was the occasional trip to teacher Robinson's small cottage at Woodhall about four or five miles away, where he took us in his horse-drawn buggy. There was a small sugar mill driven by mule power — the animal moving around in circles incessantly, converting the cane into liquor. Too few city children get opportunities nowadays to spend vacations in the country and in any event, many of these delights seem to have disappeared.

Chapelton is located many miles from the sea. Carlisle and Jackson's Bays were the closest points, and Milk River Bath involved a day's expedition. However we had the Rio Minho river and its tributaries. There was also the occasional return to the birthplace, Mandeville. These return visits were usually made mainly for the flower show, the oldest in Jamaica, the horticultural society having been formed in 1865, and in the 1930s and 1940s, still a beautiful experience. The opportunity was also taken to see old friends such as Miss Dottie Hogg Lumsden and Teacher R.A. Gordon and family: parents of Mrs. Iris Whittaker the musician and her brother, Ronald, the dentist and former Calabar football star. Nowadays, Mandeville seems to have lost some of its charm, the old English-type village with the Anglican church and green as its focal points.

The development of bauxite and alumina by the complex of corporations Alcan and Alpart has, of course, caused considerable population growth and while the town remains a cool haven, it is no longer reserved for the retired. But the approach from Melrose Hill is still a beautiful sight, especially the perspective from the new highway which by-passes Horseshoe Curve and emphasizes the pleasantly rolling green backdrop of hills: a view reminiscent of north Wales. Alpart has also contributed to the view from the top of Spur Tree at night, the plant resembling a ship at sea with lights ablaze.

Mama was second teacher to headmaster Robinson at the elementary school now designated 'All Age'. Wallace Nam of Photo Express, Norman McMorris, Manager of Kingston Ice Making Company, and Muriel ('Cissy') Rose, now Pouyatt, Buddy's wife, whom she taught during the early 1950s, have told me what a strong disciplinarian she was. We were also taught by Eddie Burke, later of Jamaica Welfare and teller of folk tales and Lawrie Lampart was a pupil teacher. Since that long ago period, Eddie Burke has served as a UN community development consultant in Africa, has been honoured with the Norman Manley Award for Excellence and been ordained a priest.

Mama supplemented the family income giving piano lessons teaching and selling milk and butter from heifers sent to her by her father in August Town. I recall well the early morning exercises on the piano scales as her pupils ran through their scales. It is incredible that elementary school teachers managed to survive on their meagre incomes and to rear families, many with signal success. Take the case of the Lloyds for example: the teacher-parents of Astley, Clement, Ivan, Hugh, Jimmy, Birtill, educator, engineer, doctor, dentist, lawyer, scientist, respectively.

This was an age when the teacher and the parson were highly respected in the community, exercised considerable influence as guide and adviser, and were regarded as role models. Some, such as my mother, also served their communities as Justices of the Peace (JP). One of the sad and disappointing developments in contemporary Jamaican society has been the dramatic decline in the status and influence of the teacher, a result, perhaps, of technological and economic changes which have left the teacher behind. Involved in these have been a breakdown of the social system and changes in the value systems, with status and respect tending to be accorded primarily on the basis of a money criterion. As a consequence, a significant stabilizing and cementing element has been eliminated from our social structure.

We were drilled in the principles of english grammar with emphasis on analysis, parsing and spelling; and this, with the foundations laid in arithmetic and geography, provided standards which placed us ahead of children groomed in preparatory school. There was a time when I was highly proficient in spelling; however, the experience in recent years of reading numerous essays and examination scripts has left me less confident, doubtful about my own competence. And even more sad is the fact that some of the worst offenders, both in grammar and spelling are teachers.

At school we struggled manfully with measurements of bushels and quarts, quatties and gills, collectively reciting responses to the teacher, while some acquired adeptness at mental arithmetic. The lessons of history were taught totally from England's perspective: history written by West Indians such as Elsa Goveia and Roy Augier would not be widely available for more than two decades.

Conditioned in a context of acceptance of British superiority as axiomatic and unquestioned, we learned of English invincibility and of countless wars always won by England, disregarding the defeat which led to independence for the American colonies. God was always on England's side. We were indoctrinated by the red-flagged areas on the world map which extended over all the continents and indicated the expanse of the Empire on which the sun never sets. We were insensitively required on public holidays to stand to attention in the school yard sun and, while saluting the Union Jack, the British flag, to sing songs such as *Land of Hope and Glory* and *Rule Britannia*.

Older generations then, developed a strong sentimental attachment to the mother country and things British: feelings which were fed by this diet of patriotic songs, and nurtured by schooling and reverence for the Union Jack and other symbols. For some of us younger ones, such affinities would be eroded within a decade and a half and superseded by increasing nationalist consciousness and a reaction against imperialism.

Periodic visits by the inspector of schools provided opportunities for preening and giving pride to the school by our performance. Also, Mrs. Kathleen Bourne, widow of a former Colonial Secretary, would come to reward with *Band of Mercy* cards those of us who could convince this little lady that we had protected a defenseless animal from injury, particularly a lizard: 'You must not kill the little bu'(ll) f(r)ogs'. We were told that in Kingston she presented a conspicuous sight on her bicycle. As in most elementary schools of the time, pupils cultivated a school garden, a practice which has since died.

We experienced other diversions in school, some enjoyable, others not as pleasant. Our Chinese school mates introduced us to a minor level of gambling in *drop pan*, but we did not graduate to the more advanced *peaka pow*: And we shared vicariously in the triumphs of local hero, sprinter, and Class 1 Champion, Herman McMorris, when news reached Chapelton, via the *Gleaner* and *Daily Mail*, that he had led Calabar High School to their first Boys Athletic Championship title's in 1930. Other pleasures were provided by women who sold at the school gate, mouth-watering bullas, coconut gizzadas, and grater cakes.

But indelibly etched on the memory was the sight of a prisoner being punished by cat-o'-nine-tails in the police station yard. In an age when corporal punishment was customary, he was strapped over a barrel (placed in a rolling position, but rendered immobile by clamps) in which a hole was cut to provide for urination, evidently an inevitable consequence of the caning.

There was the day too, almost 60 years ago, when the entire town was engulfed in gloom by news of the very serious injuries suffered by Busha Tom in a car accident on the May Pen road, when Andrew and George were babes in arms. He was most fortunate to survive, as he lay in a hospital bed for months, but emerged with a handicapped leg. And the day when, in playing cricket on a shortened pitch, a bowler tragically lost an eye permanently, as he reacted too slowly in attempting to take a return catch.

We looked forward to free days on Saturdays with the bustle of market activity: the donkeys and mules, laden with baskets (panniers) of produce and people past our gate. Above all, Saturday was the day when lunch would be based on a large bowl of beef soup, dunked with dumplings, cocoa and yam. And on public holidays after singing in the sun, we watched adults at the market fair, dancing to the mentos, led by the melodious, the sweet sounds of the bamboo fife. Feelings of nostalgia return whenever I hear this music by fife or flute today. On rare occasions we were taken to the fair and races in Vere, 15 or 20 miles away; and would meet teacher R.J.M. Lewin, head of Hayes school and father of 'Dr. Olive Lewin, the musicologist, and Dr. Monica Atkinson.

On public holidays the public buildings in the town centre were white-washed, particularly on the anniversaries of royal birthdays. The gleaming, whitened sepulchres also welcomed the rare 'royal' visit to the parish by Governor Stubbs or Colonial Secretary Arthur Jelf. On such occasions, Custos Muirhead, the Queen's representative in the parish, would act as host.

Church was a three times a Sunday custom (including Sunday School) with the seating reflecting the social hierarchy: the Custos, Resident Magistrate, property owners, doctor, police inspector and their families occupying the front pews. The parson was normally from Britain. Mama was the organist and somehow combined this responsibility with leadership of the choir; with other prominent choristers, father and mother Lampart and Miss Rosa Brash. On special Sundays there was a police parade led by my father, tall, slim and straight-backed, resplendent in his uniform. As he entered the church, removed his spiked helmet, took his place at the head of our family pew and unbuckled his sword, we felt a surge of pride.

On some choir practice evenings we boys took a turn pumping the bellows of the pipe organ for Mama the organist. This will no longer provide a pastime for present day youngsters, modern electrical bellows blowing having displaced the manual operation.

Awful memories remain too of preparations for Sunday lunch when, without facilities of refrigeration, a screaming chicken would be executed by neck-wringing. One Friday afternoon we witnessed, with trepidation, the drama of a cow, pole-axed for slaughter, but evidently at the incorrect location in the head or neck, running berserk down the road.

It was at St. Paul's Parish Church that later, young Alvin Stone, now Archdeacon, but at the time in the Chapelton police force, cut his teeth; and he took piano lessons from my mother, as would Miss Stuart, now Mrs. Percy Broderick, Miss Angelita Ricketts, now wife of former Prime Minister Barbados Erskine Sandiford, and Selvin Campbell of Cee-Foods Ltd. All three were also her students at school. An interesting social custom was the ritual after night service of some members of the congregation walking home in a group and gradually letting off group members at their respective gates after a brief conversation at each stop. As children, we looked forward to after-church ice cream which we assisted in making by turning the bucket handle. There can be no nicer ice cream than the home-made variety. Calf's feet jelly was a regular item on our Sunday supper menu.

On Christmas eve, after walking about looking at the shops, we would set out for midnight service and go to bed excited with the anticipation of waking early on Christmas morning to see our stockings hanging from our bedheads filled with presents, before walking to Grand Market; and on new year's eve, to watchnight service. During the year, in anticipation of Christmas, Mama would send off mail orders from a *Sears, Roebuck* catalogue and we children awaited with bated breath the arrival of the appropriate packages. On one occasion, my excitement knew no bounds as the parcel containing my small mechanical train and its track was being opened. Imagine my disappointment when the engine experienced difficulty in moving along the track, despite being wound. Treatment with oil only aggravated the problem; one wheel fell off as the engine continued to skid and slip and the toy had to be abandoned. The feeling of disappointment still lingers.

I have recollections of my brother and myself throwing firecrackers across the street from our front gate and one exploding in the face of a passing motorist. The consequences remain deeply and indelibly imprinted on my memory; though not elsewhere, physically. And memories of post-christmas lunch linger, of savouring the taste of gungo peas soup seasoned with ham bone. And of harvest festival, with the altar abounding with gifts of fruit and other agricultural produce.

Good Friday, the most solemn and sacred day of the year, involved dozing intermittently at the mid-day three-hour service; and setting the egg white to see what the future would hold, for instance, a ship forecasting travel. In the bushes behind our house was the plant from which, legend asserts, the cross of the crucifixion was built and which, when cut on Good Friday yielded a blood-red sap. We could never remember to test the truth by cutting it at other times of the year.

In 1931 I won a part-scholarship to secondary school from the pupil teachers' examination. The climax of the elementary school experience came later that year, when, taken to teacher Lewin's school at Hayes, to sit the Vere Trust Scholarship examination, I was able to enter Jamaica College that September as a boarder without cost to my parents. This was the initiation to more serious study and Chapelton would now become a haven for the relief and relaxation provided by school vacations.

3

A MID-VICTORIAN PUBLIC SCHOOL

To reminisce about and to recollect life at Jamaica College (JC) as I knew it, requires an effort of recall and recollection sufficient to stretch and strain the mind. And yet incredibly, much of the general atmosphere and ambience of the school as it was in the 1930s and even specific incidents are still vivid, indelibly engraved on my memory and psyche.

Half a century before, a law had been enacted creating the Jamaica Schools Commission which was assigned the responsibility of preparing and executing 'schemes for the reform of governing bodies, and the better application of endowments for education throughout the island'. Further, and of more direct relevance to JC, the Commission was named as 'the governing body for the management of a school to be called 'the Jamaica High School'. The Jamaica Free School, established in 1795 and located in St. Ann, was transferred in 1885 to Hope as the Jamaica High School and a University College attached five years later. In 1902 the School and College were amalgamated as Jamaica College.

Imagine a country boy of comparatively poor parentage, arriving at the prestigious portals of this select school as a scholarship student in the Jamaica of 1931! His first impressions were of an extensive campus (estimated size: 17 acres) encircled by a perimeter fence, a large spreading guango tree close by the main entrance and conspicuously located like sentinels, in front of the main building, two imposing old ficus trees; the last, parading their banyan paternity, their roots running like giant veins across the ground.

Behind were the hallowed halls and corridors which had been graced by distinguished old boys such as Reginald Murray, Norman Manley, Noel ('Crab') Nethersole, N.N. and Leslie Ashenheim, C. M. Morales, W.N. Dickenson, H. Laurence Lindo and K.H. Ross — all Jamaica or Rhodes Scholars between 1904 and 1931, and outstanding sportsmen. Their names and photographs were generously and conspicuously displayed on the walls of the main 'tower' building for all newcomers to see and to emulate as role models. In that era, high priority was accorded to all-round proficiency in scholarship and sport and to the qualities of leadership. Portraying the features of its parental prototype, the mid-Victorian English public school, Thomas Arnold's Rugby, at JC organized games and particularly cricket, football and track athletics were elevated to the role of a religious rite.

In a perceptive and excellent article, 'Jamaica College — the Schooling of a Colonial Elite' (*Sunday Gleaner*, October 9, 1988), Arnold Bertram has identified certain characteristics of the school during its early years under the leadership of the first headmaster, Canon (later promoted to Archdeacon) Simms. Bertram has compared the features of the original Rugby prototype and its Jamaican progeny, emphasizing the social composition of the two — the latter, 'the preserve of the white landed gentry'. Indeed, the high 'visibility quotient' reflecting the conspicuous colour composition of the majority of the boys is entirely evident from photographs of the student body over the first two decades of the school's history.

In 1931 when I entered JC as a boarder, relics of this racial and social class dominance remained. It was a time when not more than 1% of Jamaica's population of secondary school age were admitted for secondary education. JC's total enrolment numbered 133: 72 boarders and 61 day boys, as compared with the 1991-'92 figure of about 1300 (boarding now abolished). The annual fees including boarding of £55-£60 in the early thirties were well beyond the resources and reach of the combined incomes of a police sergeant major and an elementary school teacher. Hence, my brother, Don (who joined me in 1932) and I could never have attended such a school were it not for the scholarships awarded to us. Incidentally, two years before I did, our sister Sybil won a scholarship to St. Hugh's High School for Girls. It should be emphasized also, that, unlike the current situation, very few such scholarships were available 60 years ago.

The year I entered JC, only eight schools competed at the Boys Athletic Championships and five for the Manning Cup, the premier competition for schoolboy football. Kingston College was then an infant of six years. During the first thirteen years of competition in championships, JC had won the Cup on nine occasions and the Manning Cup eight times in nine years of competition, entirely monopolizing the first six years of the latter. In ten years of Olivier Shield competition, for this football trophy, they had emerged victors on seven occasions, and shared the trophy on an eighth. A performance of which we boys were inordinately proud was the winning of all seven trophies in which the schools competed in 1916; the participants, whose composite group photograph took pride of place in a conspicuous position included Leslie Ashenheim, later distinguished attorney of Milholland, Ashenheim and Stone, and Privy Councillor; Rudolph Burke, Member of the Senate, planter and president of the Jamaica Agricultural Society (J.A.S.); and Hugo C.W. Chambers, destined to spend a life-time of teaching at his *alma mater* and ultimately becoming headmaster.

Before long, we new boys were to be imbued with the spirit and inspired by the deeds of Norman Manley both on and off the playing fields. Twenty years before we arrived, in two consecutive years 1911 and 1912,he had virtually won the championship cup for JC. With five firsts and one second in the earlier year, 1911 (including the record 10 seconds 100 yards), and wins in all six events in which he competed in the next year, he contributed more than fifty percent towards his team's aggregate points in each of these years! (Note however, that the number of competing schools was even less than in 1931). And Manley's prowess in sport was not restricted to track athletics; his legendary reputation also thrived on the story handed down of his climb to the top of the school tower to address his fellow students. So we had a hero and his exploits represented exciting elements in the traditions of the school.

Among Manley's contemporaries at school were J.M. ('Fire') Hall, (the father of JBC's Dennis Hall), winner of the 100 and 200 yards in the first championship sports of 1910 and B.M. Clark, later Jamaica's golf and tennis champion, and recorded by Sir Herbert Macdonald as the first and only winner of the standing high jump. Before all of them came Sam W. Brown, a towering footballer, who would proceed to teach different generations of the same families and, *en route*, serve as head of Titchfield High School in the parish of

Portland. During the next two decades after Manley's era, the strong sports tradition was continued; the roster of distinguished names seemed endless and most of them would also graduate to distinguished careers in public life. Apart from the scholar-sportsmen whom I have mentioned earlier — the Ashenheims, Dickenson, Lindo, Morales, Ross — were individuals such as future lawyers Harry O.A. Dayes, C. Lynden Cawley, Locksley Moody, R.C. Marley (and his two brothers, engineer Noel and doctor Norvel, all three on the Championship Cup winning team of 1928) Sydney Phillips, a future St. Mary Custos, and Morris Burke, Crown Solicitor in the making. Among them also were future Chief Medical Officers A.A. ('Gussie') Peat and W. Jeffrey Wilson and Professor of Microbiology, Louis Grant; A. Noel Croswell, who would become Commissioner of Police, and R.B. Crooks, Headmaster of Happy Grove High School also in Portland; Robert C. Lightbourne, later industrialist, first Managing Director of the Industrial Development Corporation (IDC) and Minister of Trade and Industry; Hugh Miller, Agricultural Scholar and Chief Technical Officer in that Ministry; V.A. and C.H. Valentine, the former, an opening bowler on the West Indies 1933 team to England.

The sportsmen whom I recall during my first two years were Trevor Donaldson, Manning Cup goalkeeper and later, Managing Director of Sevens Estate; inside forwards Eric and Huntley DaCosta, soon to play for Jamaica; two or three of the Gore quintet (sons of James Gore, famous for 'serendipity', tobacco, tiles and Hellshire Hills); Harry Fox and Carlton Alexander, the last, at the time a mere slip and not the robust, ample adult he would become 40 years later as the honoured Chief Executive of Grace, Kennedy Company.

Nineteen thirty-three was the year of an unforgettable Manning Cup experience. St George's College, the 'Light Blues', boasted a tradition of playing skilled, constructive football. In those days the competition, comprising only five schools, involved playing at home and away, with no need for zoning as in the current competition with 22 teams participating. J.C.'s, the 'Dark Blues', reputation rested largely on the myth of invincibility on the rain-soaked, often soggy surface at Hope. In 1933 St. George's were already in the lead, had already beaten us at least once and seemed destined to emerge champions. But relative newcomers, eight year old K.C., in the guise of 'David' (led by Bunny Barber, L.K. Brown, Chester Burgess, Gresford Jones, and Ralph Holding [Michael's father] incredibly held the 'Goliath' to a draw, throwing the competition into a triangular tie between St. George's, JC and Wolmer's. Out of the drawing of lots St George's and JC were scheduled to meet at Sabina Park in the first run-off match, the winner to play Wolmer's. Few of the pundits outside of their ardent supporters gave JC a chance. At Sabina, on the appointed day, many St. George's fans (not schoolboys nor graduates) were heard to exclaim: 'College (referring to St George's) must win!'. In fact, JC won a memorable match by an incredible 7-0! St. George's had surprisingly replaced their regular keeper by Dalhouse who had not represented the Manning XI before. Captained by Winston Stuart, a future agricultural scholar and chief technical officer in the Ministry of Agriculture, JC boasted the 'flying five' forwards: advancing from the right, Audley Narcisse, R.C. ('Bob') Humphries, Earl Burrowes, Winston Shelton and R.F. ('Dickie') Kinkead; and also included W. Jeffrey Wilson and in goal, Keith Burrowes. In 1934 again winning the cup under Stuart, the forward line and goalkeeper remained intact, but fresh recruits included Horace Edwards and R.N. Lewin as halves.

Humphries was an even more accomplished cricketer than footballer. I recall seeing his classic innings of 57 at Sabina Park in a game against visiting English county champions, Yorkshire in 1936, which included Test bowlers Bill Bowes and Hedley Verity and a young Len Hutton. This seemed to be a West Indies player in the making; tragically, his potential career was cut short by war. Six years later, as an officer in the British Army fighting in the Far East, Humphries would be captured by the Japanese and languish in a prisoner-of-war camp in Singapore until the end of World War II. In a post-war career as a chartered accountant he would serve as a partner in Carman and Bruce, senior partner of Price Waterhouse and Chairman of the Bauxite and Alumina Trading Company (BATCO) of Jamaica. Earl Burrowes a 100 yards champion, would be killed in action in the war; his namesake Keith, no relation, would be recruited to the Island Treasury, where I would work with him from 1941 in the pensions section under Allan R. Abrahams and later, he would be promoted to the position of Accountant General. Of the two wingers, Narcisse would return home to medical practice from Edinburgh University, and Kinkead, graduating to the Jamaican XI, would join the family's famous pharmacy, soda fountain and icecream business on King Street and later located on Harbour Street. Horsy Edwards, one of my fellow residents at a colonial students residence in London during the immediate post-war years, would ultimately be elevated to the rank of Queen's Counsel.

My senior years were adorned by the presence of a number of outstanding sports performers, several of whom combined prowess in sports with scholarship. I recall particularly, H.A. Grant, all-rounder in cricket, football and athletics; H.L. ('Tubbin') Fox; Irving Johnson, (cricketer and footballer), later agricultural scholar and subsequently, director of agricultural planning. I recall more vividly, of course, those who were fellow members of the Sunlight Cup Cricket teams on which I played and of the Manning football team. Foremost among these last two groups were Alton ('Duke') Ellington, cricketer, footballer and long jump record holder, winner of the Jamaica Centenary Scholarship (celebrating the anniversary of Emancipation) and later as Dr. Ellington, government chemist; Ronald ('Billy') Glegg, inside forward and batsman and uncle of attorney Sonia Jones, agricultural scholar, and as Dr. Glegg, long-time member of staff and later of the Board of Directors of Eastman Kodak; and Douglas Hall, all-rounder: wicket-keeper, footballer, rifle shot, track athlete, and Professor of History at the University of the West Indies. Douglas served in the British army during the war and was among those who slogged their way through the mud, moving from the toe to the midriff of Italy as the Allies conquered Caserta and Cassino in that critical campaign.

And there was Victor Sutherland, my colleague along with Pat W.C. Burke, in form 6A preparing for Higher Schools Certificate examination; Victor, cricket vice-captain, also no doubt contemplating the horses and medical studies at Aberdeen. Pat, who shared the opening slots with Jimmy Farquharson, could be heard from his home at Liguanea, where Sangster's Bookstore was later located, hammering the pitch with his bat as he awaited the bowler, and almost ten years later he would repeat these exercises, opening the batting for the London School of Economics and London University (both also under my captaincy). Schooled partly in England before returning home to JC. — his father, famous R.M. Sam Constantine Burke and a distinguished grandfather, also Samuel Constantine, acting attorney general and ex-officio member of the old 1885 Legislative Council — he spent most of his early working years in the colonial secretariat, *en route* to promotion as permanent secretary in education and health, respectively.

Jimmy Farquharson (Miss Maud Farquharson's nephew) would be a future Jamaica tennis champion, his professional career as aircraft pilot tragically abbreviated by polio, while dapper Donald Fonseca, a member of the 1938 Sunlight squad and my successor as Manning team goalkeeper, was destined to die in World War II. Seymour James (uncle-in-law of Douglas Orane Jr.), brilliant football wing half, future Jamaica star, and cricketer and track man, would move to Addis Ababa to tend the Economic Commission for Africa (E.C.A.) library and later, practise his professional expertise on promotion as head of the UN library. Undoubtedly the most accomplished member of the 1938 Sunlight team even then at the tender age of 15 was F. Jimmy Cameron. Off-spinner and all-rounder, he would become a Jamaica and West Indies player and tour India with the West Indies and graduate as a civil engineer — constructor of the George Headley stand at Sabina Park.

In 1937 JC had lost to Wolmer's in a tie match. The latter was a much superior side which included Lloyd Kelly, among the best bowlers in the history of the competition, L.V. Dujon, outstanding opener and Jeffrey's father, and a 15 year old Allan Rae. (Rae had been a member of the team from the age of 13!) In between the formal, conventional cricket we had learnt the art of playing French cricket, and I spent countless hours plotting and placing the field on paper in preparation for assuming the responsibilities of captaincy in the following year. JC.'s turn then came when, motivated by our coach, G.C. Foster (also athletics coach), we won in 1938 after a ten year drought, without losing a game.

I recall well the ensuing euphoria on that June afternoon when, having beaten St. George's at Hope, we were assured of winning the Cup. Hoping to take advantage of headmaster Reginald ('Reg') Murray's participation in the celebrations, I asked him to allow boarder-members of the team to go to Pat Burke's house at Liguanea to listen to the live broadcast of the return Joe Louis vs Max Schmeling heavyweight bout scheduled for that evening. Two interesting features deserve comment: the absence of a radio in the school, and the head's reluctance to entrust that sort of responsibility to me not only as captain, but also headboy. Eventually, after persistent efforts to persuade him, he relented; we rushed to Liguanea, only to find that the fight had already ended, with Louis demolishing the German in a brutal revenge bout, within the first round! This would have been my first opportunity to listen to a live broadcast of a sporting event.

Incidentally in their first fight in 1936 Louis could not counter his opponent's right cross, was repeatedly hit, and eventually knocked out. Schmeling's victory provided fine fodder for Hitler's Nazi concept of the 'master race'; but his overweening satisfaction was jolted a fortnight later by the gold medals won by Jesse Owens and other black U.S. athletes at the Berlin Olympics. Viewing the film of the fight later at the Palace 'theatre', one local fan could not take any longer the punishment being meted out to Louis who, before the emergence of Muhammad Ali, was for Jamaican fans their favourite boxer on the international scene. Leaving the cinema before the end, disappointed, he shouted defiantly: 'Cho! Wait till Joe catch 'im a' Tivoli'. (A cinema in Kingston's poorer west end). Joe did so of course, in 1938, but at New York's Polo Grounds.

In the same year, we were fortunate that Jimmy Cameron's elder brother, John, an old boy of Taunton School, at Somerset in England, arranged a Jamaican tour by the school's cricket team, which included a Jamaican, fast bowler R.A. Robison. Accompanied by their Headmaster, Mr Crichton-Miller, they played against the Sunlight champions JC, the runners-up Wolmer's, and an All-Schools XI of which I was vice-captain. John Cameron would represent the West Indies against England in the following year in a tour which ended prematurely on the outbreak of war on September 3, 1939.

Memories of Manning football seasons bring to mind, too, the anticipatory butterflies in the belly during the hours preceding matches especially against St. George's away at Winchester Park; and of singing at the usual morning chapel service in St. Dunstan's Chapel, the hymn specially selected for those days, *'Fight the good fight with all thy might'*. In 1937 it seemed that the *Gleaner's* football reporter 'Effat' was much prejudiced in my favour: note for instance, the following extract from his comments on the game vs St. George's, the eventual champions, at Winchester Park:

> The most outstanding, and indeed attractive feature of the game was the performance of Mills, JC skipper-goalie. This was seen to even greater advantage during the second half, when St. George's had the run of play entirely to themselves.

'Effat's' praises were even more exaggeratedly expressed in his Review of the 1937 season:

> In Mills, this school's (JC) team had a fine leader — one who possesses all the fine qualities of a first class school skipper, and in addition to this, as a goal-keeper was *par excellence*.

1937 was also a significant year for a number of other more important reasons. At the Championship Sports Arthur Wint confirmed the potential shown earlier in his Class 2 years by becoming Class I champion, foreshadowing his future olympic stardom; K.C. won the Championship for the first of its many victories; and it was the year in which the event throwing of the cricket ball was staged for the last time.

During my tenure at school in the 1930s, two other important features characterized the approach to sport. One was the participation of staff members in mixed teams for certain competitions. Playing alongside us, but under our captaincy, either in the Minor Cup (cricket) or Junior Cup (football) or in both competitions, were one of my two heads, Reg. Murray, second and third masters J.C. ('Poogy') Sleggs and Hugo ('H.C.') Chambers, the latter's brother S.B., James Waterhouse, K. ('Soapy') Pringle and the more junior Cedric Lindo, later UWI's Public Relations Officer and Johnny P. Gyles, later Minister of Agriculture. Their involvement and the example they set served to inspire and motivate us.

The other feature was the opportunities provided for all students to take part in games at some level, if even only in inter-house matches. This is a pole apart from the present cult of concentration on the best and confining participation to a few. Presumably this change reflects partly the problem of coping with the phenomenal ten-fold burgeoning in the student population. Associated with this feature, some schools have engaged in poaching student-sportsmen from other schools.

These were the days of dominant headmasters: Rev. Price of Calabar, Rev. ('Priest') Gibson of K.C., Hon. A.E. ('Wagga') Harrison of Munro, Baker of Cornwall, William Cowper of JC. They all believed fervently in education in the widest sense; encompassing and emphasizing not only intellectual and cultural pursuits, but also sport. It was an age when great emphasis was placed on traditional values which were instilled in young girls and boys in elementary, preparatory and secondary schooling. Among these values, integrity, sportsmanship, fair play, discipline, courtesy and good manners were accorded high priority. We were expected to be gentlemen, not crude roughnecks; but it was most important to us not to seem to be sissies.

My first headmaster at JC was the forbidding grey-bearded classical scholar William Cowper, an Englishman — otherwise affectionately or not so affectionately dubbed 'Pross'. He was assiduous in attempts to inculcate in us the importance of assimilating the ethic that while we should strive with every effort, every fibre, every nerve, to win, we should eschew the temptation to do so at all costs and without constraints. In other words, that the end does not justify the means; and further, that while it is difficult to be a good loser, an even more difficult test of character centres on being a good and generous winner. Today we live in an era in which many of the values which Pross endeavoured to instil have become *passé*, a cause for denigration of those whose behaviour reflects them.

Two incidents illustrate Pross Cowper's attitude. One was the concern he expressed when, in a Manning match at Hope, he observed that the St. George's goalkeeper seemed to be unwell. The head summoned the school's resident nurse at once and asked her to administer appropriate medication to the player. The other incident occurred when JC beat another school (which shall remain nameless) 12-0 and the head responded by 'gating' members of the Manning team, preventing them from leaving the premises for a specified period, for what he considered an unsportsmanlike act! In retrospect, this appears to have been an extreme reaction.

Another expression of his views was his strong disapproval of vociferous, chauvinistic school cheers at Championship sports and Manning matches. A perennial custom practised not only at the games themselves, but also *en route* to and from, was the loud shouting and singing, not always in chorus, of the school cheer partly based on its Latin motto:

Fervet opus in campis
When we shoot, we never miss
When we cheer, we cheer like this:
Hash and roast beef, mince and pie,
N-O-M-E-R-C-Y.

Many a day on our way to Championships (and on the return journey, depending on the results) we would sing loudly, clinging to the sides of overcrowded tram-cars as they swayed from side to side like rhumba dancers, and lurched along Hope and South Camp Roads. On one occasion, Horsy Edwards was fortunate to survive, suffering only burns, when he held on to a live area on the roof of a tram while other boys also suffered shocks in their efforts to release him. The head disapproved particularly of cheers or cries which expressed disparagement of other schools, such as:

Rattle up a tin pan, shimmy up a tree,
(name of school and repeated once) tiddle diddle dee.

Instead of such cheers, Pross encouraged and made unsuccessful efforts to persuade us to utter in modest and modulated tones, the more sedate 'School! School!' He must have been appalled when, after Laurence Lindo beat the favourite, Calabar's Herman McMorris, in the 100 yards in 1929, JC fans composed and sang a ditty in celebration of the victory:

Lindo bought a bundle of grass
And stuck it up McMorris'.....

During the 1930s JC still displayed the characteristics of its parental prototype: a hangover from the traditions and customs of the mid-Victorian public school. This pattern was reflected in initiation ceremonies, often very cruel, in ragging and bullying, corporal punishment and an emphasis on a hierarchical structure of headmaster first, then second master, and other more junior masters; followed by headboy, monitors (prefects) senior, and junior or small boys. At an alumni function held not long ago, in responding to a speech made by former Prime Minister Michael Manley, I observed that I would have known him at school only so far as the headboy would have known a small boy; but added that generally, the gap would have narrowed after leaving school and in his case has extended in the opposite direction!

Initiation rites took various forms which included bumping, involving being held stretched out, parallel to and high above the ground, face upwards, by two or more boys and repeatedly dropped backwards; candle-greasing, whereby a lighted candle is allowed to drip on to the victim's head as he slept, leaving his hair totally tangled; toeing, an exercise in which one of the sleeping victim's great toes is tied by a scout knot at the end of a long piece of cord, the other end reaching the perpetrator's hands via the dormitory bannisters. In this last example, the hapless victim is pulled up to the ceiling and is suddenly released when he cries out in pain. The two nocturnal practices were also normally conducted as a ritual on end of term eve.

Those who suffered from ragging were not restricted to the students: some masters also endured the experience; for a few it was persistent. At times a master would enter a classroom to teach a form and encounter a loud banging and rattling of desks; worse, on lifting the lid of his own desk, he might be confronted with a most unpleasant smell, arising from a 'stink bomb' placed there by a boy or boys — the offensive matter consisting of carbon bisulphide. Now and then a booby trap would be set for a master in charge of a dormitory: perhaps a chamber pot filled with urine, placed precariously on the top of the door. The dormitory residents would then create a noise, attracting the attention of the master who, rushing from his room and pushing the door, would suffer the effects of the resulting shower. The more a master reacted to ragging, the more he was ragged — in an escalating process. If he was bent on punishing offenders, the alternatives were limited: an 'imposition' — the offender being required to sit in a room and write a prescribed sentence or 'lines', say, 100 times — or, for more serious crimes, referral to the head for a caning.

Ragging was taken to extremes of savagery on one occasion when the insides of an unpopular master's pajamas were rubbed comprehensively with 'cow-itch' (like nettles). On returning to his room and going to bed that night, he was reduced to a bloody condition from scratching. The boys (some involved in the escapade, others not) considered that confirmation of the justification of the act was provided by the report which appeared in the *Gleaner* not long after, datelined Cape Town, reporting that the same master (who had emigrated) was 'tarred and feathered' by students, and driven through the streets of that city!

For me, memories remain of those first 18 months of life under Pross Cowper, undying survivals of a gloomy ambience of dark, depressing days intensified by the rainy winter mornings when, in response to the six o'clock bell, we boarders were compelled to surface and rush from the comfort of warm covers in our dormitories to the cold showers downstairs. Associated with this was the atmosphere of fear, especially for the small boy, in the face of such rites and of bullying. We were seated in ascending order by form in a long classroom for evening 'prep', that is, home-work and preparation for next day's classes. For a 'small boy' to dare even to look behind at senior boys was a punishable offence which could provoke the dreaded directive: '6.02 tomorrow morning, and bring your own bricks'. This meant reporting, brick in hand, next morning to the bathroom where the dispenser of punishment would scrub the offender, using a large rough bath-cleaning brush covered with brick dust. Often the victim bled.

In his brief autobiographical notes, Rt. Excellent Norman Manley has written of the rampancy of bullying in his time at the school, during the early years of this century. The condition certainly continued into the thirties. I understand it ended in the 1950s after an end-of-term injury to a boy's eye. But in my day an incident occurred in which headmaster Pross, who prided himself on being a dispenser of justice, turned an allegation of bullying on its head. The accused was a boy from Vere, later a long-time civil servant in the customs department; the plaintiff (son of a St. Ann property owner) would become a medical doctor and serve as a coroner in England — a rare achievement for a Jamaican. On a report from his son, the plaintiff's father drove from St. Ann to see the head, who forthwith summoned the two boys to his study. Putting each boy in turn on a balance scale which he kept outside his study, he drew the father's attention to the fact that their weights were almost identical. 'And you expect me to believe that this boy bullied your son?' Without receiving any satisfaction, yet without protest, the father got into his car for the long return journey home.

In his autobiography *Boy*, Roald Dahl, the Norwegian-English novelist, famous also for his children's stories, has recounted the story of his unhappy boyhood, focusing on schooldays and beatings — the latter dubbed 'the English vice'. He devotes a chapter to the savage corporal punishment meted out by his headmaster at Repton, who was subsequently promoted from Bishop of Chester to Bishop of London, and ultimately, Archbishop of Canterbury — evidently Lord Fisher of Lambeth. Consistent with the contemporaneous context was the custom at JC of intense corporal punishment, administered by Pross since only the head could cane. His peremptory 'bend over there, lift up your coat-tail' is unforgettable. Each stroke of the cane fell with unerring accuracy in the same groove.

A classical scholar, graduate of Cambridge, he attempted to teach throughout the school, but had difficulty in imparting Latin to the lower forms. Those who could not cope, often through nervousness occasioned by fear, could accurately schedule in their timetable a caning in Latin class, and prepare accordingly. Newspapers were the popular form of padding. A contemporary of mine, a brilliant student in most other subjects, later won the Jamaica Scholarship and became an internationally renowned scholar, at one time also on the UWI staff. On one occasion he was caned on the platform in front of the entire class, the head's anger rising to boiling point when, after inserting his finger in the boy's collar from the back, while drumming in each individual Latin word and phrase, the unfortunate student, twisting and writhing, ended up facing him. The justification for the punishment was expressed thus: 'You nearly broke my finger and almost asphyxiated yourself!' Another victim developed a stammer from Latin class encounters or the anticipation of them, a condition which continued throughout his life.

Pross's ideas of justice were illustrated too when dealing with a case of a boy who was misbehaving in class, and who was sent to him, accompanied by the form head boy, the latter carrying a note from the teacher. Taking the note and putting it on a table without reading it, he directed the head boy: 'Bend over there'. The latter protested vigorously: 'It's not me, sir, but this boy; please read the note'. Ignoring the response and becoming angry, convinced that the boy was defying him, the head administered the caning. Then, he asked, 'Now, what is it you were trying to tell me?' In tears, the boy repeated what he had said earlier. Thereupon, Pross caned the real offender and, turning once more to the head boy: 'Well, you must have done many things for which you should have been caned, but were not'.

For him the urge to flog appeared to be compulsive. For instance, one Saturday morning, passing along the corridor outside a classroom on the way to his study, he observed through the window, a boy bending over a desk talking to another. Note that this was during a free period: no class, nor 'prep', was in progress. Evidently unable to resist the temptation, he called to the bending boy: 'You, Master X, just remain in that position until I return from my study'. And, returning cane in hand, he proceeded to cane the boy. Incidentally, often wearing 'sneakers', Pross moved almost silently and thus surprised many a boy.

But among the worst features of this predilection were indications of what appeared to be racial prejudice. While most boys were mercilessly beaten, others, a select group, mainly white or light-skinned, were privileged in the type of punishment they received. The head kept a light piece of board in his study, using it to pat such boys on the back, with the admonition: 'Naughty boy, you should not do this again'. One sensed too throughout the school that being a scholarship boy represented a lower form of life; even worse, if you were also a country boy. Although this thought did not occur to me at the time, in retrospect, I have at times wondered whether the head's behaviour was not symptomatic of some underlying condition.

I have emphasized the atmosphere of gloom and depression which pervaded the school during that early period under Pross Cowper. To complete the set, picture a scene representing groups of boarders, boys bedecked in obligatory black Sunday suits, confined within imposing iron gates and perimeter fence watching the tram-cars and motor vehicle traffic (then sparse) passing on their way to and from Papine. On one such occasion, but on a weekday, I witnessed the car accident which partially crippled music teacher Miss Elsie Burrough. I still remember the experience of extreme nervousness, bordering on fright, when appearing in the witness box to give evidence in the case in which Warner Bolton appeared for the plaintiff. Many years later I was told that she received a record high of damages awarded for such a case.

For a fortunate few, there was also the privilege of inclusion in a group for a Sunday afternoon walk to Hope Gardens close by, on a collective *Absit* under escort by a monitor. At the time, Latin represented a normal mode of expression. Thus, sets of brothers, for example the Gore quintet, were designated major, minor, tertius, quartus and quintus; there was the rare threesome — Philip, Lloyd and Ralston Feanny, the Matalons and Gerald, Vivian and Kenny Grant (Louis' brothers) but several sets of majors and minors including Eric & Huntley DaCosta, Jeffrey & Leslie Wilson, John & Pat Clerk, Maurice & Lloyd Facey, W.H. ('Billy') & Michael Escoffery, Lennox & Owen Munroe, Harry & 'Tubbin' Fox, Dennis & Jimmy Hall, Neville & Ronald Glegg, Clifford & Franz Brandt, Leslie and Delroy Marsh, Ossie & George Murray, Winston & A.H. ('Bunny') Stuart, Donald & Farren Soutar, Max & Michael Smith, Ivan & Ken Arscott, Richard & Edward Ashenheim, the Kyle twins, and the two Mills brothers, not four. On the visits to Hope Gardens, now sadly deteriorated, the opportunity was customarily seized to raid pineapples and luscious Bombay mangoes from the fruit area of the Gardens while a blind eye was turned by the monitors.

Our physical preparation for sport was supplemented by the perennial practice of rising very early, sometimes not long after midnight, pillow case in hand, to raid mangoes from the vast Bombay estate which extended from the Hope Road opposite to the JC front fence, across to the Mona Road. Sprint and high jump records were unofficially broken when, chased by estate rangers, boys were forced to escape by scaling the fences and running the return journey to their dormitories. Ironically, this long-standing tradition was discontinued in the mid-1950s when a team of old boys, the Matalons, created the first extensive middle class housing scheme, Mona Heights, from the Bombay property. *Sic transit gloria!*

Mentioning the Matalons reminds me that during my schooldays, I was entirely unaware that there was a distinction between Jews and Arabs. In my time, apart from the Matalons, my contemporaries included the younger Ashenheims, attorneys-at-law: Richard, track and field statistician supreme, and Edward, Athletics XI captain, Roy Levy, 1938 Rhodes Scholar, more than one Henriques, and Raymond Alberga, later sprint champion for Wolmers, the Feanny's and Mahfoods.

During the first 18 months of my sojourn at JC, apart from the head as latin teacher, we sat at the feet of a mixed group — the most outstanding being second master and science teacher J.C. Sleggs (the Head's son-in-law and future head of Manchester School), Hugo ('H.C.') Chambers who taught mathematics, a rare local, and James Waterhouse who instructed us in french. While Pross was feared, H.C. was the master whom we most respected. In addition to french, Waterhouse also assisted in teaching english grammar and devoted some attention to imparting to us the niceties of 'figures of speech', such as the alliteration, hyperbole and metaphor, while illustrating them by examples of each. The one which sticks in my mind was his graphic representation of the 'innuendo': the story of an art exhibition, with the crowds of viewers 'oohing and aahing' over a particular painting. A man then turns up, stretching to see above the crowd from behind and after viewing the work for a few minutes, exclaims: 'What a beautiful frame!'

But there were other masters whose efforts at teaching left much to be desired. Prominent among these was a history teacher, who taught entirely via a chronology of events, for example Waterloo and Trafalgar and a succession of kings and queens; and whose frequent tests consisted of filling in a word or a date to complete a sentence from the text which you were expected to commit totally to memory.

Following the Easter holidays of 1933, a red letter day occurred in our lives and particularly for those of us who were boarders. A new headmaster, Reg Murray, old boy and Rhodes Scholar, entered our lives, leaving Wolmer's to succeed Pross Cowper. I vividly recall the strong impression made on me at the time of a suffusion of light dispelling the long period of gloom, his arrival appearing to herald the advent of emancipation.

Arriving at the same time, along with a few boys who had emigrated from Wolmer's to rejoin the new head, was Miss Anna Hollar. She would have an impact on me as my new latin teacher. She was the sister of well-known poet Constance Hollar and instilled a love for latin as language and discipline and of the associated Roman history and literature. So we enjoyed our immersion in the exploits of Hannibal and Hamilcar, in the poetry of Vergil (especially the Aeneid), Horace and Ovid, and the prose of Cicero and Caesar. In fact, having obtained a distinction in latin at Senior Cambridge exams, I took this subject with chemistry and maths for the Higher School Certificate (HSC).

The abandonment of the study of latin in schools and university is in my opinion, a grave mistake: the rigorous discipline provided by the effort to master latin grammar contributes to the making of an educated mind, and would I suggest facilitate improvement in the current deplorable standard of english.

During my middle years at school we were fortunate in having two inspiring history teachers, first H.P. ('Jiggy') Jacobs, followed by E.H.J. King. In addition, Henry Fowler, a recent graduate, had been promoted to the staff to teach us British empire history while waiting to take up his Rhodes Scholarship. Jiggy who had been so nicknamed because of his peculiar jigging gait, was a prime target for ragging, promoted partly by his intense reaction to the boys' activities. But, he provided perceptive insights into European history, often with witty remarks and trigger-sharp responses to efforts made to unsettle him, generally emerging victorious in a battle of wit. He introduced his classes to the complexities of the Balkan problem, emphasizing in unforgettable nasal tones the tribulations of Bosnia and Herzegovina almost 60 years before the current crisis and civil war in Yugoslavia, brought so dramatically before us by advanced media technology. Abiding memories of Jiggy's wit are his almost reflex response to a question in class, 'Please sir, what instrument did Spain play in the Concert of Europe?' Jiggy: 'Spain? Spain played second fiddle!' And when, while ladling and serving soup from the head of a table during lunch, a fly dive-bombed into the tureen, he continued to serve, carefully avoiding the intruder. When the turn of the last boy in the line came, Jiggy enquired: 'What will you have, soup with, or without fly?' The boy, in high dudgeon, replied: 'Soup without fly of course, Sir!' Jiggy: 'Well, I am afraid there's none'. Sadly for JC, H.P. left after a brief spell to become editor of the new P.N.P. paper, *Public Opinion*, and later, General Secretary of the

Jamaica Imperial Association; his wit continued to flourish in *Gleaner* subsidiary leaders and under the nom de plume Hobb Nailes, in the *Jamaica Times*. In one of the latter columns he suggested that Headquarters House on Duke Street, the former venue of parliament, would more appropriately be named Hindquarters House as the seat of government.

A master who also made a significant impact was english teacher K.R. ('Soapy') Pringle. He was a quiet, unassuming, not too articulate man, but he seems to have been the principal stimulus to the blossoming of potential poets and prose writers who emerged between the latter part of the 1930s and the early 1940s all contemporaries, either formmates or in forms not far below, and who continued to write and publish long after graduating. They included M.G. Smith, H. ('Dossie') Carberry, Neville Dawes, John Hearne, Mickey Hendricks, Ken Ingram and Basil McFarlane. No other school can boast such a contemporary collection, nor can JC at any other period. This particular set of boys was no doubt also stimulated by the coincidence of the circumstances and events of the time: the social-political upsurge of 1938 which seemingly sparked the first real stirrings of nationalist consciousness and a nascent artistic, literary and intellectual ferment, inspired by Edna and Norman Manley and expressed in the early works of George and Ralph Campbell, Henry Daley, Albert Huie, Roger Mais, Vivian Virtue, and Philip Sherlock.

In a somewhat lesser way, I too was influenced by Soapy Pringle. I owe to him a deep and wide interest in English literature, which he stimulated: until his arrival (1934/35) the Senior Cambridge syllabus consisted exclusively of a few 'set' (prescribed) texts. An alternative syllabus, General English Literature was introduced and we opted for this; and so, we read very widely: poetry Shakespeare of Milton, Blake, Coleridge, Keats, Shelley, Wordsworth, and the novels of Dickens. But leading the assembly of outstanding teachers from 1933 with the arrival of new headmaster, R.M. Murray was the head himself, simplifying the complexities of dynamics, mechanics, and hydro-statics for us as we were promoted to the 5th and 6th forms. His hearing was impaired, a consequence of shelling in World War I trenchbattles, and his characteristic teaching style included placing the right forefinger on his lips when emphasizing a point, leaving a chalk-mark running vertically down both lips. A man of few words, whether in speech or on paper, Reg spoke and wrote in almost staccato terms like Jingle of Dickens' Pickwick Papers. He possessed closely concealed sensibilities which surfaced occasionally, such as the time when, entering the assembly hall, he found my brother Don playing the piano. Forefinger on lips, he requested: 'Play "Capri" ('The Isle of Capri') for me'. A poet, nature lover and mountaineer with considerable knowledge of the Blue Mountains and their environs, he settled after retirement in the small village of Millbank in Portland. No greater tribute can be paid to him than that bestowed by N.W. Manley, crediting this brilliant mathematics teacher as the source of the inspiration which changed his life.

On the domestic staff, I had two relatives: my only aunt, Mrs. Rhoda Spence (my father's sister), who was the resident nurse, and a cousin, also on his side, Miss Lannaman. Two matrons served during my tenure, Mrs. Bond and Miss Noad and we had most attentive and long-serving maids (now referred to by the more dignified title 'helpers') in the persons of Iris, Beryl and Agatha. Many years later, JC old boys on the U.W.I. staff would be fortunate in meeting the first two of these again, at the Senior Common Room bar. On the grounds and as general handyman, was McGowan. Sixty years later, I can still hear Pross calling out his name in those stentorian, nasal tones. Rounding off the scene, though not on the staff, but a fixture nevertheless, was Campbell, peddling peanuts, his presence anticipated by us, and proclaimed by his whistling cart.

In the Senior Cambridge examinations I had tied for first place (boys) in the island with Leo Jones of Wolmer's who later, became head of the science unit, a colleague at UWI. Coincidentally, as I discovered more than 40 years later from my mother's scrap-book of Gleaner clippings, my wife to-be, Winnifred Moss, then at St. Andrew High School for girls, placed third among the girls in the same year.

Among my most memorable recollections of life as a boarder at JC are of afternoons of bun and lemonade and of the ritual of meal times. We would line up for the dining room, entering in ascending order, form by form. After the boys were seated on their benches and the masters had moved to the head table on the platform or to head tables crowded with boys, the head would appear. Most of my fellow students quickly learnt the technique of eating quickly in a highly competitive situation; the alternative was to go hungry. I never learnt. It seemed to me that only a few minutes would elapse between the head's introductory grace and his final words when we were obliged to get up and troop out of the dining room; this time in the reverse, descending order.

In between, I had barely begun my meal, and I survived those school years only through the good fortune of Aunt Rhoda's presence. So, often I dropped in at her cottage to supplement my meal. Even today, I am teased at times about my excessively slow eating, a habit which has persisted: shades of the 'Mills of God?'

The turbulence which had erupted in the society in May-June 1938, particularly at Frome and on the Kingston waterfront, were almost alien events to many of us at Jamaica College. We were not aware that such events had been taking place in other West Indian islands since 1935. Not only were we preoccupied with Sunlight Cup cricket and preparations for Higher School Certificate examinations, but for those of us who were boarders, this condition was accentuated by isolation and insulation from the significant and vital events taking place within a few miles of Hope. And communications media were non-existent at the School: the small local radio station ZQI would not be established for another two years, and we boys did not see the *Gleaner*.

I do not recall that we were sufficiently conscious of the deplorable social and economic conditions in which so many fellow Jamaicans subsisted, though some of us lived in poor rural communities and had spent years at elementary school. Moreover, Papine and August Town were almost within a stone's throw of JC and for years, there were bare-footed boys — the so-called 'toes' — from these communities and Matilda's Corner, who stood behind the football goals, kicking back the ball on to the field as it went into touch. The one who has stood out in my memory from my own goalkeeping days was dubbed 'Scuffler'; and for many years after leaving school, I would see him, sometimes at UWI where his wife Imogene was employed for a long period, coincidentally in the faculty of social sciences. Two of their sons also worked at the University of the West Indies, one who at the time of writing still does, at the campus bookshop, the other at Irvine Hall. He died tragically in 1991. Their most famous son is Norman Washington Jackson, popularly known as 'Tiger', the dance hall music man ('D.J.') and composer of *Wanga Gut* and *When*.

Efforts were also made by Headmaster Murray to develop in us a social consciousness and a social conscience. For instance, he inspired and initiated for under-16 boys, cricket matches in which we were hosts to two elementary schools, one of them Half-Way-Tree, then under Mr Wesley and Mrs Dalton James. This was an unprecedented step for an elite school of 55 years ago. Nevertheless, I certainly left school very much an innocent that end of July 1938.

As I reflect on the harsh and severe conditions in which we lived at JC, especially in the years under Pross Cowper, it occurs to me that perhaps such experiences contributed towards forging a toughness of character which was partly responsible for producing so high a proportion of outstanding leaders of the country during the 1950s and 1960s. A partial list of these would include in earlier years: Norman Manley, the Ashenheims, Rudolph Burke, Ernest Johnston, G.G.R. and H.R. Sharp, Harry Dayes, Douglas Fletcher, the Marleys, Carlton Alexander, all of the private sector and some as legislators; public officials in the Morales brothers, Robert Lightbourne, Laurence Lindo, Earl Maynier, Allan Abrahams, Jeffrey Wilson, Louis Grant, Hugh Miller, Morris Burke, Winston Stuart. And not long after: Clem Tavares and the Matalons; and in the civil service, the Clerk brothers, O.H. Goldson, Percy Beckwith, Irving Johnson, Pat Burke, Neville Glegg, Ossie Murray, Alton Ellington, Horace Barber, Dossie Carberry, and Don Mills.

Did these men rise to become significant leaders, their character shaped by the tough circumstances in which they were nurtured? Or did they emerge in spite of this conditioning? But, we should note that JC continued to produce such leaders into the 1980s in a variety of areas.

Graduates since the 1960s would not have experienced the harsh conditions which existed during the first 50 years of the School's history and included my tenure there. Within the past three decades, the school has not repeated its academic successes of earlier years, nor have its graduates assumed as dominant a position in the society as before. I would suggest that a major part of the earlier successes is attributable to the elitist nature of education at the time, providing for a minuscule percentage of the secondary school age population. The democratization of education has altered the situation significantly.

As I prepared to leave JC, Mr Murray, sitting on a tree stump by the new swimming pool invited me to return to teach. I was sorely tempted by a seemingly irresistible urge to return to this place where I had enjoyed considerably, the past five years. However, my uncle J.J. Mills, speaking from a lifelong experience of teaching, strongly advised me to enter the civil service. And so, I parted with regret, from the imposing buildings and portals, from the twin ficus trees, the giant guango and the 'butts', at nights, illuminated by fireflies going on and off in unison as though being drilled by a fellow sergeant. Alas, the 'butts' are no more, overtaken by 'development';

while the ficus, their roots stifled by concrete have died but fortunately have left offspring now struggling for survival.

The old guango tree, long-serving landmark at the main gate, a victim of Hurricane Gilbert has also been resurrected but in a new form. Its trunk has been cut and shaped into plaques for presentation to distinguished alumni in memory of one of JC's most distinguished old boys, the late Carlton Alexander. In 1990 Douglas Fletcher and Louis Grant were the first recipients. The following year broadcaster Dennis Hall and I were the proud honourees. Retired Prime Minister Michael Manley received it in 1992, in the following year the Honourable R.C. Lightbourne together with the 'Flying Five' forwards of 1933 and 1934; and in 1994, the Honourable Aaron Matalon and Dr H.D. Chambers, the oldest surviving alumnus.

4

IN THE SERVICE OF THE CROWN

Leaving the cocoon of boarding school I ventured into the world of work on the day after Emancipation Day in 1938. This day marked the centenary of the abolition of slavery in the British colonies; a highly, significant historical landmark which, strangely, is no longer celebrated in Jamaica. I have found that some West Indians display a penchant for attributing most of the present problems and ills of their societies to the long experience of slavery and colonialism despite the fact that emancipation occurred more than a century and a half ago and more than three decades have elapsed since some of these states became independent. On the other hand, some strongly condemn such attitudes as reflecting an obsessive preoccupation with the past, and argue the need to forget these evils and concentrate on improving the present and the future. There is merit in both points of view. Historians remind us that in order to understand the conditions of the present and the needs of the future, it is essential to understand the past.

The validity of this advice is strengthened in the case of the Commonwealth Caribbean because the heritage of slavery and of colonial subordination appears to have left deep social and psychological imprints which persist in current attitudes and behaviour patterns. Centuries of slavery, the plantation system and of colonial rule contributed significantly to the generation and perpetuation of ideas which emphasized the dominant and the dominated. This conviction was bolstered by the injunction anointed by the church, 'You must be content with the position in which it has pleased God to place you.' It seems that the attitudes and systems which gave expression to these ideas have persisted beyond emancipation and into the age of independence.

Any realistic recollections of Jamaica during the closing years of the 1930s and the early 1940s must focus on the riots and civil disturbances of 1938 and their aftermath. They represented a watershed in West Indian history and set the stage for fundamental social, economic, cultural, political, constitutional and administrative changes.

As boarders at Jamaica College (JC) we were scarcely conscious of the events at Frome and the Kingston waterfront, and of the turbulence and trauma which were tearing the society apart. Several years would elapse before we would become aware that Alexander ('Busta') Bustamante had been an inveterate letter writer to the *Gleaner* during 1935 and 1936 on the economic conditions experienced by workers and the problem of unemployment. Strangely, I do recall that we knew of governor, Sir Edward Denham's death that summer of 1938. The individual, personal tragedy might have made a greater impact on the mind. We knew of Norman Manley because for us he was a hero. His name conjured up a reputation redolent of legendary deeds and feats performed at J.C. more than a quarter of a century before. This reputation was enhanced by reports of his considerable skills of advocacy, illustrated by tales of his triumphs in securing acquittals in murder trials against seemingly overwhelming odds. The Alexander and Southby cases, left indelible impressions on many and were still spoken of with wonder.

Those of us who left school in late July of 1938 did not remain ignorant for long of the troubles afflicting the society. We read in the *Gleaner* and *Jamaica Standard* of the exploits of Bustamante and later, the formation of the Bustamante Industrial Trade Union (BITU), of St. William Grant and 'Father' Coombs; and of Busta's early association with Manley, primarily as lawyer for Busta and the protesting workers. We read also of the creation that same year of the People's National Party (PNP) with British Labour Party's Sir Stafford Cripps, a future minister, on the platform when it was launched at the Ward theatre. These two giants who would later be designated national heroes and who bestrode centre stage at the time, were destined to dominate political life for the next three decades. The middle and upper classes were divided about Manley: for many, his socialist ideas, though democratic, were hated and appeared threatening. Others, especially those in their teens and twenties, were impressed and attracted by his reputation as an advocate.

Busta created greater impact with his tall, rangy physique, unruly shock of hair, flamboyant style and picturesque speech. His charismatic attraction and courage displayed in confrontation with police weapons galvanized the workers into a condition of enduring loyalty, summed up in the song *We will follow Bustamante till we die*.

Ambivalent attitudes were also displayed towards Busta. Even some who were fascinated by his personality, contemptuously dismissed him as an uneducated rabble rouser. When some of these people eventually met him, they were captivated by his charm and generosity, and surprised at his innate intelligence. For me, among his most impressive and enduring traits was his recollection of those he had met. In later years, whenever I was in his presence he would ask about my mother whom he had met in Chapelton years before.

Those who were fortunate to get to know Manley would realise and recognize that his external appearance of arrogance and aloofness belied his real attitude and character. When later I worked with both as chief ministers and as premiers, I learnt to respect their differing styles of leadership and decision-making.

During the 1930s, for entry to the civil service an applicant was required to have passed the Cambridge School Certificate examination with a G ('Good') or C ('Credit') in english and maths and to hold a certificate of the London University matriculation examination. The applicant was also required to submit a recommendation from a member of the privy council, the custos of his parish of residence, a member of the legislative council, or the head of a civil service department, certifying him as a fit and proper person for admission to the service. In addition to these there was a competitive examination, arranged once each year, comprising precís writing, composition, dictation, handwriting, arithmetic and bookkeeping, general knowledge of Jamaica and correction of errors in expression.

The successful candidates were interviewed by a public service selection committee consisting of the colonial secretary and two members appointed by the governor and, if considered suitable, their names would be placed on a list of selected candidates, awaiting appointment when vacancies arose.

Incredibly, the rules precluded married women from being appointed to the service, unless, in the opinion of the governor, there are 'exceptional circumstances which justify such an appointment.' If a woman married while in the service, she was liable to be called upon to 'vacate her office without having any claim to pension, compassionate allowance or gratuity.' So much for equality of the sexes! These regulations were amended in 1942 to provide that where the governor exercises his discretion, he 'may appoint or retain a married woman as a female clerk.'

At that time women, even of single status, were certainly not seen in senior positions, unlike the present, where, ironically, the head of the civil service, the permanent secretary in the ministry of the public service and the chairman of the Public Service Commission are women. Moreover, also held by a woman, is the position of permanent secretary of the ministry of education, the largest ministry. As far as I can remember, the only woman who held a fairly senior post then was Miss Edith Clarke (the anthropologist and author of *My Mother who Fathered me* and *Gleaner* chairman Oliver Clarke's aunt) as secretary of the board of supervision and, later, assistant secretary in the colonial secretariat.

The profession of solicitor was closed to women, and they were precluded from articleship. These disabilities were abolished in 1944 by the enactment of the Sex Disqualification (Removal) Law 20 which stipulates in clear and unambiguous terms:

> A person shall not be disqualified by sex or marriage from the exercise of any public function, or from being appointed to or holding any civil or judicial officer post, or from carrying out any civil profession or vocation, or for admission to any incorporated society...

In 1948 Miss Daisy Chambers became the first woman to qualify as a solicitor. She had been performing clerical functions in N.N. ('Crab') Nethersole's law office and was subsequently accepted for articleship. The disqualification suffered by women in respect of a bar to admission to the legal profession was presumably derived from British custom, as was the case generally of most elements of the constitutional, political and legal systems in Jamaica and across the British Empire. In English case law, women were traditionally not eligible to enter the legal profession. When, early in this century an Oxford graduate was refused admission and lost the case which she took to the courts, undeterred, she succeeded in having the issue raised in parliament and legislation was subsequently enacted in 1919 effecting abolition of the bar. It should be noted that certain disqualifications relating to Jews and Roman Catholics in Jamaica were also removed by legislation in 1944.

A recommendation that I was a fit and proper person had been generously provided by Mr. Frederick Bond of the audit department. Having successfully surmounted the other hurdles, I was inducted into the service on probation as a temporary assistant/temporary clerk in the criminal division of the office of the clerk of the courts subject to the provision of a certificate of medical fitness, and, as was customary, the attainment of a typing speed of 30 words per minute within the first year of appointment. The salary amounted to the princely rate of £100 per annum or £1 18s 6p per week. To prepare for that test, I enlisted at the Durham College of Commerce, also undertaking a book-keeping course.

Having passed the test, I was given a permanent appointment about twelve weeks later. Through 22 years of life in the civil service, I was never required to use my typing skill, a source of satisfaction since I disliked the process. To my great surprise, the typewriter keyboard appears to have made an indelible impression, buried deep in the recesses of my mind. On looking at my computer's keyboard, the rubric 'QWERTYUIOP' returned immediately, without any conscious effort at recall.

My first job in the criminal division of the resident magistrate (R. M.) court at Sutton Street required me to write up indictments for the clerk of courts. It was a boring, clerical copying chore which I considered most unchallenging and inappropriate to exercise and test the mind and mettle of a Higher School Certificate secondary school graduate. In retrospect, I appreciate that the chore, calling as it did for considerable care and accuracy, provided disciplinary training in attention to detail which laid an important and valuable foundation.

The resident magistrate was J.E.D. Carberry who would later be knighted as chief justice, with Peter Gunter of Mandeville as clerk of courts and deputy clerk, William Swaby. After a start in the colonial secretariat, Willie would become the first director of public prosecutions after Independence, and ultimately an appeal court judge.

After a brief two month spell I moved to the parcels post office, then located on Barry Street, behind the main King Street post office headquarters. Veteran R.H. Fletcher, (father of Douglas, Attorney and former Ambassador to Washington) was about to retire as postmaster general to be succeeded by W.A. Campbell.

For a neophyte in the world of work this was not an inspiring ambience, assessing duty, accepting and delivering parcels at the counter. Some older colleagues, barely subsisting on their meagre salaries, hiding from debt collectors, made weekly efforts to eke out their incomes by gambling, greedily anticipating opportunities and occasions for overtime pay. The Christmas season, of course, presented the principal opportunity for this; a time memorable for the massive mountain of mail and of sometimes working beyond midnight.

Fortunately for me, there was an escape to playing cricket for Kensington Cricket Club. In addition, in the desert of the work situation, an oasis of literary light was provided in the apparently paradoxical person of Del Lumsden, a well-read, highly intelligent and interesting personality, who introduced me to Aldous Huxley and Somerset Maugham via *Point Counterpoint* and *Cakes and Ale,* respectively. I recall too one unique essay in spelling by the sender of a small package to an overseas destination: the declaration form read '1 1b *KARPHY*' — not even one letter correct! Among our clients appearing to collect their commercial imports at the counter were Mr. Harold Vaz, father of Douglas, a J.C. alumnus and George Townsend, the Lucas Cricket Club Senior Cup bowler, on behalf of Reginald Aitken Co.

The Moyne Commission was appointed by King George VI, through the Secretary of State for the Colonies, Malcolm MacDonald, on Aug. 5 1938. Its mandate was to investigate social, economic and political conditions in the British West Indian colonies. Members arrived in Kingston by boat, at the beginning of November and began visiting sites and taking evidence. These processes would be repeated over and over as the team moved throughout the region from British Honduras to the west, through the islands, across to British Guiana. Lord Moyne and his fellow commissioners eventually returned to London in April 1939 to take further evidence there and complete the writing of their report, which would represent a significant landmark in West Indian history.

The report was completed in 1939 but was not published until after the war. Evidently, the British government considered that dissemination of the facts disclosing the atrocious conditions in which most West Indians existed would provide fodder for enemy propaganda, and be capitalized on by Dr. Goebbels, Hitler's propaganda minister. However, the Government set about implementing the recommendations in 1940 with the creation of the Colonial Development & Welfare (CD&W) Organization based in Barbados, under a comptroller, Sir Frank Stockdale. Under the CD&W Act, funds provided by the imperial government through the colonial office would be spent during the 1940s and 1950s on education, health, housing, labour matters, social welfare, community development. As Gordon Lewis later put it, 'This was a period of welfare phobia.'

For the first time, also under CD&W auspices, organized training programmes were introduced, designed to provide some of the skills which would be required for future development of the countries. Regional social welfare courses were conducted in Jamaica and scholarships in social work to British universities were provided. The regional courses were directed by Professor Simey of Liverpool University, assisted by Miss Dora Ibberson, both CD&W advisers and later by Philip Sherlock and D. Thom Girvan. Locally, classes were held at Gibraltar Camp where on the former Mona estate, World War II refugees from Gibraltar and Malta and some German and Italian nationals, considered aliens, were housed. The camp was presided over by former Jamaica and West Indies cricketer, early trade unionist and later, K.S.A.C. councillor, commandant Ernest Rae. His son Allan, until recently President of the Jamaica and West Indies Cricket Boards, spent his early adult years in the large, old, wooden commandant's house.

On these same grounds and beginning in the camp huts, another educational and training institution, the University College of the West Indies (U.C.W.I.) was etablished in 1948 with a group of 33 medical students — the campus retaining Gibraltar Camp Road and still making use of some of the old wooden huts in the 1990s.

Like the Moyne Commissioners, the tough and redoubtable 'iron man' Sir Arthur Richards had also arrived in late 1938 to replace the late Governor Denham. He would shortly declare a State of Emergency, engage in skirmishes and battles with Bustamante and Manley, and within a year of the beginning of World War II, would detain and intern Busta at Up Park Camp under Defence Regulations, and afterwards, the 4 H's: Frank and Ken Hill, Richard Hart and Arthur Henry.

Governor Richards (later elevated to the peerage as Lord Milverton), on his assignment to Nigeria, would leave a reputation for *bon mots* such as 'armchair economists' and 'fire-side financiers'.

More concretely, his lasting legacy would be the leaking Richards Reservoir, close to the U.W.I. Mona.

As the war progressed, another notable Jamaican was to be incarcerated, for endeavouring, by publication of an article in a newspaper, to influence public opinion in a manner likely to be prejudicial to the efficient prosecution of the war. In a famous *Public Opinion* article on July 1944, entitled 'Now We Know', multi-talented Roger Mais, author of *The Hills Were Joyful Together* and *Brother Man*, asserted reasons why the proposed new Constitution of 1944 was designed to perpetuate Jamaica's dependent status. In trenchant terms he attacked the Colonial Office and, as a consequence of this breach of the Defence Regulations, was sentenced to six months in the St. Catherine district prison. A fine illustration of justice during the colonial period!

During the colonial period the civil service hierarchy reflected the wider West Indian societal pattern. In this rigid stratification of whites, creole whites, browns and blacks, the last were confined to clerical positions. They were restricted to assembling papers and passing them up the line to expatriate officials who monopolized the ultimate decision-making positions.

The colonial secretary's office or the Secretariat was the dominant, prestige agency among an agglomeration of departments and was staffed exclusively from the three top layers of the ethnic-complexion hierarchy. This was the department which serviced the policy makers. It also had responsibility for the establishment of civil service posts, for filling them, transfers, career advancement, promotion (except for those higher posts for which personnel were recruited by the Colonial Office in London). Until the mid-nineteen forties, a few years before the introduction of real ministerial government, it seemed more difficult for a black West Indian to enter the Secretariat as a member of its staff than for a 'camel to pass through a needle's eye.'

Propelled by the responsibility for administering the significant new inputs of public expenditure via CD&W investment, the Treasury began to challenge the Secretariat's position of supremacy. New opportunities were opened for able and experienced men, long held in the lowly positions to which the colonial system relegated them. Among these were J. E. Clare McFarlane, future poet laureate and author of *Voices from Summerland* and *Sex and Christianity* among other books; John Mordecai, Hector White, and Noel Holtz. There were also bright younger ones including Egerton Richardson, Allan Abrahams, George Phillips, Percy Beckwith and Lloyd Collins.

All would rise rapidly thereafter, and especially following introduction of the 1944 Constitution and of the ministerial system in 1953.

In offices adjacent to our long room were our associates: on one side the currency commissioners, supported by Jackie Lewis and Misses Icy Cappé, Lena Hamilton and Elsie Sanguinetti. On the other side, the defence (finance) board, then responsible for exchange control, whose staff included Horace Tame, the board chairman, and Miss Faith Dignum. Others would join us shortly, Viv Carnegie, Ashton Wright, later high commissioner and the first contractor general; and Joe St. Elmo Hall, currently reader in obstetrics and gynaecology in the faculty of medicine at the University of the West Indies, Sam Carter, O.D. Marsh, Lawson Coore and Don Mills. Among the ladies: Joyce and Hazel Burke, Norma Marsh, Gloria Fraser, Madge and Carmen Smith.

Presiding over this empire was English Financial Secretary and Treasurer the tough A. H. Hodges, like Churchill's 'inverted Micawber, waiting for something to turn down.' He was depicted by a cartoon in an issue of the civil service magazine, tied to a pawpaw tree, evidently proposed as part of the softening process! Hodges died in office during the war and was succeeded by bluff Sir Robert Taylor.

Work in the pensions section was quite challenging, mostly involving unravelling knotty policy problems while taking care to preserve precedent. This was interspersed, however, with days of frustration and boredom, burrowing deep into dusty records stored in basement vaults, checking on service records of retired civil servants whose careers commenced in the early years of the century. After acquiring some experience, I was also assigned responsibility for assisting in the administration of the Workmen's Compensation Act. This was designed to provide for payment of compensation by employers to employees for personal injury arising in the course of such employment. This assignment often entailed consultation with the Crown Solicitor A.B. Rennie, later Sir Alfred, who would become a High Court Judge.

On that fateful first Sunday of September 1939, news reached us by radio of Britain's declaration of war on Germany, following Hitler's invasion of Poland. We followed the war news avidly, ears glued to the BBC, in the *Gleaner* and from 1940, on the new local radio station ZQI, precursor of Radio Jamaica and Rediffusion (RJR). The horrors were softened somewhat by the soothing, cultured voice of its announcer, Denis Gick.

This was a time for belt-tightening, improvisation and innovation. Although the war was being fought thousands of miles away, U-boat submarine activities in the Atlantic drastically restricted imports of food, oil and raw materials. Middle and upper income Jamaicans were forced to resort to local foods, to coal and wood stoves and to bicycles, tramcars and simply shanks's mare (foot), since scarce gasoline supplies were available only for essential purposes.

From the early days, as part of the war restrictions, a blackout had been decreed for residences and other premises, in Kingston, to be enforced by teams of wardens. At the time I was boarding with my uncle J.J. who was acting Principal of Mico College. As one of the wardens, my beat covered the area between Wolmer's and Upper Camp Road, under a chief warden, A.J. Newman, then substantive Principal of Mico but on leave with the British Army, and promoted from Captain to Major.

One incident from that experience remains engraved in the memory: while patrolling one night during the early 1940s, I observed the lights blazing in a house set within spacious grounds on Leinster Road (not far from St. Hugh's High School). Entering the premises, I reminded the householder, who turned out to be Commissioner of Police Owen Wright, about the 'regulations'. He expressed great displeasure at my effrontery, reminded me of his position, and indicated his intention to report me to Mr Newman, the Chief Warden. However, I stuck to my guns and was supported in my stand by Uncle J.J.; there were no further developments. On reflection from time to time, I am astonished at the attitude of persons in positions of authority, with responsibility to see to the implementation of the law, regulations and rules, who behave as if these do not apply to them.

For one who spent the first six years of his working life in downtown Kingston, it is sad to see its decay and the exodus to New Kingston and the Constant Spring Road; hopefully the restoration project will be successful and already its beginning augurs well. Nostalgic memories remain of the marvellous marshmallow coated and nut-filled sundaes savoured at Kinkead's down the road on King Street. And within a stone's throw of the Parcels Post Office and the Treasury were the Plaza, a favourite Chinese grocery and restaurant with Lloyd Hosang, also a part-time singer; and the cluster and complex of shops: Hanna's, Issa's and Nathan's. In those days government departments were open on Saturdays until mid-day. Leaving office and following well-worn and long established custom, we young men, and others not so young, would station ourselves at the corner of Barry and King Streets outside Nathan's where N.C.B.'s Training School now stands, to view and pass comment on the passing parade of girls. Alas, another custom consigned to the storehouse of history.

Although the War was in full force, we did not suffer from a shortage of entertainment; in fact, we were sated with such facilities and opportunities. The Jamaica Library Service would not be developed under the dynamic direction of Hon. Joyce Robinson for another decade and a half; yet, we were not deprived of reading material — and the sources were accessible within easy reach of the office. We made use of the reference and lending facilities of the Institute of Jamaica, then under the direction of Frank Cundall, and our needs were charmingly and efficiently catered to by Misses Campbell, Sybil and Beryl Fletcher. Coincidentally, the first two were daughters of former Postmasters: Sybil Fletcher, sister of Hon. Douglas, attorney; and Beryl very active until recently, at UWI's Social Work Training Centre.

In addition, two other lending avenues were available: One was the Kingston Athenaeum, situated on Church Street, near Water Lane, providing the opportunity for associated membership with the Institute, and under the guidance of my former teacher, historian H.P. Jacobs and librarian, Miss Morais. The other was located in the Coronation Buildings on Tower Street, where Miss Doris Duperly's Phoenix Library also supplemented our reading. Perhaps most significant of all, this period also saw the birth of Sangster's Bookroom, with Ferdie Sangster (assisted by Miss Cunningham) bicycle-borne, tempting us successfully with books — my brother and I numbered among his first customers.

In addition, we were stimulated by the Sunday afternoon discussion group meetings at Henry Fowler's, Rhodes Scholar lately returned from Oxford; and the Youth Movement, the latter, a vibrant organization led by young men and women including Viv Blake, Pansy and Leacroft Robinson, Lucille Walrond (Mair), Hector Wynter, Richard Hart (Pansy's husband), and Don Mills. All these strands were woven into the warp of the fabric fashioning self-government and contributing towards the creation of the University College in 1948. Blake and Robinson would become distinguished barristers and PNP ministers; Hector Wynter, Registrar of UWI and JLP minister; and Lucille Mair and Don Mills, ambassadors, Lucille also serving before this, as the first Warden of UWI's Mary Seacole Hall;

while Hart would make headlines a decade later, as one of the famous 'Four H's' of the PNP.

A welcome addition to the theatre scene was the birth of the Little Theatre Movement (LTM) and the now well-established annual pantomime, created and nurtured by Greta Bourke (Fowler), which hit the stage on Boxing Day, 1941, with 'Jack and the Beanstalk', based on the English prototype.

'Moving pictures' were in full bloom with the old, open-air Gaiety and Palace on East Queen Street and Victoria Avenue, and the enclosed Movies at Cross Roads — all still in operation. The imposing Carib had been constructed in the late '30s with its elegant, glamorous interior, with Morris Cargill as manager, and its enchanting theme tune as the curtain unfolded. In those days many patrons dressed up for the Carib on Saturday and Sunday nights as if for the theatre. Tivoli had also entered the scene — in Kingston's 'west end'.

For up-towners the popular night club venues were the Glass Bucket at Half-Way-Tree and Silver Slipper at Cross Roads. Dudley MacMillan's Colony Club, also in Cross Roads, would join these not long after, as would Lewis Kelly's Morgan's Cove — the latter on the Spanish Town Road, a stone's throw from the present three-miles roundabout. These were the intimate ones. By the latter part of the 1940s Lord Kitchener would grace The Colony and Sugar Hill at Red Gal Ring on the Stony Hill Road with his presence and the inimitable 'Kitch Come go to Bed' and 'Tie-Tongue Mopsy'. Later, he would move for a prolonged period to London.

Kingston also boasted much more spacious clubs; venues for swimming, such as Bournemouth and Springfield, both in the Rockfort area, which doubled as very large dance halls, glittering with kaleidoscopic revolving lights, especially on festive occasions such as Christmas and New Year's eve. I recall, too, the considerable popularity of Wembley Cricket Club on Old Year's Night, obtaining a berth on such occasions, by the good graces of the late Sidney Abrahams and Frank Allen. Reference to swimming pools of Springfield and others reminds me of long-time resident, the late Walter Lowi, Austrian accountant but more famous as Jamaica's swimming coach. Recollections return too, of Saturdays, Sundays and public holidays spent sun-basking at one of the grey-black pebbled beaches — Barned's, Cable Hut, Copacabana — in the east, towards St. Thomas. Perhaps colour discrimination, moving against historical trends, has now made these less popular to the middle classes than the white sands of the north coast?

In the 1930s and 1940s, the Ska, Rock Steady and Reggae were musical sounds and forms of an unforeseen future, though their paternal or maternal source, the mento, remained prominent and popular in the performances of Stanley Lyon, Baba Motta, and George Moxey, Bahamian, but very long-time and popular resident in Jamaica. Of this genre, the popular tunes of boyhood years remained evergreen — 'Donkey Wan' Water, Hole 'Im Joe, 'Manuel Road', 'Matches Lane', and 'Sly Mongoose'.

Immediately after leaving school, I had become a member of Kensington Cricket Club. In my first Senior Cup match, in 1939, as one of the opening bowlers against the strong Lucas team captained by J.K. Holt Snr., I was fortunate to play in the company of Jamaica opening batsman O.J. Cunningham, the stylish all-rounder Lennie Lawrence, West Indies left arm spinner George Mudie and H.B. Young. After scoring over 300 for the loss of three wickets, of which Cunningham made a not out century, Kensington caught Lucas on a wet wicket the following Saturday. Some very experienced colleagues taught me the lesson of keeping the ball up to the batsman on a pitch in that condition, maintaining a good line and length and forcing him to play. We won handsomely and I was fortunate to emerge with three inexpensive wickets.

I remember many years later, playing in a game at the small Stony Hill Approved School ground on a damp pitch with Roy Gilchrist, on the eve of his first tour of England, bowling flat out but short of a length. The ball continually flew over the stumps and on one occasion actually produced six byes! After the game, with diffidence, I mentioned to him that based on my experience, English conditions would often be similar, and suggested that it might be better in such circumstances to reduce his pace and keep the ball up to the batsman. A lesson passed on, at a higher level!

On one or two mornings each week before going to the office, along with a few other members of the Club, I used to travel by bicycle from Mico to Kensington for practice in an effort to secure a regular place on the Senior Cup team. Usually among our small group was Noel Silvera, wicket-keeper and later lawyer, PNP minister of Home Affairs during the '70s and long-serving President of his old club, Kensington. In that age, playing Senior Cup Cricket, moreso for Jamaica, was a great privilege — an honour, an ambition and accolade to be achieved and seriously sought and striven for. It is so different nowadays when some players are reluctant unless strong financial inducements are offered.

Graduating eventually to a regular Senior Cup place in 1941, I recall vividly my two best and most significant performances at this level, both in 1942. The first occurred when, against Unifruitco (at the ground adjoining Sabina, now called Emmet Park), in a game reduced to one day by rain, I was successful in capturing all six wickets which fell for 42 runs. Unifruitco's team included future West Indian fast bowler Hines Johnson, Jamaica opening batsman L.V. Dujon, spinner D.P. Beckford Snr., and perennial spinners Reuben Riley and H. Ivan Meikle. The other event occurred in March 1942, fifty years ago as I am currently recording it. This was our first match of the season, against four year champions Lucas — a powerful team which included George Headley, certainly Jamaica's greatest batsman ever, and among the world's three greatest at the time. In 1939, on the last tour of England, he had scored a century in each innings in the Lords Test: a feat not equalled since. In addition, there were Ken ('Bam Bam') Weekes and former W.I. pace bowler Leslie Hylton. We batted first and had lost eight wickets for 117 with Myers still not out when I came in. Though never a batsman, I managed incredibly, to remain until we had put on a level 100; my score was 32 (and Myers 80 + Not Out), the wickets shared by Hylton and googly bowler, Ferguson.

When Lucas's turn came to bat, as opening medium pacer, I bowled Wesley Alexander (the Judge) early. As usual Headley came in at No. 3 and, as I ran up to bowl, he proceeded as was customary, to shuffle across the wicket. But, instead of the ball moving in from the off, it straightened without any intention on my part and, missing it, the great man was adjudged L.B.W. by 'Fifi' Smith to the first ball he received: out for a duck! Ken Weekes entered on a hat-trick. By that time, I could hardly continue bowling, although going through the paces, I was running up to the crease as if transported, feet off the ground, in a state of euphoria. The sensation is unforgettable. Small wonder, then, that I consider Headley the best batsman in Test cricket history, and this match, in its entirety, the zenith of my cricket career.

During the war, I became one of the Dr. Laubach's brigades of *each one teach one* literacy tutors, spending some afternoons at Boys Town, for which I also played cricket. The most challenging venture of those war years involved preparation for the London external bachelor of science in economics. For many years, a number of

Jamaicans and other West Indians who lacked the resources for study abroad, and in the absence of a local or regional university, had studied at home for London University degrees. Perhaps the most prominent of the Jamaicans was Sir Philip Sherlock, later Vice-Chancellor of the University of the West Indies, who obtained First Class Honours in English.

Lawson Coore and I, both working in the Treasury, studied together for economics, economic history, British constitution, economic geography and french. We met for discussions at each other's home several nights a week. After nine months of part-time reading, Coore and I were successful in passing the Intermediate Bachelor of Science in Economics examinations in 1943. Coore secured one of the CD&W medical scholarships awarded later that year and went on to Durham University. I continued in the social sciences, going to the London School of Economics on the Issa scholarship of 1944.

I was promoted to the grade of second class clerk in April 1943 (salary ranging from £225 to £325 per annum), and was given leave to take up the scholarship in August 1944.

In 1946, during the tenure of the scholarship, I received further promotion as first class clerk and returned to service in the Treasury in November 1947, following a two-month attachment to the commercial relations and supplies department of the Colonial Office, to gain further experience in applied economics. The head of the Department was D. Kelvin Stark, and our principal assignment was to deal with the allocation of materials whose supply had become scarce during the war and the immediate post-war years. Meanwhile, Sir Robert Taylor had been succeeded as financial secretary by a friendly, unpretentious Scot, Sir Norman Strathie, whose adaptation to Jamaican life and customs was unusual.

I had left Jamaica on the eve of momentous events in the country's constitutional history. Following the Moyne recommendations and General Elections of December 14, 1944 — the first conducted on the basis of universal adult suffrage — a new Constitution was introduced, ushering in the embryonic ministerial system. For the first time too, elected members were brought into the policy-making Executive Council (Ex. Co.) and also into close contact with civil servants and with the administrative machinery, under a system of tutelage in the art of administration.

Thus, the new 'ministers' (in name, but not in terms of authority) led by 'chief' Alexander Bustamante, and including H.E. Allan (later,

Sir Harold), Dr E.R. Evans, J.A. McPherson, and Frank Pixley, solicitor, joined the ex-officio members: Colonial Secretary, Hugh Foot; Attorney General, T. Henry Mayers; Financial Secretary, R.W. Taylor; and the Governor's nominees, Robert (later, Sir Robert) Barker, and O.K. Henriques of Henriques Bros., in the Ex. Co. presided over by bland Governor Sir John Huggins who had replaced the dominant Sir Arthur Richards in 1943. The new Governor's wife, Lady Molly, extrovert, ebullient and dynamic, soon succeeded in creating an independent image of her own, in the initiation, with Lady Edris Allan, of the Jamaica Federation of Women and the mass wedding ceremonies of common-law unions.

During my absence, the civil service was undergoing fundamental changes. Eric Mills, a British civil servant, had been commissioned to examine and make recommendations for improvement of the structure and efficiency of the public service. In his Report of December 30, 1949, Mills observed:

> An educational background restricted to secondary schools is not large enough for the performance of administrative functions. Furthermore, clerical duties performed over many years do not of themselves foster the development of decisiveness, initiative and responsibility which are the pre-requisites of successful administration.

In his message to the House of Representatives of July 5, 1950 which accompanied the Report, Governor Huggins, commenting on the need for a fundamental change in the system of recruitment and career advancement, stated:

> This system where candidates work their way up by stages of promotion through the various clerical grades has operated more successfully than might have been expected, and there are many officers now in senior and responsible posts who have risen during the course of a long official career from the lower ranks. However, the system is now outmoded and will not meet the exacting requirements of present day conditions.

Thus was the foundation laid for approval and introduction of the new system in which the civil service was divided into two classes: retention of the clerical class and creation of a new administrative class, the latter consisting of individuals holding honours degrees, and candidates among the clerical group, who displayed potential for undertaking administrative functions. Officers like Clare McFarlane, John Mordecai, Hector White and Allan Abrahams, who had served in clerical positions for inordinately long periods, were now catapulted into senior administrative posts on the basis of outstanding ability.

Significant changes were taking place in the Treasury: these began with the creation of a development division in the Secretariat and the transfer of officers including Richardson, Mordecai, George Phillips and Eric Patterson, to man the new division. Gradually, other sections of the treasury were merged with the Secretariat, the remainder being converted into the Accountant General's Department. Strathie had been followed by Robert Newton as financial secretary and Treasurer. After another two years, poet laureate Clare McFarlane assumed this position, as its first native holder. In June 1950 while still at the colonial office in London, I was promoted as senior clerk in the secretariat and after another three months, as administrative assistant; the first of these appointments a consequence of the promotion of A.B. Smith who would later serve for many years as chief personnel officer and subsequently, chairman of the public service commission.

Donald C. MacGillivray, the colonial secretary, had been asked by the new governor, Sir Hugh Foot, to formulate proposals for the creation of a set of ministries. His report was completed at sea on his departure from Jamaica. The MacGillivray proposals were to set the stage for the ministerial system which came to fruition in May 1953. Governor Foot had set about with characteristic initiative and energy to lead the hurricane Charlie recovery programme and had put in train plans for the creation of the Yallahs Valley Land Authority. This was the context to which I returned at the end of September 1951, after the colonial office experience of three and a quarter years. The colonial secretariat which I joined on my return, was housed in the old Headquarters House building on Duke Street, the seat of the Legislature from 1872 until the construction of Gordon House in 1960.

Old timers on the Secretariat's staff were Jamaica College Rhodes Scholar and former Inspector of Schools H. Laurence Lindo, sensitive, kindly and meticulous Vincent McFarlane and three J.C. alumni of my period at school: brothers John and Pat Clerk and Pat W.C. Burke — the last, a member of our Sunlight Cup winning squad of 1938. In the new economics section, brusque, 'no nonsense', English Under — Secretary J.B. Clegg was supported by G. Arthur Brown who had returned from LSE the year before. Clegg would be succeeded by mild-mannered John Stewart.

It was clear that since the end of the war the Secretariat had seen a conspicuous change. Was it a spin-off of the decolonization process? Three or four years before, Richardson and Mordecai had broken through the barriers and when I joined the staff there, I was surprised to find others such as Ossie Murray, Horace Barber, later financial secretary and governor of the Bank of Jamaica, and Neville Dawes.

At the end of May 1952 I was seconded to the Department of Commerce and Industries as Acting Assistant Commissioner. This spell of service and experience, lasting for a year, was to prove one of my most interesting and rewarding. At the time, the head was Commissioner Earle Maynier, with deputy R. C. Bridge and my fellow Assistant Commissioner, accountant A.C. Carter. Also there were Eric ('Rico') Polack, marketing officer, who would establish an enviable reputation in British Honduras; Vin A. Valentine, senior accountant and former West Indies fast-medium bowler; Frank Francis, future ambassador and foreign ministry permanent secretary; Ken Lloyd, who would move into the frozen lobster business; and two bright young men Marcus Garvey Jnr., younger son of the National Hero, and Noel Moo Young.

The Department's responsibilities included cornmeal processing, control over banana and scrap metal exportation, internal marketing of certain crops, and administration of pioneer industry encouragement legislation, before the Industrial Development Corporation (IDC) got off the ground. Several issues and events remain deeply imbedded in my memory. The most important concerns the nature and style of management of the head of Department.

Among the subjects assigned to me were examination and submission of recommendations on applications for pioneer industry incentives. This involved an assessment of the projected socio-economic benefits and costs and a recommendation to the Commissioner. Time and again Commissioner Maynier would forward my memorandum to the secretariat for ultimate consideration by the Executive Council, with a short covering letter: 'Honourable colonial secretary, I forward a memo prepared by Mr. G. E. Mills, Assistant Commissioner, with which I entirely agree.' Action of that nature was most refreshing and almost abnormal: it ran counter to the general practice where a senior officer would merely substitute his own name at the end of the memo and address it to the Secretariat as though he himself had written it. Alternatively, as in the case of some individuals, the latter would devote an inordinate amount of time to re-writing the memo, or draft letter in his own words. As a result, he would spend nights and weekends at the office and on entering it was difficult to see him, hidden as he was behind a mountain of files.

A more fundamental consequence was the demotivating, demoralizing effect of this reluctance to delegate. I have often wondered whether this syndrome is partly a consequence of the hangover of the conditioning of slavery and the colonial system. Yet, there were the few like Earle Maynier, who had the confidence to give junior officers their head, not worried that they might make mistakes but contributing significantly to personnel and personal development.

With the introduction of the ministerial system, I was promoted as Assistant Secretary and moved to the Ministry of Finance on All Fools' Day, 1953. A number of former Treasury stalwarts were now holding senior positions in that ministry: Hector White, Allan Abrahams, George Phillips and P. W. Beckwith; and among the younger group, former school colleague, Ossie Murray — with sociable, down-to-earth Englishman, Frank D. C. Williams as financial secretary. At the helm was minister Donald Sangster whose bland, affable, easy-going appearance belied a surprising firmness and capacity for hard work.

Working as an assistant secretary in the ministry of finance, which coincided with the inception of the real ministerial system, served to consolidate and develop the foundation in administrative training and experience laid in the Department of Commerce and Industries. This experience was more direct and involved closer contact with the ultimate decision-makers.

Perhaps the most memorable event during these first two years at the ministry of finance occurred during my assignment as Secretary to the Commission of Enquiry into the Match Industry in 1955. In 1935 the Henriques Brothers had been granted, under the Safeguarding of Industry Law, a monopoly licence to manufacture matches. Two additional protective measures were handed to the company, Jamaica Match Industry Limited, in order to ensure not only survival, but unequivocal profitability: first, to cut out competition from imports of the Swedish match, *Vulcan*, which had hitherto been popular in Jamaica, the tariff was set at a prohibitive rate, almost at the level of the selling price of the product. Secondly, the company was provided by the government with a guarantee of a minimum profit of ten per cent after tax; and in any year in which profits fell below this rate, public revenue was handed back to the firm. In fact, such refunds were made to the tune of £800,000.

In 1955, when the PNP took over the reins of government for the first time following their success in the general elections of January that year, the executive council decided to appoint a Commission, to investigate the operations of the company and the terms of the franchise. By that time JLP minister of finance Sangster had been succeeded by genial N.N. ('Crab') Nethersole. The Commission consisted of barrister David Coore who had not yet entered politics as Chairman, Paul Goldson and J.P. Wynne, distinguished accountants, A.F. Earle, an economist from Alcan Jamaica Limited and later head of the London Business School, and D. D. Bean Jnr., an experienced match manufacturer from the USA, recruited by A.D. Little Inc. of Boston. (Bean, in a line of match manufacturers from Jaffrey, New Hampshire, later established a plant which produces 'Comet' matches in Kingston, ably assisted by H.A. ('Charlie') Braham.

In preparing for the Commission's hearings, I delved into the history of the safety match business in Jamaica from the 1890s, including the reactions by the government to imports, and prepared a memorandum which formed the basis of my evidence when I was called as the first 'witness' and cross-examined by N.N. Ashenheim who represented the company. I recall going to a young Hugh Shearer's house to deliver a subpoena directing his attendance to answer questions in relation to the employees, who were represented by the BITU.

The Commission noted that the company was a member of a group of sister firms with inter-locking directorates (all forming part of the Henriques Brothers enterprises) which supplied goods and services for the match operations: Kingston Industrial Garage (motor vehicle supplies and maintenance) Kingston Industrial Works (plant and machinery) and Kingston Industrial Agencies (raw materials). It was therefore 'notoriously difficult to discover the true profit earned by the match enterprise.' This pattern was to be repeated during the next two decades, especially in respect of public utility undertakings with overseas majority ownership.

The match plant was serviced primarily by hand labour provided by semi-skilled and unskilled employees, the latter mainly women. The Commission found that a more mechanized operation could produce matches at a lower selling price without the need for a government guarantee or a subsidy. But this would have rendered 80 per cent of the labour force redundant. Questions arose as to who would be responsible for compensating workers released in such circumstances, and eventually the firm closed during my absence on post-graduate studies in the U.S.A. Another interesting and significant feature of the case, a pattern also repeated later, reflected the dual positions held by O.K. Henriques, the managing director of the company originally, who served also as a member of the colonial privy council which granted the concessions and privileges to the company.

A four-year stint in that department was to be broken half-way through by an assignment to the new Central Planning Unit (CPU) on promotion as a principal assistant secretary, followed by a year of post-graduate studies. I returned in 1958, on further promotion, to one of the three newly-established posts of assistant under-secretary, in the new investment division. The last five years of the 1950s were an exciting period, particularly in the early activities of the CPU initiated by George Cadbury, and the initiatives taken by Crab Nethersole, ably assisted by new financial secretary Egerton Richardson, in the development of financial institutions.

I arrived at Harvard to study for the MPA at a very interesting period of United States' history. The attempt to integrate a school in Little Rock, Arkansas (President Clinton's state capital) and the launching by the USSR of satellites 'Sputnik' and Mutnik triggered significant reactions from the government and people of the USA.

I was fortunate to be taught by Professors J.K. Galbraith, John Gaus, Arthur Smithies and Edward Mason. Galbraith, stimulating and provocative, was engaged in completing *The Affluent Society* in which he coined the felicitous phrase 'the conventional wisdom' and which was later assimilated into the language. Gaus applied the concept of 'ecology' to the field of Public Administration.

The investment division was headed by Welshman E.T. Nevin. The staff also included a number of young men who would graduate to service in other areas: D.R. ('Jack') Clarke, to the World Bank; Roy Jones to the Bank of Jamaica as director of research; Trevor Da Costa to Washington as a diplomat in the Jamaican embassy, and later, to the Inter-American Development Bank; Roy Dickson, then recently returned from Oxford as Rhodes Scholar who would become the Gleaner's special projects manager. Thus, we were involved in the creation of the Development Finance Corporation, precursor of the Jamaica Development Bank, the modernizing of commercial banking legislation, the initial ideas which eventually culminated in the establishment of the Bank of Jamaica (BOJ) and the Stock Exchange, and the use of Treasury Bills as a major mechanism of monetary policy. This was the period too, in which legislation was introduced setting up the small businesses loan board. Among the most significant breakthroughs was the entry into the New York market by a British colony for the first time!

The quiet and charming PNP Secretary, Vernon Arnett, had been elevated to succeed Nethersole who died in office in March 1959. I spent my final year at this ministry, in charge of the budget and dealing with revenue remission applications. I worked with P.W. Beckwith, who would succeed Arthur Brown as financial secretary, and with Ossie Murray. Assisting us were highly efficient secretaries in the persons of Mrs. L. Terrelonge and Miss Dorothy Williams, later Weller, who moved to the Bank of Jamaica. Along the way I had also been involved in negotiations with Mayer Matalon on mortgage insurance arrangements concerning the West Indies Home Contractors housing scheme at Harbour View.

Immediately after the PNP's victory at the polls in January 1955, new Chief Minister Norman Manley, fulfilling an election campaign commitment, rushed to New York to seek United Nations technical assistance in the form of a senior economic adviser. One of the principal responsibilities of this adviser would be the creation of a Central Planning Unit (CPU). George Cadbury was specially selected by Manley for this role. A Fabian socialist, he was the *white sheep* of the prestigious chocolate family of Bournville, Birmingham. Cadbury had served in a similar capacity to Saskatchewan Premier Tommy Douglas of the democratic socialist Cooperative Commonwealth Federation and to a number of Asian governments.

Initially seconded to the new C.P.U. as its first civil service recruit, I was joined later by Raphael ('Raph') Swaby, Gloria Fraser-Scott (a former L.S.E. colleague), and Mary Winch Guilbride, a Jamaica Scholar with G. Arthur Brown as Director. Raph, a highly intelligent man, had been an Income Tax Department assessor and then had been appointed the first Bursar of the University College of the West Indies, having obtained the London Diploma in public administration, externally, and gained first place internationally in the Corporation of Certified Secretaries (C.C.S.) examinations.

Located in the office of the chief minister and minister of development, the CPU's terms of reference centred on providing the minister and executive council, later, the council of ministers, with advice on social and economic matters and on drafting of the first long-term Development Plan of 1957-1967. Each member of our small staff was allocated a sector for research, investigation and policy formulation in consultation with the appropriate ministry officials. The preparation of a paper for a discussion among CPU staff was required, with the refined, collectively formulated paper then moving to the chief minister and thence, to the executive council. We met the expressions of envy, prejudice and criticism of our group, dubbed the 'brains trust, ivory tower boys,' by adopting a participative approach. We would insert the name of a top sectoral ministry official as joint author of the paper, although he or she had not written any part of it. This strategy proved successful.

It was out of these deliberations, and on the basis of ideas generated by the CPU, that fundamental policy recommendations emerged initiating development in areas such as education and health, and which laid the foundations of current policy approaches and development patterns. Here began the movement towards democratization of secondary education, with provision for admission to secondary schools, of an expansion above the level of one to two per cent of the population of secondary school age who enjoyed such opportunities at the time: thus the new education programme launched in 1957 and presided over by minister Florizel Glasspole.

In the health sector priority was placed on preventive health, implemented via an island-wide distribution of health centres, presaging the current approach with its emphasis on primary care.

A number of significant initiatives were taken in the development of infrastructural facilities and in providing a framework for such development. Foremost among these were the beginning of swamp drainage and of highway construction to provide improved access to development in Negril.

Town and Country Planning legislation was enacted, bringing physical and socio-economic planning into the portfolio of the chief minister and minister of development. The commissioner of the New York State Park, Robert Moses, visited to advise on the development of Palisadoes. A most interesting tax measure was also introduced: new Land Development Duty legislation represented an attempt to recoup, by a capital gains or a betterment tax, part of the windfall gains accruing to landowners in specific areas where property values had appreciated significantly.

Director Arthur Brown played a prominent role in the formulation of this proposal, as he did in the first bauxite royalties re-negotiation exercise of 1957, with significant support in expertise on the marketing of bauxite and alumina, provided by UN technical assistance consultant Sam Moment.

Norman Manley had a vision of a publicly owned broadcasting institution designed to display our national cultural development with dignity and to serve as a medium for educational purposes. In 1956 David Dunton, Chairman of the Canadian Broadcasting Corporation, was invited through the CPU to survey the broadcasting scene with special focus on the government broadcasting service. Dunton's report laid the foundations for the creation of the Jamaica Broadcasting Corporation in 1959. Our experience of the 1970s and 1980s suggests that the fulfillment of Manley's vision was vitiated, his dream denied.

Among Cadbury's other 'brainchildren' were the creation of the Jamaica Youth Corps (JYC) and the institution of a ministers' meeting and of a ministers' retreat.

The rationale for the Youth Corps was to postpone entry to the labour market of young boys, aged about 16, while providing them with a modest level of technical training, a sense of discipline and character building.

The JYC was based partly on the model of Franklin Roosevelt's New Deal Civilian Conservation Corps (a 'domestic Peace Corps') of the 1930s with the boys required to contribute as a national service group. My contemporaries will recall that when the JYC was created, excessive indiscipline had not yet become the significant social problem so evident currently in Jamaica.

In implementing these ideas, Cadbury was supported by two valuable allies in the persons of Vin Lawrence, father of Vin Jr., the engineer-Chairman of the Urban Development Corporation, an energetic, dynamic Mico College graduate who was principal of the school attached to Boys' Town, and later, by Raph Swaby. Beginning with the Cobbla camp situated in the Christiana Spaldings area, and extending two months later to Chestervale in the hills of St. Andrew, the Corps expanded within a short time to a complement of over 1000.

The Corps was administered by a Board of Management which included Hugh Sherlock, Glen Owen, Wesley Powell, L.A. Henriques and Raph Swaby. Under the direction of Vin Lawrence, assisted by Owen Batchelor and Geoff Brown, subsequently, director of UWI's

Social Welfare Training Centre, it became a success story. During the 1950s and early 1960s several private sector employers, notably The Hon. Abe Issa, selected graduates from the camps for employment because of their character and disciplined behaviour.

The first ministers' retreat, initiated on Cadbury's suggestion, was held, not at a luxury north coast hotel, as has become customary, but at the old homely Pine Grove Guest House. There, around 1956, the ministers spent a very fruitful week-end, cut off from telephones and other distractions, discussing salient social and economic issues and development plans with Cadbury, Richardson, Brown, Swaby and me.

At a time when the executive council and later, the council of ministers, still included a few non-party nominated and ex-officio members, an arrangement was introduced for a regular Friday afternoon meeting of elected ministers only, with Cadbury as secretary, to collate a collective view and approach on items appearing on the executive council agenda for the following Monday. On occasions when Cadbury was away, I was asked by him to deputize. But I discovered to my embarrassment as a civil servant, that the meeting often turned into a purely party discussion after completion of the formal agenda. So, finding finance minister Nethersole, the extrovert, easier to talk to than N.W.Manley I asked to be relieved of the acting assignment and this was done.

During the ministers' meeting, copies of the *Star* evening newspaper were usually brought in and on one occasion the paper was delivered while a minister was making his presentation. As Mr.Manley began to read, the speaker, became angry and blurted out: 'Mr. Chairman, I am going to stop, because you are not listening to one word of what I am saying!' In response, the chief minister detailed, 'You said 'A. B. C...;' thus deflating the minister.

In 1956 the chief minister asked me to represent the government as a member of a delegation to a conference on Planning in Port of Spain Trinidad under the auspices of the Caribbean Commission. My colleagues on the delegation were Jimmy Lloyd of the ministry of local government and housing and Bill Hodges, assistant government town planner. We were interested in the notion of a broad-gauged approach to planning, in which the socio-economic and physical facets would be integrated. Among other participants were Paul Southwell, who would become Premier of St. Kitts, Joe Crookes, Trinidad's government town planner, who would serve as the United Nations Development Programme's resident representative in

Jamaica; and Andrew Rose, a future People's National Movement (PNM) minister. In Port of Spain I was intrigued by the complex of traffic roundabouts on which the planners were focusing at the time.

A few months before, Dr. Eric Williams' PNM had won an historic landslide victory in general elections and N.W. Manley arranged for me to meet and brief him on the structure and operations of our year-old CPU. The new chief minister invited me to lunch and proved a charming and gracious host. I was disappointed to learn how irascible he became later. I was also impressed by the sight of someone wearing dark glasses within the confines of a darkened dining room and lounge. The government of Trinidad and Tobago set up a planning unit not long after.

Despite the obvious contribution of the civil service to my personal and professional development, the truth is that I was quietly chafing and becoming irritated and frustrated by a number of incidents and experiences in the ministry of finance. I was tempted by the offer made by a contemporary at school of a lucrative position with his firm coupled with a place on the board of directors. However, my response was negative, since I was aware that the business world was not my *métier*, and I confirmed this in a conversation with him a few days later, having been asked to give the offer further consideration. At times I reflect on the fact that had I accepted and remained with that firm these 30-odd years I would have become a millionaire. But I am still convinced that I had made the right decision.

And so, I left the civil service in June 1960, to embark upon a new and exciting career at the fledgling University College of the West Indies. Looking back, I have never regretted this decision; indeed, I have been most fortunate in the breadth, depth and range of interests and experiences enjoyed from these two careers.

5

STUDENT DAYS IN BRITAIN

In August 1944 a small group of us came together at a Kingston wharf to begin a journey on a small cargo vessel. It was wartime and we travelled in hush-hush conditions. We bade goodbye to parents, relatives and friends who were unaware of the route to our final destination. My recollections of that sea trip to Tampa, Florida are of the smell and taste of oil, bringing continuous feelings of nausea and the cramped and confined accommodation on the cargo vessel.

Whiling the time away in Tampa, then a small town, awaiting our train to New York, we decided to watch a film. In the context of the colour bar — of 'Jim Crowism' especially in the southern USA below the Mason-Dixon line — and in a moment of mischief and bravado, we strode deliberately and boldly to a cinema, labelled with the clear and conspicuous caution, 'For Whites only'. The female ticket-seller, was momentarily surprised, but on hearing our accents presumably assuming that we were ignorant strangers/foreigners, admitted us without an expressed demur or question.

In New York, our West Indian background was to be of benefit in obtaining berths on the Britain-bound Queen Elizabeth. The Cunard Line's application form included a question intended to identify the racial background of the potential passenger and when we inserted 'Negro', the official remonstrated with the reaction: 'No, no! Say 'British West Indian!' Thus, were our feelings of superiority over the 'coloured' American nurtured, and these attitudes were bolstered by the latter's seemingly servile and cowed behaviour. We were oblivious of our own inferior status as second class colonial British subjects.

Most of the students who boarded the *Queen Elizabeth* with us in New York were on Colonial Development and Welfare (CD&W) medical scholarships. In 1943 when the first CD&W medical scholarships were awarded, 14 scholarships apparently intended for distribution throughout the West Indies, were all inadvertently allocated to Jamaica. Benefiting from this bonanza, the government decided to assign one to each parish. The awardees were selected by a committee comprising the custos, member of the legislative council and chairman of the parochial board of the parish. Inevitably, a number of highly qualified persons were passed over, while a few with mediocre qualifications were selected. A few of the latter experienced considerable difficulty in staying the course. Some dropped out and others moved to lower qualifications. However, those 1943 awards produced notable successes in Henry Shaw, Lawson Coore, Ronald Lampart, Roy Ebanks, Leslie Williams , Oswald Forbes, A.F. Brown and Locksley Gordon.

As the QE sped on its zigzag route across the Atlantic to avoid German U-boat attacks, we were summoned to daily survival boat drill at the siren's sound, wondering, whether we would make it to Britain. Our journey was incident-free and entirely unexciting. Escorted by destroyers on each side, the QE docked at Gourock, Scotland. We arrived in London in September, three months after *D Day*, to become the first residents of a colonial students hostel in Collingham Gardens, Earls Court.

I recall vividly going to bed on the fifth floor following the watchman's words informing us that the air raid shelter was in the basement. Physically and emotionally exhausted from the tension of the preceding six days, I was in a deep sleep when I heard the air raid siren. I jumped out of bed, rushed six flights down to the basement, and was greeted by the watchman's quiet, 'That was the all clear!'

London was a grimy, smoggy, dark, drab and depressing city. At times, buses could merely crawl because of poor visibility and the conductor would walk in front with a lantern. Very little motor traffic moved on the streets because our arrival coincided with the regular attacks by the dreaded flying *doodle bugs* or *buzz bombs* and soon after, the V-2 rockets.

This was the age of austerity and all resources were rationed in the interest of winning the war. Allocations of meat, sugar, bacon, tea, were each less than one pound per person per week. Bread, sweets, soap and utility clothing were also heavily rationed. We were served powdered *ersatz* eggs and reindeer and whale steak. My favourite food, ice cream, was a travesty of corn flour and powdered milk.

Not long after September 1939, West Indians began trekking to Britain to join up the armed forces. Some sought adventure and excitement. Others sought opportunities for further education which were not available to them in the Caribbean. Many were fired by sentiments of patriotism towards the empire, and others were motivated by a mixture of all of these concerns and hopes.

Most of the West Indians active in the fighting services were members of the Royal Air Force (RAF). Included in this group were future prime ministers Errol Barrow, Milton ('Bob') Cato and Michael Manley. There were also other future barristers like Eric Frater, Arthur Dujon, John Burke, Dudley Thompson, Uriah Parnell, W. ('Derry') Marsh, Ulric Cross, C. ('Dusty') Miller, and Derek Knight. Other RAF veterans were future Olympic athletes McDonald Bailey and Arthur Wint, broadcaster Dennis Hall, E. K. Powell, Ralph Brown, Ernest Peart, Vernon Lindo, Roy Augier, novelist John Hearne, and my Chapelton neighbours, Frank Smith, Tom Abrahams, and Jimmy McMorris.

There were also the rare ones who served in the Army (Infantry) such as Keble Munn, M.G. Smith and Douglas Hall. A few servicemen from this region were decorated for their exploits and special acts of heroism. No West Indian serviceman was more highly decorated than squadron leader Ulric Cross who was awarded the Distinguished Service Order (DSO) and the Distinguished Flying Cross (DFC) with bar. The award of the DFC was also made to Jamaicans Robert Rubie and John Blair. John Ebanks, President of the Royal Air Force Association received the Distinguished Flying Medal (DFM). Rhodes Scholar Ron Sturdy of the Royal Naval Reserve was decorated with the Croix de Guerre.

The recruitment of 'coloured' West Indians to officer rank in the various branches of the armed forces was a significant breakthrough. Barrow, Cross, Thompson and Wint, who attained these positions in the RAF, could not have done so at the beginning of the war. Marika Sherwood's *Many Struggles* has unearthed facts about the discrimination experienced by West Indian workers and service personnel during the War. Sherwood exposed the colour bar which denied commissions to British subjects who were not of pure European descent. Indeed, she discloses that on these grounds, Jamaican Leo March was originally denied an RAF commission in September 1939. A colonial office official had advised that he should not be encouraged to re-apply since it was 'unlikely that the RAF will give a commission to a black dental surgeon'. He eventually became 'the first coloured person to receive a commission as an officer in the British Army'.

For the same reasons, an application from Arundel Moody, son of Dr. Harold Moody, founder and President of the League of Coloured Peoples, was originally turned down by the army's tank corps. All the cases concerned, including those involving a few Africans, were strongly fought by the league through the colonial office, with eventual success.

As the War dragged on, West Indian women volunteered for the armed services, mainly for the Auxiliary Territorial Service (ATS). Included among the volunteers were Ena Collymore Woodstock who was Jamaica's first female judge, Norma Marsh , Esther McMorris, Nellie Forrester, Ursula Burnett, Aileen Lynch Fraser, Inez Salmon and Marjorie Valère.

Before 1943 the recruitment of 'coloured' women to the armed forces was impossible. The British war office had declared, 'we cannot agree to accept coloured women for service in this country.' A further revelation from Marika Sherwood, from the minutes of a meeting between the war office, the ATS and the colonial office earlier that year reveals the characteristic hypocrisy, cynicism and subterfuge: it was essential that this discrimination should appear a matter of selection and not of racial distinction. At least the American colour bar was more frank, forthright and honest than the British.

Against this background, some Jamaican servicemen acquired the accolade of hero in more bizarre situations. Observers from other parts of the region and even some of their own countrymen who themselves enjoyed benefits from such exploits were ambivalent about these attainments. They welcomed the beneficial results but deplored the means and manner of their achievement. Generally considered crude, excessively aggressive and militant, some of these Jamaicans taking very decisive physical action broke the colour bar established by white American GIs who attempted to transport their 'Jim Crow' system to Europe. The Jamaicans created the path for black Africans, Americans and West Indians to set foot on the soil of infamous *Rainbow Corner*, a section of Piccadilly Circus access to which had been denied to blacks for a long time.

During this turbulent period, the London School of Economics (LSE), where I was a student, was evacuated to the less vulnerable area of Cambridge. In this haven, situated about 60 miles from London and sheltered from the bombing, we scarcely remembered the war. We lived a quiet, untroubled life in beautiful surroundings of imposing old college buildings and of the River Cam. Our consciousness of the war was kept alive only because of news reports, rationing and the presence of a large United States General Issue (GI) camp in the town centre.

The British adopted an ambivalent attitude to the American GI soldiers who had 'invaded' in hordes. They were welcomed as essential support for the war effort but some Englishmen expressed doubts about their capability as soldiers and airmen. Their intrusion was resented, partly because of insecurity and anxiety about their presence as sexual competitors. They flaunted their prosperity in money and goodies, especially nylon stockings, steak, fresh eggs, and chocolate. In popular parlance, 'they are over-paid, over-sexed and over here.'

Apart from freedom from fear, we were fortunate in having access to a constellation of eminent scholars from both LSE and Cambridge. They included Austrian emigré Friedrich Hayek, later Nobel laureate in economics, Harold Laski, Lionel Robbins, and the brilliant St. Lucian Arthur Lewis who would become the first West Indian Nobel prize winner.

Other stars in this galaxy included economic historian R.H. Tawney, author of *Religion and the Rise of Capitalism*, Nikki Kaldor, K.B. Smellie and Evan Durbin.

From Cambridge university we endured boring lectures from Joan Robinson, famous for the long-running controversy with Harvard's E.H. Chamberlin over her theory of imperfect competition versus his of monopolistic competition. Occasionally we had the rare fortune of listening to the erudite philosopher and mathematician, Bertrand Russell, and the highly influential John Maynard Keynes, both subsequently raised to the peerage. Hayek introduced us to what seemed at the time to be the extreme complexities of contours in constructing indifference demand curves. At the time, he was writing *The Road to Serfdom* — a condemnation of socialism.

Among these great scholars, Laski was a particularly stimulating and witty teacher. One of his courses, Social and Political Theory, which also attracted Cambridge students and servicemen from the GI camp, was usually so crowded that if you did not arrive at least 20 minutes before the lecture, you had to resort to standing or sitting on the floor. On the issue of 'equality', he would advise: 'If you wish to be a success, to make your way in the world, you must be careful in the choice of your parents!'

In 1947 Laski brought a suit against the *Newark Advertiser* and the Beaverbrook *Daily Express*. As Chairman of the Labour Party during the 1945 election campaign, he was reported by these papers as advocating violence in one of his speeches. These reports were accompanied by cartoons depicting him as a bogeyman. Counsel for the newspapers, the eminent Sir Patrick Hastings, based the defence primarily on portions of the text of Laski's famous *Grammar of Politics*, one of the prescribed texts for our programme in Politics. When Laski lost the case, the costs of £13,000 were over-subscribed by donations from well-wishers in Britain and by some of his former American students but he never recovered from the defeat.

Primarily because of Laski's conspicuousness and influence, LSE has had a reputation as a seed-bed of *leftists*. In fact, the liberal and conservative elements, led by Robbins and Hayek respectively, have always been very strong. The notion that the School has produced an inordinate number of left wing leaders like Pierre Trudeau, Michael Manley and Errol Barrow is highly exaggerated and founded on ignorance. This is so, especially when considered in light of the contributions made by Oxbridge to the education of leaders such as Nehru, Gaitskell, Richard Crossman, Harold Wilson, and Trevor Munroe. Moreover, it is also significant that a number of West Indians who could scarcely be described as 'left wingers' are products of LSE, including Oliver Clarke, Senator Oswald Harding, Mrs. Shirley Miller, Hon. G.Arthur Brown, O.D. Marsh, Mrs. Sybil Francis and Sir Randolph Douglas.

Fellow students at LSE included Nora Sifleet Mailer who would join the staff of the Development and Planning Unit at the University of the West Indies (UWI). There was Kari Polanyi (Levitt) who would become a professor of economics at McGill and a regular visiting teacher and researcher at the UWI's St. Augustine and Mona campuses. My classmates in politics, Ralph Miliband, John Rees and Bernard Schaffer would in later life be appointed professors at Leeds, Swansea and Sussex, respectively.

The West Indian community was well represented at LSE. There were Jamaicans Odel Fleming, a future chief probation officer,

Rudolph Cousins, later chairman of Jamaica Broilers, Sybil Hill (Francis), Gloria Fraser, and Jean Oppenheim, my immediate predecessor as Issa scholar. Gloria Carpenter was studying law at Girton College, Cambridge. Jack Dear of Barbados, also reading law, would be appointed Queen's Counsel. Other law students, Lionel Seemungal of Trinidad and Fred Kelsick of St. Kitts would also attain similar eminence.

While we were cloistered away in Cambridge, the war in Europe was moving to a climax following the allies' opening of the 'second front.' Victory came on May 8, 1945, *V.E. Day*. It was an experience of absolute euphoria and work and classes were cancelled. Some of us rushed to London to join the crowds of thousands that packed the Strand, Piccadilly Circus and other popular parts of the city. We observed the intoxicated behaviour, not all drink-induced, and the extrovert expressions of conduct by so many of a reputedly reserved and inhibited people.

A few months before our move to London and Nutford House, the victorious Allied leaders and their supporters had emerged from a meeting in San Francisco in a mood of euphoria and confidence flowing from the decision to create the United Nations. A year before, other leaders in the economics and financial fields had come together at Bretton Woods to forge international institutions in these fields — the IMF and World Bank. Following a phase of warm welcome by the 'underdeveloped' colonial world, they would become prime targets of attack three to four decades later, from the same countries, now dubbed the 'developing third world', confronting conditionalities imposed as an imperative of structural adjustment.

In July 1945, Clement Attlee's British Labour Party, against all odds, had incredibly won a landslide electoral victory (in which many of us solidly supported Labour), denying Winston Churchill, the war-time leader, 'the tools to finish the job' which he had begun. As one of its first acts, the new government, through Fabian Socialist Colonial Secretary Creech Jones, had enunciated its decolonization policy, thus setting the stage for the liquidation of the British Empire. Certainly, Churchill had fulfilled his vow that he would not preside over this liquidation process! In retrospect therefore, this was a propitious period and the environment a seedbed for the germination, and the emergence of future colonial leaders; though I do not recall that we focused specifically on such opportunities at the time. Indeed, Britain of that period became an incubator of such potential leaders: in politics, the professions, the academic and other areas of activity.

At the end of that summer LSE returned to its London home and we moved back to the impersonal environment of the big city with more than a tinge of regret. Our numbers were significantly augmented by demobilized ex-servicemen and new students arriving for study throughout Britain. About 200 of us, from Africa, Asia, the Caribbean and the Middle East, moved into a new residence, Nutford House, conveniently located between Marble Arch and Edgware Road. In this warm cocoon of comfort, we provided psychological support and protection for each other in the face of a cold, unfriendly and hostile society outside. There were lighter moments too. For instance, among the rules of the house, set out on the notice board, was one which prohibited residents from entertaining female guests in their bedrooms. A resident inserted an addendum relating to the entertainment of male guests from the colonial office. This was a reference to the rumour about homosexual members there.

Fellow residents from Jamaica included cricketer Allan Rae, Odel Fleming, Rudolph Cousins, Reg. Phillips, Pat W.C. Burke, Horace Edwards, Basil Rowe and John Hall, Mickey Roper, Vernon Spence. The last three would later become distinguished members of the medical fraternity and of the Kingston Public Hospital. We met daily at meals, in the lounge and on social occasions, with future prime ministers Forbes Burnham of Guyana and Milton Cato of St. Vincent and the Grenadines and governor-general (G.G.) Rupert John, also of St. Vincent. The Guianese residents were former football and hockey player, Ivor Robinson, O.A. 'Johno' Johnson, Fred Charles, 'Sweetie' Hart, and Richard Allsopp, whose precise diction foreshadowed his career in linguistics at the UWI. Earl Seaton, a Bermudan, would serve in the High Court in East Africa, and become chief justice of the Seychelles. The lone Bahamian, Harold Munnings, civil engineering student would become permanent secretary, moving through a range of ministries and later, a member of the Public Service Commission.

From Trinidad and Tobago there were Lloyd Braithwaite, medical students Bernard Warner, Horace Charles, and Jack Armstrong, social science student Ken Sealy, later Industrial Court judge, and language student Rae Charles, who would become an interpreter at the United Nations.

The Leewards were also represented by law and medical students respectively, Basil Diaz and Ersdale Jacobs, both Kittitians. From the

Windward Islands were Telford Georges of Dominica, Barry Renwick, Carol Bristol and Raphael Fletcher of Grenada, Guy Alexis Mathurin and Vincent Floissac from St. Lucia and Eric Rawle and C.G. ('Pat') Huggins of St. Vincent. Renwick would become legal adviser to the Organization of Eastern Caribbean states (OECS), while Fletcher was appointed head of the physics department at St. Augustine. Georges would serve as chief justice of Tanzania, Zimbabwe and the Bahamas and as professor of law at Cave Hill. Floissac would attain a similar position in the Eastern Caribbean supreme court.

Mathurin had a brilliant legal future forecast for him but tragically died in a motor accident. Rawle also died young, but as a murder victim. Pat Huggins would serve a long period as Labour Commissioner. Barbadian Eric Bishop would sit on the High Court Bench for the Eastern Caribbean States and Frank Ramsay, a medical specialist, would join the University Hospital staff for a short period.

Ignoring Caribbean boundaries, our company included Veerasamy Ringadoo, a future minister of finance and first president of Mauritius, Peter Fernandez of Gibraltar, and Sam Jegasothe and Bertie Senevaratne of Ceylon. A practical joker, Bertie became fascinated by the famous Jamaican word 'r—s.' One day, he suggested to an English girl fellow student at L.S.E., that when next she saw Sybil Francis, she should greet her with what he told her was a Jamaican salutation, 'Hello, Sybil, r—s!' the girl dutifully did so next morning and Sybil, proper lady that she was, reacted in consternation.

From Africa there were Abubaka Tafala Balewa who was Nigeria's Hausa prime minister and Charles Njonjo a future Kenya attorney general. Frank Torto and Mike Bentill of the Gold Coast, and Thomas Marealle, a Tanganyikan chief, were also members of our company.

At Cambridge I had been closely associated with Davidson Nicol of Sierra Leone, later director of the United Nations Institute of Training and Research (UNITAR). In addition, there were Cambridge students in agricultural economics, Twum Berima and Assem from the Gold Coast. My teammates on the LSE cricket and football teams included Godfrey Amachree, who would become Nigeria's attorney general, F.J. Idigbe, a law student from Nigeria, and Sam Crabbe of Gold Coast, a future chief justice there. Roy McCaulay of Sierra Leone and 'M'Chauru of Tanganyika would be heads of important social services agencies while Raymond Njoku would become Nigeria's Minister of Transport.

The African connection had been initiated earlier in the century, when members on both sides of my family — father's first cousin, Laura Dawes (Neville's mother), and my mother's cousin, Rhona Douglas (Enid's and Daphne's mother), had spent several years in Calabar, Eastern Nigeria with their missionary-teacher husbands. They were among a larger group of Jamaicans who had enjoyed this valuable experience, including Sam Hart, F.E. Jones, James Manderson-Jones (father of attorney, Dr Ronald), Canon Walter Brown and the Reverend gentlemen R.A. Llewellyn and Henry Ward. My mother used to tell of one or two visiting Africans to her parents' home in August Town during the earlier years of the century and of several missionaryteachers engaging in practice preaching at the family church, St. Cyprian's.

So, long ago, we had been fortunate in gaining some authentic knowledge of so-called 'dark Africa'. The connection was bolstered by the strong link forged by my godfather, Archdeacon Lennon, a long-time resident of Eastern Nigeria (as mentioned in Chapter 1) and Reverend Fraser, famous Principal of the foremost Gold Coast educational institution, Achimota College (whose son 'Sandy' became an equally famous Headmaster of Jamaica's Munro). Some of our African colleagues in London told us (West Indians) that they had been students of Lennon or Fraser and of the contribution made by these men.

One of the most interesting incidents which occurred during my time in London concerned Seretse Khama, chief-designate of the Bamangwato people in Bechuanaland. He was the centre of a political and international storm over his friendship with a white English girl, Ruth Williams. The blossoming romance between the two was accompanied by feverish activities by the colonial office, represented by secretary of state Gordon-Walker, John Keith, director of colonial scholars, and by the South African authorities. When Seretse, in defiance of his uncle, Chief Regent Tshekedi, and the British government, married Ruth in 1948, he was banished by the British, in deference to South Africa.

Ruth was well-known to us at Nutford House. She visited Seretse there and attended our dances. Within a decade and a half, Seretse would be restored to respectability, becoming Prime Minister and then president of the newly independent Botswana, acquiring a knighthood *en route*. In 1975 he would visit Jamaica, with Ruth and their grown-up twin sons, for the Commonwealth heads of government meeting, and a Nutford House old boys reunion.

On returning to London in 1945 we frequently met the Shackleford brothers, 'Bank' and 'Akin', born in Lagos of a Jamaican father. Bank would come to Jamaica, work with Seprod and teach in the engineering department of the College of Arts, Science and Technology .

Future West Indian leaders were cutting their teeth as students, beginning in 1945 and 1946: Eugenia Charles of Dominica and future governor general of the Bahamas Gerald Cash, at the Inns of Court; and a demobbed Michael Manley at LSE. There was tall, slim Forbes Burnham. He impressed everyone as a highly intelligent, articulate, witty and urbane young man and gave indications of the oratorical skills which would be developed later. On occasion, signs appeared suggesting characteristics which some would consider essential prerequisites for a successful political career. On my visits to British Guiana from 1960 onwards, I used to get in touch and be entertained by him, but I did not do so in later years when I became critical of his actions. We must remember, however, that leaders are partly creatures of context and circumstances. One wonders whether he would not have seemed an entirely different personality and type of leader in a different context.

Other notable scholars were Elsa Goveia, brilliant Guyanese historian who was the University of the West Indies' first female professor and first professor of West Indian history, and Lucille Mair, a future ambassador and United Nations assistant under-secretary general. Phyllis MacPherson-Russell who was Issa scholar the year after me, and future minister of education, joined Leslie Robinson, Elsa and Lucille at UCL. Before these, came medical students Lenore Harney and Gwyneth O'Reilly of St. Kitts and Antigua. Sharing accommodation with Leslie and of similar stature, were two medical students from Trinidad, Mervyn Henry and Harold Hamilton. Two or three years later, others would join this company, including Arthur Brown, Don Mills, O.D. Marsh and Jack Harewood at LSE, and David Coore and Hector Wynter at Oxford. Other noteworthy students were Viv Blake, Douglas Manley, and Leacroft Robinson.

Impelled by the growing number of West Indian students in the British Isles and the significant development then taking place at home, a few students began to discuss the desirability of developing a connecting link for the promotion of 'cooperation and unity among the peoples of the region.' So a group of students gathered at St.

Peter's Church Hall, Belsize Square in north-west London on December 28, 1945, and decided to form the West Indian Students Union (WISU). Initiated by an executive committee led by president Ken Sealy, WISU organized a range of activities. These included talks by visiting West Indians such as N.N. ('Crab') Nethersole, presentations by members, and a study group led by Arthur Lewis and organized by Elsa Goveia.

Perhaps the most significant event in which WISU was engaged was sending a deputation, including Guy Mathurin, Forbes Burnham, Dossie Carberry, A. ('Bunny') Cunningham, and Winnie Birkbeck, to discuss the proposed University of the West Indies with secretary of state for the colonies, Arthur Creech Jones. Among the issues raised by the delegation was the importance of having a university 'which fulfilled our social, economic and political needs.' Also discussed were the need to increase the proposed ratio of female students and the question of academic freedom for the university. On this last issue, the WISU suggested a system of grants to avoid the university being embarrassed by the annual wrangle of passing the estimates in the local legislatures. The deputation also sought an assurance that qualified West Indians would be appointed if available. They warned that it would be all too easy for the university to become a little English college quite out of touch with the community around it.

By 1946 a new executive committee had been elected which included, apart from the members of the deputation to the Colonial Secretary, Gloria Fraser Scott, Frank Williams, and Hilda Gibbs Bynoe of Grenada, a medical student, destined as Dame Hilda to become the region's first female governor general. The WISU later branched out, with the formation of an Oxford group, convened by David Coore.

Early in its life, the WISU also moved to forge international relations, especially with the World Students Union, and sent delegates to a number of conferences, festivals, work camps in several European countries. The first of these was the world students congress held in Prague, August 1946, at which the union was represented by Winnie Birkbeck. In the following year, the youth festival, also convened in Prague, and was attended by a delegation led by the new president Forbes Burnham.

It should be noted, however, that not very long after these events there was a split in the youth movement, which produced two organizations, one communist, the other 'free world'.

Despite the rigours and shortages of war-time and its aftermath, students found avenues of entertainment and relaxation. As in Jamaica, the big jazz and dance bands were at their best. We enjoyed student dances at Nutford House and spent many a Saturday evening at Hammersmith Palais. We were fascinated by the formalized and unspontaneous English dancing, uni-directionally circumnavigating the floor as if drilled by a sergeant. To the English, the West Indian *rent a tile* dancing style was a travesty. We became acquainted with Jamaican poet Una Marson, and a number of West Indians in the music world such as Edric Connor, bass vocalist and pianist Winnifred Atwell, both from Trinidad. We met Cy Grant of British Guiana, Nadia Cattouse of British Honduras and Grenadian Leslie ('Hutch') Hutchinson. Reg Phillips and I visited Hutch's home through our friendship with his daughter Leslie, a law student at LSE We learnt that during his pre-London stay in New York, Cole Porter wrote some songs for him. In London, as a café pianist and singer, he was very popular in high society circles, particularly with the ladies. We were also shown the crater left by the bomb which destroyed the famous 'Cafe de Paris' in London's west end, killing many of its socialite patrons flocking to hear and see West Indian 'Snake-hips' Johnson and his band — when the leader himself perished.

We enjoyed excellent films involving actors and actresses such as Louis Jouvet, Raimu, Michèle Morgan, and Jean Gabin. Directors Vittorio de Sica (*The Bicycle Thief*), Jean Cocteau (*Orphée*) and Marcel Carné were also unquestioned attractions. One of Carné's films, Les Enfants du Paradis, with Arletty and the famous mime Jean-Louis Barrault, is unforgettable. It is certainly among the three best films I have seen. I emphasize that view after having seen it in the middle 1940s, again during the 1960s and for a third time in 1975. It seems to me that those of a younger generation who have been brought up almost entirely on a diet of Hollywood productions and have not been exposed to the varied fare which we enjoyed in its breadth and depth have suffered a deficiency and missed an important ingredient in their intellectual and cultural development.

For the school, Rudolph Cousins and I formed, if I say so myself, a formidable pair of opening bowlers, while Pat Burke was one of the opening batsmen. In addition, our university cricket club included Abbott, who played for Essex, Rusi S. Cooper, and David Atkinson, a medical student from Derbyshire and Dr Monica Lewin's husband.

I was also selected to play for the combined English universities team against the Scottish Universities. Our team included Leslie ('Bunny') Williams, studying at Newcastle, and later chief of Jubilee maternity hospital. Coincidentally too, Bill Robertson, a member of the Scottish team, would join the staff of the University hospital. In our game against Liverpool, both captains were Jamaican, the other Henry Shaw, the future Kingston Public hospital surgeon. My successor as captain of the London University team was medical student Bertram Ross of St. Kitts, who would captain the Leewards in Jamaica at Sabina Park in 1958.

I was also President of the Sports Union and played football and LSE reached the finals of the Cambridge inter-collegiate soccer league. When we played at Christ's College, I noted photographs of cricket and football teams which included goal-keeper Rolph Grant, later of T.Geddes Grant Limited, Trinidad and the University of the West Indies's finance and general purposes committee. Some two decades later, Franz ('Gerry') Alexander would emulate Grant's record as Cambridge 'double blue', West Indies cricket captain and member of England's amateur football team. When LSE played UCL at football, there was Leslie Robinson, the future University of the West Indies pro-vice-chancellor, opposing me from his position as right winger. Engaged in rare sports activities for West Indians were Randy Douglas of LSE in rowing and Vernon Lindo who played rugger for his London hospital. Randy Douglas would become chief justice of Barbados, ambassador to Washington and high commissioner to the United Kingdom.

A highlight of an altogether different kind centered on my first trip to Paris, as captain of the school's football team against our French counterpart, L'Ecole des Hautes Etudes Commerciales. A long-standing annual event, the venue alternating between the two cities, but suspended during the War, it was revived in 1946. We also played a match against the champion club of Chartres where the beautiful stained glass windows of the famous Cathedral had been removed for safe keeping during the war. There, the local newspaper billed our team as including three internationals, namely two African colleagues and myself.

My last winter before taking Final exams in 1947 was recorded as the worst in the century up to that time. The records reveal that between February 2 and 22, 1947 there was not one hour of sunshine! There was a critical shortage of coal which represented 90% of the fuel used for industrial and domestic purposes and the severity of the weather aggravated Britain's financial crisis, influencing United States aid to the country. The country's foreign exchange situation was in a parlous state. Without coal for heating or electricity and with heavy smog, we suffered not only dire discomfort, but considerable problems in preparing for exams.

That winter was a metaphor for the harsh realities of some aspects of the life we endured in London. Yet we were happy in each other's company. Those early stirrings of West Indian integration provided a nest of warmth and security against a cold society. I shall never forget the spirit of brotherhood among us students especially at Nutford House.

6

LIAISON OFFICER IN LONDON:
Taking care of future leaders

In the late 1940s, the British colonial office persuaded colonial governments to establish posts of liaison officer to look after the welfare of their students in the British Isles. In 1948 I was appointed to represent the West Indies. I was seconded from my post in the Treasury to which I had returned from studies at LSE nine months before, and was based in London, at the colonial office.

This appointment was significant in two respects. It represented the first realistic effort at regional representation, ten years before the founding of the ill-fated Federation; and the West Indies boasted the only native liaison officer. All the other countries had recruited retired colonial service officers who had served as district commissioners in those colonies.

Travelling to London on that banana boat, I would meet Winnifred Moss, of the colonial secretariat, bound for Westminster Hospital as student nurse and later to become Mrs. G. E. Mills. Another fellow traveller was Ewart Forrest, a future Solicitor General and Privy Councillor.

I arrived in the United Kingdom early June 1948. My constituents during my term of office, 1948-1951, numbered approximately 1200 to 1500 students distributed throughout the British Isles including the Irish republic.

The liaison officer's responsibilities ranged from assistance in securing admission to tertiary educational institutions and in providing accommodation, resolving financial and other problems, helping with vacation employment, to contacting regional governments in advance, in efforts to ensure employment on the graduate's return home.

During my tenure, I was assisted for different periods by Colin Bryan, Norma Marsh Wint, Willie Richardson of Trinidad and his wife Leslie. Other colleagues served temporarily as liaison officers for colonial servicemen, dealing with the problem of demobilization at the end of the war. Among them, Dudley Thompson, Ulric Cross and Johnny Smythe of Sierra Leone who would become his country's attorney general. It was in that office, too, that I first met Aubrey Fraser of British Guiana, who was earning pocket money in the filing room.

In London, where the majority of the students was concentrated, the British Council provided accommodation in residences at Nutford House, Hans Crescent and Collingham Gardens, and at intransit hostels at 77 Wimpole Street and Hallam Street. Other organizations, notably the Methodist Church which established a set of international houses, supplemented these British Council efforts on behalf of overseas students.

A significant number of students were on scholarship, having payment of their allowances disbursed by the colonial office. Queen's counsel Emil George, once reminded me of his request, on arrival as a young Dominica Island Scholar to Oxford, for my assistance in managing his quarterly allowance. The majority, however, were private students, some barely eking out an existence and anxious to secure part-time employment.

One case of unforgettable desperation is that of Dalip Singh, a Trinidadian, studying dentistry in Edinburgh. He appealed for financial aid to complete his studies, stating that both his parents had died recently in a motor accident. An enquiry relayed to his government evoked the brief response: 'Both parents of person named alive and well.' Some years after returning home to practice his profession, he was convicted of murdering his wife and executed.

Unlike the situation in North America where it has long been the custom for students to complete their tertiary education from earnings obtained by working during term time and vacations, opportunities for such part-time employment in Britain were not as widespread.

The liaison officer was also expected to provide a roster of doctors, dentists and lawyers, from which students could select if they needed such professional services. My medical list included David Pitt of Grenada, later elevated to the House of Lords, long-time Barbadian resident in England, Belfield Clarke and C. Bertie Clarke, also of Barbados, a member of the W.I. cricket team vs England in 1939. Contacts were maintained with students, via correspondence and through regular tours of all five component countries of the British Isles.

Among the less pleasant responsibilities of my job were assignments associated with the illness or death of students and acting as friend and supporter in cases involving legal action against a student. Such incidents involved getting in touch with parents and attending inquests and funerals. My first contact with the family of A.N.R. Robinson, former prime minister of Trinidad and Tobago, followed the tragic death by gas poisoning of his older brother, a London law student. I also attended an inquest following the death of an English boy who had impaled himself while playing on an iron railing. He had been treated and sent home by Nobel Sarkar, one of our medical students at Sheffield. Since the parents were threatening to take legal action, I went up for the inquest and stood as *amicus curiae* for Sarkar. Fortunately, the matter was not pursued.

An unwelcome incident was the visit paid to me by an officer from the special branch of Scotland Yard. His mission was to enquire into the political attitudes and activities of students and he wanted information about any West Indian student who appeared to be on 'the left'. He was quite upset by my sending him packing on the basic principle that I was there to represent and assist students and took a very dim view of being expected to act as informer.

There was also an embarrassing experience which taught me a lesson in dealing with the media. Following my tours of student locations and meetings with constituents, I would feed information to a free-lance journalist on the successes, achievements and problems of our students. After visiting Dublin and Cork, I mentioned that students felt somewhat isolated, being far away from colleagues and without access to West Indian newspapers. Within a fortnight, I was asked to see Mr. Keith, director of colonial scholars. He produced a letter written by the angry Archbishop Ryan of Port of Spain, enclosing a clipping from the *Port of Spain Gazette*. The clipping had a headline which read, 'West Indian students in Ireland unhappy'and implied that I had reported that they were distressed and subject to very poor treatment by their Irish hosts. As a result the irate prelate threatened to discontinue his practice of providing opportunities for scholarships to Irish universities.

The liaison officer had responsibility for both scholarship holders and private students. Some were winners of the Rhodes, or other prestigious national scholarships, such as the Jamaica, Barbados, Trinidad, the Jamaica Centenary, and CD&W scholarships. These scholarships were available in diverse fields, from economics to forestry to medicine. The British Council awards were made primarily in the arts and cultural fields.

I recall that many of these scholars arrived in pairs: Francis Xavier Mark and A. Knolly Butler of Trinidad, Haynes of Barbados and Harry Phelps of Trinidad, both for engineering. Among my most vivid memories is that of two bright and brash young law students arriving in 1950 *en route* to Cambridge: one was Ian Ramsay, Jamaica Centenary scholar who would be famous for surrendering his Queen's Counsel status: the other, Oliver Jackman, Barbados scholar, a future ambassador and Inter-American human rights activist.

I have already referred to those future prime ministers who were my contemporaries as students: Burnham, Cato, Charles, and Manley. There were some who came during my tenure as liaison officer and were numbered among my charges: Errol Barrow, Linden Pindling and John Compton, of Barbados, the Bahamas and St. Lucia respectively. Future attorney general and opposition leader of The Bahamas, Kendall Isaacs, always seemed too sensitive, modest, and quiet for the rough and tumble of politics. Nor did I foresee that Ivo Heath, medical student in Belfast, would also embark on a similar political career in Antigua. Early associations with these future leaders in politics and other arenas would facilitate access and support for the University of the West Indies' public administration education and training programmes on my visits to their countries during the 1960s and 1970s.

Law and medicine were the most highly represented groups, as the traditional, prestigious professions throughout the region. The majority of these did not need my services. Among the contenders for the Bar were future chief justices such as Ken Smith of Jamaica, Denys Williams of Barbados, attorneys general Shridath ('Sonny') Ramphal and Fred Wills of B.G., Fred ('Sleepy') Smith of Barbados, and Paul Adderley of the Bahamas. Those destined for the high court bench included Aubrey Fraser, Clifford Husbands, Chappie Marsh, Charles Perkins of Trinidad, and Dossie Carberry. At Bristol was Arthur D. Hanna of the Bahamas, a future minister of finance and deputy to prime minister Pindling. Destined either for the private bar, or for practice as solicitors were David Coore, Richard and Edward Ashenheim, Ronald Williams and Emil George all like Carberry, also at Oxford. A particularly interesting member of the law group was H.O'.B. ('Mac') Fernandez-McCartney. Studying part-time and working at the Millbank offices of the Crown agents for the colonies, Mac was most active in organizing and getting financial sponsorship for West Indian student cricket tours of northern England. Another member of that group Colin Moore of the Bahamas would emigrate to Australia as a university lecturer. When I visited Canberra in 1981, he had been appointed head of the federal electoral system and entertained me at lunch.

The medical students were to be found in schools throughout the British Isles and most of them were on CD&W scholarships. There was a strong contingent in Dublin, especially at the Royal Colleges, including H. W. and A. W. Eldemire, the former would become minister of health, Ossie Tomlinson, now custos of St. Ann, Carol deLisser, Stuart Gray, Keith Stanley of Mandeville, Ernest Wells, John Williams. It was in Cork that I first met Matthew Beaubrun of St. Lucia, subsequently, physician to prime minister Manley and Ambassador to Venezuela.

Among the large number of nurses were future matrons such as Cislyn Lambert of the University hospital of the West Indies, and Doreen Margetson of Montserrat's premier hospital. Gertrude Swaby would become senior tutor in nursing for Jamaica and Olive Ennever would be appointed principal tutor of the University hospital. Grenada was represented by Monica Munro Clyne, their future chief nursing officer, and Joan St. Bernard Bierzynski.

There were the media men like the inimitable A.E.T. Henry of Jamaica. He was premier Norman Manley's public relations officer and was bound for the British Broadcasting Corporation (BBC). Calvin Bowen of the *Daily Gleaner*, had been awarded a Commonwealth journalists scholarship, and A.F. Raymond, Trinidad's information officer. A story is told of Henry's first weeks at the BBC, when an Irish colleague heard a voice from behind him bubbling with the blarney. Spinning around and coming face to face with Henry, he exclaimed, 'Begorra! A smoked Irishman!'

Those representing the arts included Louise Bennett Coverley, Cecil Baugh, Ivy Baxter, and Noel Vaz, who were all on British Council scholarships. There were two artists who would become famous beyond their own territorial boundaries: Denis Williams of British Guiana and M.P. Aladdin of Trinidad. It was in music that the arts flourished at that time, boasting in that group, Hazel Lawson Street, Julien Barber, Billy Pilgrim of British Guiana and later the Jamaica Broadcasting Corporation, Pat Vermont, Lloyd Hall, Dennis Brown, Sheila Anderson, Olive Lewin, Fay Hale Lindo and Daphne Segre. Segre returned to Jamaica decades later, to direct the school of music. Olive and Fay assisted me in organizing a concert for the opening of a Colonial Exhibition by King George VI. Rita Inniss-Coore of Trinidad would bless Jamaica with her incomparable skills as music teacher and the genius of her son, Stephen ('Cat') of the Third World band.

We had language specialists in Rae Charles, Frank Abdullah and Eustace Seignoret, all of Trinidad, and Hector and Sylvia Wynter, Probyn Marsh, Pauline Christie of Jamaica. Charles would hone his skills on the United Nations staff, while Abdullah, Seignoret and Marsh would employ theirs as diplomats. The first two served their government as permanent representative to the United Nations, and permanent secretary to the ministry of external affairs, and the third as ambassador to France. Hector Wynter enjoyed a variety of careers at the University of the West Indies, UNESCO and the ministry of education. Pauline was appointed later dean of the faculty of arts and general studies at Mona. Sydney Scott would become headmaster of Glenmuir High School.

Studying the natural sciences were Alfred Sangster, president of College of Arts, Science and Technology, and Dennis Irvine who would become professor of chemistry at Ibadan University in Nigeria and vice-chancellor at the university of Guyana. There was also Eric Frater who would serve as headmaster at Rusea's High School and the University of the West Indies as senior assistant registrar.

During this period administrative training for members of the civil service began. This training was to prepare them for the responsibilities of self-government and independence and was undertaken at Oxford, Cambridge or LSE. It was only then that the colonial authorities acknowledged that civil servants required special training to assume administrative responsibilities. This neglect reflected the traditional British attitude that administrative skill is an art which could be learnt only by 'picking it up on the job.'

Among those who went to the United Kingdom in the late 1940s to participate in this programme were future permanent secretaries and chief technical advisers, such as O.H. Goldson, Vin McFarlane, Pat Clerk, Horace Barber, Ashton Wright all of Jamaica, Bernard ('Chess') Gibbs, Keith Alleyne, later attorney general of the Windward Islands, Gavin Kennard and Arthur Abrahams of British Guiana, the last subsequently burned to death with his family in the racial riots of 1964. Usually I attended the preliminary seminar and at the request of the West Indian department, I also arranged for British Guianese participants to meet representatives of the department regularly for discussion.

Serious efforts were also initiated towards training an officer cadre for the police service at the Metropolitan police school in Hendon. My charges included Nathan Houston, Ken Mayne, A.C. Foulkes, a future assistant commissioner, Sidney Anderson who would become St. Vincent's impressive colonel and chief of police in 1954. Two others, Orville Bernard and Fred MacIntosh, were both destined to become assistant commissioners and, tragically, to be killed similarly by gunmen. Arriving shortly before my departure was Basil Robinson, who would create history as the first to rise from the ranks to leadership of the force, and eventually to even loftier heights as custos and deputy governor general.

A significant proportion of students were men and women who by virtue of their war service and the required admission qualifications were awarded education and training grants by the British Further Education and Training Programme (FEVT). Many careers were moulded via this route. Arthur Wint and Vernon Lindo studied medicine. Errol Barrow, Ena Collymore Woodstock, Roydel Lawrence, Ulric Cross, Uriah Parnell, Dusty Miller, Arthur Dujon, John Blair were all trained in law. The non-traditional areas of study were represented by Roy Augier and John Hearne in history, Ivo deSouza in administration, M.W. ('Ruddy') Austin in construction, Victor Beek in quantity surveying, John Clarke, W.S. Richardson, Fred Barrows, Alvin Chapman, Lloyd Johnson, N.W. Mills, all in accounting, Bunny Rae in electronics and Stanley Thomas in social work. Among those in economics was U.V. Campbell who, after adding law to his professional qualifications, would move to the courts of appeal in Jamaica and the Bahamas. There were also St. A. Clarke, later of the Economic Commission for Latin America and the

Caribbean (ECLAC), Douglas Collins, who would serve as Jamaica's Cabinet Secretary, Clive McMorris, Hutton Griffith, later British Guiana's deputy director of civil aviation and Julian Marryshow. Ena Collymore would move to the High Court bench, Roydel Lawrence taught at the University of Papua-New Guinea, and Richardson worked with the Colonial Development Corporation and later Peat Marwick.

Perhaps the largest single group consisted of those who studied engineering. This large group included E.K. Powell, a future minister of state, Douglas Wint, Dennis Anderson, Hugh Brand, C.F. Batts, Terry Higgins, Alvin Mair, Victor Panton, Keble Williams, John ('Cleve') Lawrence and Dennis Mendez. Many of these would return to establish businesses in Jamaica. Wint, Batts and Lawrence would all serve in the public works department, the first ultimately becoming director of the department, and the last, deputy contractor general.

The welfare and students department's outpost in Edinburgh had responsibility for Scotland and the north of England. Edinburgh and Glasgow had been traditional educational centres for West Indian medical and engineering students respectively. After the war the range of institutions and subject areas had widened to include Aberdeen, St. Andrew's and Newcastle and the humanities. At St. Andrew's were Gloria Cummins of Barbados, Gloria Constantine, Glory Robertson (St. Hugh's High School's first Jamaica Scholar), Mary Jones Langford, and Roy Augier. Located at Newcastle were dental student Leila Gibbs Augier and medical students Rolph Richards and Quintin Bynoe, all of Trinidad. Rolph would become professor of medicine at the University of the West Indies.

In addition to the medical students, were veterinarian Lyndon McLaren, Hester Field Rousseau and architect-in-training Hal Lawson. The most distinguished of all, Phil Lecky, father of the Jamaica Hope cattle, who was completing his Ph.D. Edwin P. Minnis of the Bahamas, an economics student would follow this with a professional accounting qualification, later becoming a senior lecturer at Strathclyde university and a member of the 1993 commission of inquiry, investigating allegations of fraud and corruption in certain prominent Bahamian public institutions. In Glasgow, Don Martin and Dennis Mendez of Jamaica and J.N. Supersad of Trinidad continued the engineering tradition while C.L. (Peter) Bent would become a veterinarian.

A young and debonair G.E. Mills circa 1960.

Uncle J.J. Mills, one of three men who most influenced the author's life. The other two were Earl Maynair and Allan Abrahams.

Mama Josephine Mills.

Papa Gilbert Mills.

4 Grist for the Mills

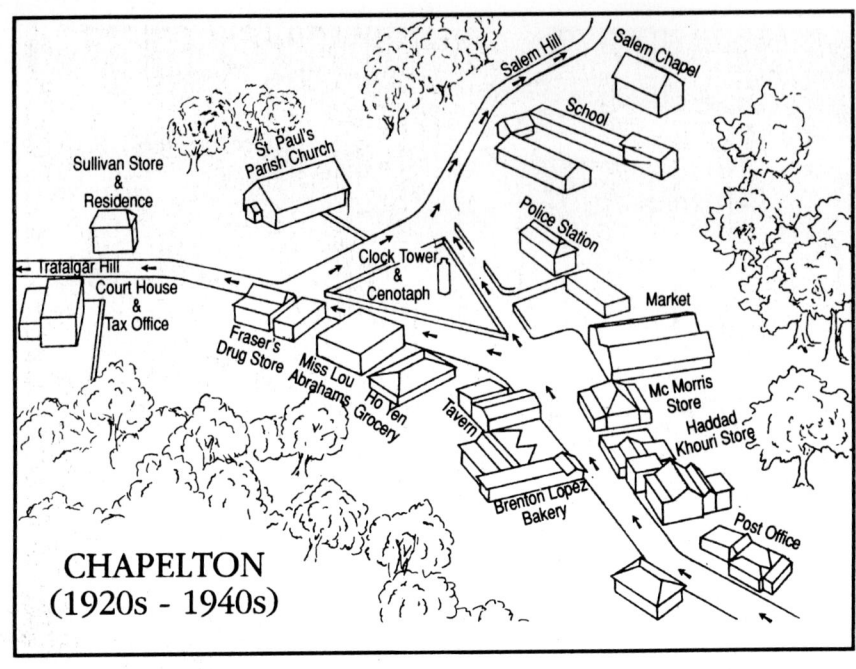

CHAPELTON
(1920s - 1940s)

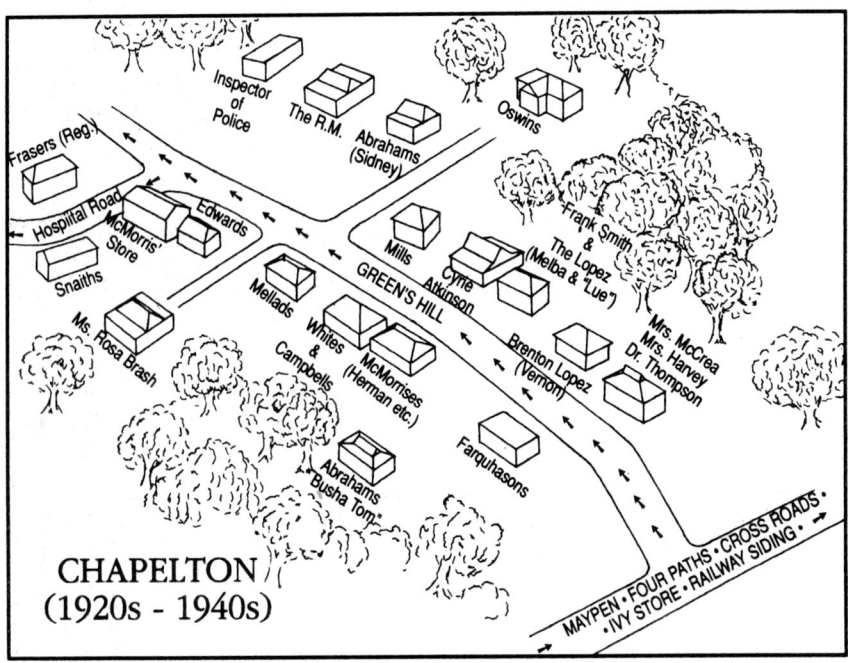

CHAPELTON
(1920s - 1940s)

Grist for the Mills 5

A modern aerial view of Chapelton. The Cenotaph and St. Paul's church are clearly visible, in the centre of the picture.

Reginald N. Murray

William 'Pross' Cowper

Above and Right,
Formidable headmasters of the 1930s.

Below,
Jamaica College in 1937.

Right,
Gladstone and Winnifred after their wedding at St. Martins in the Fields, London 1949

Below,
The Mills brothers and their wives in London.

8 Grist for the Mills

Residents of Nutford House 1945/46.

With one of many Diploma in Public Administration groups, U.W.I. 1963 - 64.

The Brandenburg Gate and a section of the Berlin Wall, 1966.

10 Grist for the Mills

The Berlin Wall under construction.

J.C.'s victorious Sunlight Cup team of 1938 with G.E. Mills as captain.

L.S.E. Cricket team 1945.

L.S.E. Football team 1944/5

With staff members of the West Indian department of the Colonial Office about 1950.

In cricket circles with members of the 1971 touring Indian Test team.

Four O.J.'s at Kings House in 1989. Left to right Leslie Robinson, Gladstone Mills, Joyce Robinson and Harold Milner.

Celebrating the 10th anniversary of the Electoral Advisory Committee.

Receiving gifts at a farewell function hosted by U.W.I. Vice-Chancellor Alistair McIntyre.

Most staff members of the colonial office seemed sympathetic and supportive, facilitating efforts by the liaison officers to assist students in surmounting problems of admission, housing, finance and employment. Among those in the West Indian department were Douglas Smith, who would later spend a year on secondment to the Ministry of Finance in Jamaica, and Barry Smallman, who was later appointed British high commissioner to Jamaica. The director of information services was Mr. Kenneth Blackburn, before his promotion to governorship of the Leewards, and later, of Jamaica and subsequently, Jamaica's first governor-general.

By far the most helpful person in the Welfare Department was Ivor Cummings who performed legendary feats in securing admission for students, especially through the almost closed doors of medical schools, and also in obtaining part-time employment for others. There are many professionals now practising throughout the Caribbean and West Africa, who owe their career opportunities to Cummings, not all of whom have shown their appreciation for his significant assistance.

At the other extreme were those officials administering the FEVT scheme who, themselves without the benefit of tertiary education, resented and resolutely reacted against the idea of such higher educational opportunities being afforded to so many blacks. This attitude tended to be expressed in an automatic cancellation of grants, and immediate booking of berths for transportation home, following even a minor failure in examination, with such action often being taken without calling the relevant institution for comment or recommendation. Even now, more than 40 years later, I can recall my confrontations with these gentlemen and my hackles rising in reaction to their attitude and actions.

An incident which occurred indicates the typically aggressive Jamaican response to insensitive treatment. An ex-serviceman (not a student) armed with a payment voucher, after waiting for hours in the reception room at the welfare department, was shunted on to the air ministry as the proper disbursing agency. After travelling by bus to that ministry and subjected to another long wait, he was sent back to the colonial office. When he eventually arrived upstairs again after another waiting period and the official whom he had seen originally came out to the counter, our compatriot reached over, grabbed the official's tie and with a sharpened pocket knife severed it, leaving only the knot, demanding in a threatening voice, 'Gimme my r..s money!' In a jiffy the payment was disbursed, all doubts about appropriate disbursement and jurisdictional agencies being deferred to be resolved by adjustment vouchers later.

In the late 1940s and early 1950s in Britain racial problems were not yet widespread, beyond the black seaport enclaves such as Cardiff and Liverpool. The effects of the 'Empire Windrush' invasion, which heralded a great wave and flood of immigrants, had not yet burgeoned, and our elite group of colonial students still possessed a high visibility quotient. Britain could still sustain its superior posture towards the USA in its attitude to race relations. There were incidents, albeit isolated ones, though some assumed serious dimensions, such as the case brought by Learie Constantine in 1944 against the Imperial Hotel in Russell Square for refusing him and his wife a room which had been reserved.

Another memorable incident focused on a British Overseas Airways Company (BOAC) display window on Regent Street, depicting in life-size dimensions, an English traveller in the jungle, helmeted and in khaki shorts, being transported on the shoulders of four natives, unclothed in 'G-strings'. Since a number of angry African and West Indian students were threatening to throw bricks at the window, my colleague flight lieutenant Johnny Smythe, and I decided to intervene.

Enlisting the support of Smythe's friend, member of parliament John Lewis, we visited the BOAC offices on a Friday afternoon. The manager proved reluctant to see us but Lewis successfully invoked the name of the minister of civil aviation. He retreated under pressure, from a position of 'doesn't the display in fact, depict a real-life situation?' to a plea for understanding. Cigars and drinks not proferred initially, were now volunteered in response to Lewis' insistence on immediate removal of the offending display. On Lewis's suggestion we visited the scene next Monday morning and observed the English traveller on foot, trudging along, transporting his bags, natives no longer around!

By the 1960s, racial animosity had intensified, following the influx of West Indians, Africans, Indians and Pakistanis. The movement began with the return to the United Kingdom of many West Indian demobilized ex-servicemen, disillusioned and frustrated by the absence of employment opportunities at home. I was down at London docks to meet the relatively few students arriving on the 'Windrush', on that landmark occasion in 1948 when Louise Bennett's *Colonization in Reverse* began.

The change in overtly expressed attitudes, especially on the part of young British men, was evident in their hostility on seeing one of us driving a fairly expensive car. I discovered this during a visit in 1966 when I bought a Rover 2000. And such attitudes were also displayed by the police, 'Is this your vehicle?'

I have been the target of similar attitudes and actions in the United States. The Americans tended at times to be more brutal than the British. These attributes were well illustrated by an unforgettable experience early in my sojourn in Cambridge, Massachusetts on postgraduate studies at Harvard. I shall never forget that night in 1957. It was my first real experience of American racism. That night Aneurin Bevan, the famous Welsh left-wing firebrand of the British Labour Party, was scheduled to speak in Harvard Yard. Bevan was regarded as one of the most eloquent of orators in recent British history and was considered by Churchill to be a worthy rival. Unable to get in because of the crowd, I suggested that we go to a nearby café for a cup of coffee. Only one fellow student, a white girl, accepted the invitation.

While sitting, sipping coffee and talking, I heard an angry growling sound nearby. I was at first entirely unaware that the voice was addressing me, until I noticed a young white man hovering by. 'What you think you're doing sitting with a white girl?' I was taken totally aback, having assumed that New England was free of such overtly expressed prejudice. I replied, 'Where I come from, I am accustomed to sitting with girls, whether white, brown, black.' Responding angrily, 'I couldn't care less about what you do where you come from; you don't sit with a white girl here.' He grabbed me and ripped my shirt down the front. It seemed that the stocky, black waiter had sized up the situation, and scaling the counter, he came to my rescue. I am ashamed to say that I stood by witnessing the battle of fists and chairs, not participating but leaving the attack totally to my supporter. In the meantime, two other young men, companions of the attacker, showed signs of entering the fray. Someone telephoned the police, and they decided to make a run for it.

The police took all four of us to the station and, after hearing the story, informed me that they could take no action. The only recourse would be a suit formally initiated by me. My attacker pleaded with me, by gestures, not to pursue the matter by such an action. Significantly a policeman who entered the station later enquired aggressively what we were doing there, and on hearing the story, his remark virtually implied, 'Well, what were you doing sitting with a white girl, anyway?' On my return to the apartment, Leslie Robinson who was my roomate, startled at seeing my face and clothes in such a condition, knew immediately that some dire incident had occurred. I kept that shirt as a souvenir for some 25 years.

Another experience occurred *en route* home from Harvard in August 1958 following a short stay in Washington D.C. We travelled to Miami to board the 'S.S. Evangeline' and while waiting at the pier along with Dr. Horace Bramwell and his wife, the doctor and I decided to buy hot dogs and drinks for our two families. The manager at the counter refused to serve us unless we went to the back. We refused to do so and left without food. As we walked back to the pier, a white beggar approached us. We gave him about two dollars and suggested that he should go to the same café and tell the man at the counter the source of his gift.

Returning to the United Kingdom, I found that very pleasant assignments and opportunities were open to me as liaison officer. First, there was the good fortune of deepening my West Indian consciousness. I also enjoyed the advantage of gaining a wide knowledge of the British Isles which very few of the natives possessed.

A special privilege of being a liaison officer was an opportunity to meet and hear the great singer-political activist Paul Robeson in 1949 when he stopped briefly in London. A few months before, he had given a free concert to crowds estimated at 50,000-80,000 at the Kingston race course. In an intimate setting, seated on the floor in a London room, we listened with rapt attention as he sang and spoke in his deep resonant voice which held us spell bound. Already being hounded by the American authorities, his passport would soon be taken away in an imposition of travel restrictions.

The principal entertainment event provided by the liaison officer was the annual Christmas dance sponsored jointly by all the liaison officers for students. The guests numbered thousands, and included appropriate colonial office staff and representatives from organizations with which we worked closely. Among the distinguished guests in 1948 were secretary of state Creech Jones and his wife. For such a large crowd, we were obliged to hire the spacious Porchester or Seymour Hall.

Always assisting us in a voluntary one man cabaret performance was singer and guitarist Ivan Browne of Montserrat. Ivan would graduate from the Norman Manley Law school four decades later, as perhaps their oldest student. One doctor-designate demonstrated early entrepreneurial ingenuity at these dances, by photographing participants, rushing back with proofs and securing orders from patrons intoxicated by the euphoric atmosphere of the dance. Indeed, he adopted a similar strategy successfully to finance a return trip home on holiday, on that occasion exploiting the susceptibility of captive boat passengers.

For West Indians the Continent was our oyster. Although most of us were island dwellers, we did not share the insular attitude of the English, expressed and epitomized in the newspaper headline, 'Fog Over Channel. Continent Isolated!' I took full advantage of these opportunities; and recall among other pleasures, enjoying black American Josephine Baker's scintillating performance at the Folies Bergère and sopranos Lily Pons and Kirsten Flagstad; and the dancing of Roland Petit and Renée Jeanmaire. An additional source of pleasure was a holiday in Juan-les-Pins, at the time, still a small unspoilt village. We also enjoyed many a driving-camping trip on the Continent.

Occasionally I was invited by the West Indian department of the colonial office to join in discussions with visiting officials especially on the subjects of student welfare and employment opportunities in the West Indies. The highlights of my first year as liaison officer, both occurring in the summer of 1948, were certainly the visit by Chief Minister Alexander Bustamante of Jamaica, and the London Olympics.

I was invited by John Southgate, head of the Jamaica desk in the West Indian Department, to join him in meeting Mr. Bustamante on arrival for his first visit to the United Kingdom. We travelled to Liverpool and early next morning met the banana boat which had brought the 'Chief' and Miss Longbridge. It was difficult to get into his suite. The room was crammed with media men who were being entertained and were fascinated by stories of his exploits, some dramatized, depicting him with guns blazing as he lay on the cabin floor.

He had brought his Buick 'Straight 8' and while the car was handed over to a liveried lady from the ministry of transport to be driven to London, Southgate and I accompanied the visitors on a train journey to the city in a specially prepared compartment. The visit seemed to have been singularly successful, quite apart from the Chief Minister's official discussions. Wherever he went, representatives of the press followed, especially when he distributed bunches of bananas among poorer people in London's east end. His leonine locks fascinated everyone and one daily paper published a cartoon of him, focusing on his hair and the 'new Bustamante wave!'

Bustamante possessed a charming personality and great wit. One evening he was invited by the West Indian Students Union to speak to their members. During question time, a number of students remonstrated at the ludicrous salary offers made by the government to Jamaicans who had recently acquired doctoral degrees. Feigning ignorance, the Chief Minister enquired, 'Ph.D.? What is Ph.D.?' A chorus of exclamatory replies arose, 'Doctor of Philosophy of course, sir!' Without skipping a beat he asked, 'Philosophy can grow yam?'

On the eve of his departure for Jamaica, an informal party was held for him by John Keith, director of colonial scholars. The honoured guest explained that because of a scheduled audience with King George VI he would be late. When he arrived and we quizzed him about the audience, he replied, 'Fine! George is a charming fellow.' From his account we inferred that he had virtually hinted that the appropriate time for termination of the audience had arrived: 'Your Majesty, I know that you are a busy gentleman, and I am too. So let's call it a day.'

One benefit of my position as liaison officer was the opportunity to witness the 1948 Olympic games. There I had the pleasure of seeing the incredible performance by the 'flying' Dutchwoman, Fanny Blankers-Koen, which earned her four sprint gold medals. The Czech Emil Zatopek won silver and gold in the 5,000 and 10,000 metre races respectively, and was greeted by the crowd chanting his name whenever he was on the track. I recall also, MacDonald Bailey of Trinidad, the black British hope in the sprints, who disappointingly, took sixth place in the 100 metre race.

We saw firsthand the triumphs and disappointments for Jamaica. There were great expectations of Arthur Wint, the tall, gangling, ex-RAF officer and medical student. He was well-known and very popular throughout Britain but relatively unknown outside. The overwhelming favourite for the 400 metres gold medal, however was Herb McKenley who held the world record and best time at several distances. During the quarter mile race, following his initial breakaway from the group, Arthur, with consistent, long strides passed Herb, not to be overtaken again. This was a classic example of the tortoise and the hare. Wint was followed by the favourite, to the latter's disappointment but for Jamaica it was gold and silver.

And as they stood on the rostrum, the British National Anthem, 'God Save the King', and flag, the Union Jack, appeared for the first time at those Games! No special Jamaican anthem or flag were heard or seen until Independence in 1962. More vividly, I remember the culmination of McKenley's disappointment in the 4x400 metre race when Arthur unfortunately developed muscle trouble and Herb was left waiting for the baton and for gold. I can still see Arthur, off the track on the grass, limbs flailing in frustration and pain.

Cricket was an integral part of this life. In 1948 I had the good fortune to be in England during a tour by an Australian aggregation of Bradman, Lindwall Miller, and Harvey. This was among the best test teams of all time and they steam-rollered over England. Unfortunately, my sole glimpse of the great Bradman was his farewell test innings at the Oval where he was dismissed for a duck!

Local West Indian teams playing regularly included players like the famous Learie Constantine, Allan Rae, Bertie Clarke, Ernest Eytle, John Figueroa, Ken Ablack, Peter Bynoe. Michael Manley captained a side which played frequently in Regent's Park and he has never allowed me to forget a catch he took one-handed in the slips off my bowling, more than 40 years ago. Peter would become external examiner for the College of Arts, Science and Technology's architecture degree and diploma programmes,white Ablack and Eytle were pioneers of Caribbean broadcasters of cricket on the BBC radio.

Perhaps the most interesting of these cricket experiences occurred on the summer tour of Derbyshire, Lancashire and Yorkshire by a group of students, organized by H.O'.B. Fernandez-McCartney, and which I usually joined. Cricket and hospitality in the north normally lived up to their reputation. Our group included Barbadians Oliver Browne, Eric Bishop and Clifford Husbands; all three would become highly placed legal officers or sit on the High Court bench. In addition, there were Grenadians Raphael Fletcher, medical and law students, Rupert Japal and Carol Bristol, Arthur Dujon of Jamaica, and George Stoll and Fred Wills of British Guiana. Wills and I opening the bowling, usually gave the batsmen problems in the heavy northern atmosphere. Wills would later become attorney general and minister of foreign affairs, captain of Demerara cricket club, and a patron of the young Clive Lloyd.

Throughout the summer of 1950, we basked in the triumph of the West Indian Tour of Rae and Stollmeyer, the three 'Ws' and the 'two pals', Ramadhin and Valentine. We especially enjoyed the euphoria of that victory at Lords, our first on English soil, and the ensuing calypso dance on those hallowed grounds. England's humiliations that summer were heightened by defeat by the United States in the World Cup football tournament in Brazil.

In a pre-tour one-day match played at London university's Motspur Park, West Indians living in England led by Learie Constantine gave the touring side a good game. J.K. Holt Jr., then playing in the Lancashire League, scored 50+ for us and opening the bowling with Constantine, I took the wickets of Stollmeyer, Weekes and Goddard for 12. This is not intended to provide a chronicle and record of my own performances; but it would be less than human not to mention how proud I have always been of that achievement.

In 1949, invited by the World Federation of Democratic Youth to participate in their Festival in Budapest, W.I.S.U. selected a delegation to be led by its secretary, Arthur Brown. Attendance was to be subsidized by the hosts. On arrival the team discovered that they were expected to march bearing placards with slogans and make speeches denouncing Imperialism and to pose for photographs with clenched fists. 'G. Arthur' objected to doing so, on the grounds that the group comprised persons of mixed political persuasions, that the delegation was representing the entire student body and in the circumstances he was opposed to the adoption of extreme positions. He was accordingly vilified, accused of insulting the hosts, and fired as leader.

On returning to London, it was decided that Brown should be 'impeached and tried' for these 'sins'. From all accounts this was a dramatic and memorable occasion, attended by a large turnout of students. Ranged on the prosecution side were the more radical students, including future Professors Elsa Goveia and Rawle Farley of B.G. and if memory does not mislead me, Max Awon, architecture student from Trinidad. Appearing for the defence were Arthur Wint and Michael Manley, advised by Allan Rae and also supported by Don Mills; in the 'judge's' seat, the then WISU President, H. Dossie Carberry, later 'Mr Justice'.

In the event, Arthur was acquitted, but the series of events emphasized a polarization of the student body. Incidentally, the C.O. had advised Arthur against attending the Festival, but, independent-minded, he decided to proceed.

One of the most fascinating student cases encountered by our group of liaison officers was that of Chike Obi. He arrived in London from Nigeria on a scholarship near the end of the 1940s, having been successful in the London university's bachelor and master of arts degrees as an external student. This had been accomplished by recourse to the library of, and discussions with, Dr. Francis Bowen, a long-time Jamaican teacher in Nigeria. Chike was convinced that he had solved a complex mathematical problem which had baffled the experts since the mid-17th century. So, he registered for a doctoral degree on this topic, at University College, London. Within a short time, he made representations to the colonial office through his liaison officer, alleging that his supervisor was attempting to steal his solution and insisted on being transferred to Cambridge. Although the case was not proven, his application was approved. He obtained the degree but on a different topic. Later, Chike would become Professor of Mathematics at Lagos university and be imprisoned during the 1960s as a consequence of his political activities. Such were the trials of a liaison officer that I was soon to leave behind!

In January 1951 our first-born emerged at Westminster Hospital, where Winnifred had been in training as a nurse. Our son was christened Charles Wade at St. Martins-in-the-Fields. His god-parents were Arthur Wint, David Carmichael, a colonial office colleague, and Ruby Welds, Winnifred's student nurse colleague at Westminster. Among our congratulatory telegrams on his birth was one from my LSE alumni football team-mates, 'Congratulations, four more a forward line.' One of our most frequent and faithful volunteer baby sitters during the first six months of his life was Howard Cooke who was at the time on a teacher post-qualifying scholarship at London university's Institute of Education.

Seven months after Charles' birth and after three unforgettable years as liaison officer, I returned to Jamaica. I shall always feel fortunate to have been granted this phenomenal opportunity to serve the region.

7

ESCAPE TO CLOISTERED ACADEMIA?

I left the civil service in June 1960 after 22 years, to become one of the founding grandfathers of the department of government at the University College of the West Indies. My departure took place on the eve of the referendum which signified the break-up of the ill-fated West Indian Federation. I was attracted partly by the challenge of contributing towards the creation of a new department and faculty of social sciences.

Admittedly, however, there were other motives and foremost among these was the prospect of spending a period engaged in reflection and contemplative pursuits away from the pressures of the political environment inhabited by a senior civil servant. The illusion that a significant psychic income would accrue from this sequestered life of study, teaching and research was soon dispelled. Disillusionment came with the discovery of partisan behaviour and activity, which appeared in a different guise from the politics of party professionals, but were no less real, and at times, more deceptive and more vicious.

The teaching of politics had begun in a very limited way, a year or two before the establishment of the department, with the appointment of Francis Xavier Mark of Trinidad. Arriving at the same time as I did were Brian Chapman, author of *The Profession of Government*, and Og Buchan, political theorist from Scotland. Arthur

Lewis, the new principal and professor of political economy, used his influence to ensure Chapman's recruitment as professor of government and director of training in public administration. I assumed the position of associate director, at the senior lecturer level. Two new programmes were added to the offerings in the social sciences, namely government as a subject of specialization in the Bachelor of Science economics degree, and an in-service Diploma in Public Administration (DPA). Simultaneously, optional course offerings in the Bachelor of Arts programme were increased. Before actually moving to Mona, during the summer of 1960 I spent a few weeks visiting the contributing territories to the UCWI, informing appropriate ministers and officials about the forthcoming DPA programme and encouraging them to nominate candidates. At the same time, also funded by the Carnegie Foundation grant which financed the initiation of the DPA programme, a Social Administration programme leading to a certificate in social work was introduced in the new department, which brought Douglas Manley, Adele Wint and later, June Dolly-Besson of Trinidad as colleagues.

The department introduced a Masters programme in 1964 and by 1971, had established a hierarchy of programmes, from the certificate level, through undergraduate Bachelor of Science degrees, in political science, public administration and international relations, the diploma in public administration (DPA), and the Master's and Doctoral programmes. Among the most far-reaching developments was the extension of the Certificate in Public Administration (CPA) to the non-campus countries in 1983, which has enabled a larger number of junior public officials in all the contributing countries to be exposed to education and training at home and therefore at lower cost to their governments.

Among the students in that first year of the DPA programme in 1960 were Oscar Hammond and Wilton Solomon, who would both become parish council secretaries, Marcel Knight, who would direct the Project Analysis and Monitoring Company (PAMCO), G.K. Lee, who would be appointed postmaster-general of Trinidad, and in the following year, Gloria Rose Edwards the future registrar of companies. Not long after, the class included Charles Maynard of Dominica, who was promoted to permanent secretary and subsequently crossed over to the ministerial ranks. There were Maisie O'Reggio Alexander and Allan Kirton, both future permanent secretaries in Jamaica, and Harcourt Lewis and Orville Durant of Barbados would rise to ministerial status and leadership of the police force respectively. Kirton was my first Ph.D. student, drawing on his training and experience in the fisheries field and the administration area. In 1965 Probyn Inniss of St. Kitts-Nevis-Anguilla, joined the select group who achieved the rare honour of obtaining the DPA with distinction. He would be elevated to the rank of permanent secretary, and later to the position of governor of that territory while still in his early 40s. Others who have completed the course with distinction include Mrs Marie Slyfield, director of Jamaica's administrative reform programme and Mrs Judith Maloney of the ministry of the public service. No student has done so since 1977!

Within the first five years of the Bachelor of Science programme, those graduating included Henderson Downer, later high court judge, K.G. Anthony Hill, ambassador and later, permanent secretary to the prime minister, Roderick Rainford, a future Rhodes scholar, former Caribbean Community (CARICOM) secretary-general and governor of the Bank of Jamaica, and W.H. McKell of Trinidad, who would become director of personnel administration. Interestingly, of ten students specializing in government in the graduating batch of 1964, five were Grenadians, including George Briggs, future director of Jamaica's administrative staff college and permanent secretary to the ministry of the public service, future Grenadian ambassador Mario Bullen, and Patrick Emmanuel, later, a colleague at Cave Hill. That batch was also distinguished by the presence of Harold Lutchman of British Guiana, and C.A.P.S. St. Hill of Trinidad. Trevor Munroe, of the 1965 graduating group, had already begun to cut his teeth as a radical leader before continuing at Oxford on a Rhodes Scholarship. A decade and a half later, he would found the University and Allied Workers Union (UAWU) and not long after, the associated Marxist-Leninist Workers Party of Jamaica (WPJ), while holding a senior position in the department.

Among those members of the wider faculty of social sciences, who were in the first degree graduating class of 1962 were Orlando Patterson, renowned novelist and author of works on slavery, who would become a distinguished professor of sociology at Harvard, Norman Girvan, professor and director of UWI's Consortium Graduate School of Social Sciences, and Joycelin Byrne-Massiah, director of the Institute of Social and Economic Research at Cave Hill. Graduating over the next two years, there were Richard Fletcher, Rhodes scholar, minister of state in the People's National Party government of the 1970s and Manley's brother-in-law, Dale Anderson, high commissioner to Canada, Errol Anderson, Jamaica

Labour Party minister, Douglas Folkes, managing director of Mutual Security Bank, and Leroy Brown, internationally accredited boxing judge.

The department has received considerable assistance from external sources. The process began with the Carnegie Corporation grant which provided the platform for the launching of the department after a five-year series of annual public and business administration courses conducted by the Henley-on-Thames administrative staff college. For two to three years the Canadian government's external aid programme brought visiting teachers from the University of Toronto's Political Economy department, including Federalism expert professor Alexander Brady, Elizabeth Wallace, George Heiman and Peter Silcox.

Not long after my attachment to the department, I was appointed a member of the three-man Manktelow commission set up by the Federal government of the West Indies, to examine staffing problems in the public services of the Commonwealth Caribbean region. The commission, noting the problems of administrative management associated with political self-determination, reported a grave shortage of competent and trained public service personnel, especially in the Leeward and Windward Islands. Against this background of training inadequacies, the UWI sought and obtained a generous grant from the Ford Foundation in 1964 for the purposes of improving the skills in administration in the public services of Barbados, British Honduras, the Leewards and Windwards, and of conducting public administration research of a pragmatic nature in these territories.

This project was implemented by two tutors, both from Trinidad. C.A.P. St Hill was based in St. Lucia, while Urias Forbes was based in Antigua, under my direction. Among the most significant initiatives taken by the project was the mounting of two colloquia (a euphemism used to avoid the sensitive term 'training') in the British Virgin Islands and Montserrat, in which ministers, permanent secretaries, heads of departments and other senior administrative and technical personnel were brought together for week-end discussions on salient issues and problems. For these highly successful colloquia St. Hill, Forbes and I served as resource personnel, supported by Crispin Sorhaindo, financial secretary of Dominica and later, a vice- president of the Caribbean Development Bank (CDB), speaker of Dominica's house of assembly and more recently president of that state.

Assistance also came from the Rockefeller Foundation in 1965 through a grant for the development of international relations programmes, and the recruitment of visiting teachers. Thus, Uwe Kitzinger of Nuffield College, Oxford, Fred Warner Neal of Claremont Graduate School, California and Maurice Waters of Wayne State University, Detroit, all taught in the department during the 1960s and 1970s. However, when Prime Minister Eric Williams of Trinidad secured the support of the Swiss government and the Geneva Graduate Institute of International Studies for establishing an Institute of International Relations at the St. Augustine campus, the diploma programme was transferred to that campus in 1966, after one year at Mona, with the department continuing to conduct undergraduate and higher degrees in this subject. Among the highlights of that period, was a highly successful international conference which we organized on 'The Role of Small Countries in a Big World' and which brought together Caribbean and North American scholars in the international affairs field, including Hans Morgenthau, John Stoessinger, Kalman Silvert and a number of ambassadors to the United Nations.

These manifestations of support were highly appreciated since they contributed significantly towards the development of the department in its formative years. They facilitated the birth and early nurturing of the three inter-related areas of its intellectual and scholarly activities namely politics, public administration and international relations. If the department was to survive and sustain its development, it was essential to encourage institution building. This objective was accomplished through a staff development scheme which linked us with our counterpart department at Manchester University and was funded by the Inter-University Council with no cost to the UWI.

The scheme facilitated the training of future teachers of and researchers in political science and public administration and of potential administrators, by selecting each year, one or two of the best students who had completed their Masters degrees and sending them to Manchester to complete doctoral degrees on Caribbean topics. Correspondingly, but not as regularly, a few Manchester graduates arrived at Mona to undertake research on Caribbean issues for Ph.Ds under our joint supervision. On a smaller scale, a staff exchange component enabled two teachers from each institution to engage in teaching and research at the counterpart institution. Following a discussion with Ali Mazrui, then head of the department of political science at Makerere University in Uganda in 1970, the link arrangement was extended to that university. Unfortunately, after one UWI graduate, Ralph Gonsalves of St. Vincent and one Ugandan, Paul Barongo, participated in this exchange scheme, the accession to power of Idi Amin aborted that link in the chain.

Much later, during the 1980s, the United States Agency for International Development (USAID) in collaboration with the American Public Health Association (APHA) and the University of Pittsburgh's Graduate School of Public Health, would provide a grant for mounting a diploma in health management (Dip. H.M.) with responsibility for its management assigned to myself and Edwin Jones. This was carried out in association with the other departments of the faculty and the department of social and preventive medicine.

Chapman had returned to Manchester in 1961, after a year and I was left to act as head until a new appointment was made to the chair. In 1961 he arrived in the form of larger than life Jan Jelle DeJong, a big, barrel-chested Dutchman. One of his favourite pastimes was appalling colleagues and students with tales of his activities during World War II, including the lining up of captured enemy personnel against a wall and shooting them. News of his impending arrival was accompanied by a reputation that he was at the frontier of the development of political science. When a very senior member of the appointments committee remarked, 'Charles, I understand that the department is getting a giant,' I responded that I didn't think so, from what I had read on his résumé. He clarified his comment, by saying he was referring to De Jong's physical proportions. These were vividly demonstrated whenever he plunged, belly-flop style, into the senior common room swimming pool, producing effects seemingly of tidal wave dimensions. In the classroom, he introduced two terms with which his students still identify him, *Politicology* (for political theory), and the *Pisthic Component*. In commenting on almost any academic subject one mentioned, he would assert, 'I have teached that.'

From the beginning, we moved through a succession of strange and eccentric expatriate colleagues, especially those who were specialists in political theory. Most of these and a few other staff members did not last the course, either resigning or having their tenure terminated before the formal end of their contracts, thus creating a condition of great instability. On occasions following the departure of a colleague, we revised our opinion of him in light of his successor's behaviour and concluded that the former now seemed surprisingly sane.

One early recruit engaged in his reading and writing while soaking in a full bath for most of the day except when meeting his students. One Saturday evening I dropped in for a brief visit at his Mona Heights home and discovered that his wife was away for the week-end. He offered me a drink and while reaching for ice from the freezer, informed me that the family's pet hamster had died during her absence and the corpse had been placed in cold storage awaiting her return. Thereupon, I immediately changed my mind and asked to have my rum absolutely neat!

One of my most vivid memories of Jamaica's first Independence week, 1962, concerned DeJong. At the time, our house guest on West Road, UWI was a friend, Amadeo Francis, an economist with Puerto Rico's Economic Development Administration and a former national athlete, who had accompanied that country's team to the Central American and Caribbean Games then being held in our new national stadium. Returning home one day before lunch, we found the head in the process of finishing a bottle of my best Mount Gay Rum. I asked Amadeo to distract his attention while I switched bottles, substituting an ordinary Jamaican rum. As DeJong lingered despite hints and was clearly outstaying his welcome, I resorted to a more direct approach. At that point, he rushed angrily out of the house into his large, heavy, yellow Rover 70, reversed rapidly on to the lawn over the large stones bordering it, and gunning the engine, dashed forward at great speed through the gate, narrowly missing one of the concrete posts. I was nevertheless, relieved by De Jong's departure, until a few minutes later, when another colleague, Bob Benewick phoned to say that the head's car had broken down on the Mona Road, the petrol having drained out from the tank which was damaged by the border stones; and could I come and help. J.J.J. lasted for less than two years, his resignation accepted almost before the ink of the letter which conveyed it had dried.

After a rapid succession of short-term successors as lecturers in political theory, Marx scholar Bertell Ollman was recruited. Though he survived a bit longer than any of his predecessors, including DeJong, his tenure was cut short when student protest was triggered by his allegations against the campus bookshop of short-changing students in the pricing of books. Ollman reported that he discovered this by systematically lifting the price tags and noting the original prices. His name would hit the headlines in foreign papers and magazines during the 1970s when he was denied appointment as chairman of the political science department at the University of Maryland. This action by the university would lead to a lawsuit.

There is the story of a visiting professor who, in the course of organizing an international conference by telephone, experienced some difficulty in getting through to Peking. In frustration and anger, he slammed down the telephone, splitting it down the middle! When he was leaving the UWI to return to the USA, I arranged to take him to the airport, but needing petrol, I had gone to the SCR pump. On returning to the office to pick him up, I was surprised to find a crowd of faculty colleagues who expressed alarm that the departing professor was seen running around in circles like a red ant, shouting repeatedly, 'Charles Mills, help!' Some of them wondered whether he had been attacked by Bert Ollman and was appealing for my assistance. But it transpired that the confusion was caused by my being five minutes late.

Partially alleviating this instability were elements of continuity in the persons of Archie Singham and Ann Spackman. Archie and Ann virtually became West Indians. Archie, Ceylonese, a behavioural scientist and a stimulating and provocative personality would spend ten years with the department. Ann, who was English arrived in 1963 after teaching at Sierra Leone's Fourah Bay College; she was an institutionalist who provided solidity to the staff. Tragically, she would collapse while lecturing during the first week of term in January 1979 and die within a few days. In addition, we were fortunate in having a set of part time lecturers, who were distinguished professionals such as G. Arthur Brown, Gladstone Bonnick, Lloyd Barnett, Dossie Carberry and Emil George, who provided continuity for the DPA programme. They came to the classroom year after year, late afternoons or on Saturday mornings, from their own very busy substantive occupations. This tradition would be continued later, by Roald Henriques, Asgar Ally, Huntley Manhertz and David Logan. Ally, a former Deputy Governor of the Bank of Jamaica would return to his native Guyana as Minister of Finance in Dr. Cheddi Jagan's government in 1992.

By the early 1970s, the composition of the staff began to stabilize, influenced to a great extent by the return of our graduates from overseas, and from the department's consciously planned policy of staff development primarily through the Manchester link scheme. Singham and I maintained contact with these postgraduate students and with others among our outstanding graduates who were studying at Oxford, Michigan and Yale. A few months before completion of their work, we made efforts to ensure that positions were available for those who were interested: not only at Mona but at our new sister departments at St. Augustine and Cave Hill, or at the University of Guyana.

Thus Harold Lutchman, the first to be awarded a Master's degree in government, joined the University of Guyana staff and subsequently became professor of government. Louis Lindsay, Edwin Jones, Ralph Gonsalves, Paul Ashley, Trevor Munroe, Carl Stone, Paul Robertson, and Rosina Wiltshire were recruited by the Mona campus. John LaGuerre and Patrick Emmanuel went to St. Augustine, and George Belle to Cave Hill after a stint of teaching at Mona. Jones, Lindsay and LaGuerre had obtained First Class Honours at the 1967 Bachelor of Science Final examinations, a record for the faculty. Others recruited included Vaughan Lewis who would move from the department at Mona to become director of the Institute of Social and Economic Research, Fitz Baptiste who later moved to the history department at St. Augustine, and Neville Duncan a future head of department of politics at Cave Hill and Dean of the faculty.

There were other participants in the link scheme who did not return to academic careers. Denis Benn entered the Guyana foreign service, moved to the United Nations Development Programme and later, assumed the position of that agency's resident representative in Jamaica. Richard Cheltenham of Barbados would practice as a barrister and serve as minister of agriculture. Kenneth John of St. Vincent would, like Cheltenham, enter the arenas of law and active politics, and also become chairman of the public service commission.

Some of the Manchester graduates who travelled in the opposite direction, that is to Mona for their doctoral research have retained an active interest in Caribbean politics. Of particular note is Anthony Payne, now a professor in Sheffield University's department of politics, and Paul Sutton, at the University of Hull. Both have continued to publish books and articles on the region, and Payne visits us regularly. However, we have lost touch with Terry Lacey, who, in the late 1960s, produced a startlingly frank and revealing analysis of the direct connection between certain politicians and the development of gun crimes, in his thesis, 'Violence and Politics in Jamaica.' It was later published but in an expurgated version.

At the staff exchange level, two came to Mona from Manchester, Christopher Clapham, an Africanist and specialist on Ethiopia, and the larger than life Ken Post. Ken was a stimulating teacher who spent two years with us, and produced several interesting books bearing intriguing titles such as *Arise Ye Starvelings* and *Strike the Iron*, based on research on protest movements and the 1938 labour rebellion in Jamaica. Ken left Mona to become deputy rector of the Institute of Social Studies in the Hague.

Archie Singham from Mona spent a year as a Simon research fellow at Manchester, and I was appointed a Simon professorial fellow there in 1978. These fellowships were awarded from a bequest left by the late Lord Simon, a Manchester engineer, and we were accommodated in his former home 'Broomcroft', an elegant house in Didsbury. An account of the Manchester scheme would be incomplete if due appreciation was not paid to the significant contribution made by two professors from that University, Dennis Austin and Bill Tordoff, who managed that end of the link and gave considerable and sympathetic support to our students and Simon fellows.

Some years ago, a Jamaican critic who holds a Ph.D. in politics, in an article published in the *Sunday Gleaner*, condemned the department of government for the high proportion of its staff which was represented by its own graduates. In fact, on the eve of my retirement in 1990, all members of the Mona staff except myself were graduates of the department, though most had completed postgraduate studies elsewhere. This did not however, preclude other distinguished scholars, for example, Vaughan Lewis, Locksley Edmondson or Eddie Greene, from joining the staff. Moreover, by the mid-1980s the deans of social sciences on all the campuses were our graduates. I make no apology for this out turn, which, as I have emphasized, is the result of a policy decision and its implementation.

From the moment that I joined the UCWI staff I was the senior West Indian member of the department and became acting head, then head for a period of 17 years beginning in 1963. The responsibility therefore fell primarily on my shoulders to keep things together and not allow the department to disintegrate during that period of instability. To add to this burden, when Hector Wynter, then director of extra mural studies was seconded to the government as high commissioner to Trinidad in 1963, I was asked to double up as acting head of both departments. Despite the additional responsibilities, there were compensations. In my new acting capacity I enjoyed the weekly staff meetings with Adolph Thompson, Rex Nettleford, Sybil Francis, Hugh Morrison, Noel Vaz, Trudy

Hamilton, and in that year the Trade Union Education Institute was created with Rex as its director of studies and Frank Gordon as a member of its advisory board. I recall presiding over the function which marked the opening of the Kingston extra mural centre on Camp Road, with Prime Minister Dr. Eric Williams of Trinidad performing the opening rites.

I also visited other branches of the department's far flung empire. On one such occasion I enjoyed my maiden experience of the Trinidad carnival. It was an unforgettable experience, of a surfeit of sound and colour, with the winning road march tune on the steelbands running through my head for many months after. Performing these dual roles and functions proved too much and I asked to be relieved of the extra mural position after a year.

This action provided only temporary relief. By the next year I was appointed vice dean of the faculty of social sciences. Following a year's absence on sabbatical leave, I was elected Dean, retaining that position for three years and continuing as head of the department.

During this latter period the university, and this faculty in particular, experienced a series of serious and painful events which must be unforgettable for those who were members of the staff or student body at the time. The troubles began in October 1968 with the action taken by the Jamaican government to bar Guyanese Dr. Walter Rodney from re-entering the island and re-assuming his lecturer post at the university. The resulting protest march into Kingston by enraged students and academic staff members sparked general unrest in the city and triggered rioting, the overturning of buses and burning of a few buildings. As a consequence, the Jamaica Defence Force (JDF) entered the scene, their men and armoured vehicles standing guard at the university gates and helicopters circling above, while members of the academic community barred the gates against intruders. For me, a person not normally prone to violent behaviour, these actions provoked an unusual reaction of aggressiveness and militancy.

The Rodney crisis was followed a few months later, by the demonstrations against the exclusion of another Guyanese lecturer, Dr. Clive Thomas of the social sciences faculty. During this period of crises, sit-ins, teach-ins, newspapers and newsletters mushroomed, the latter set including the radical *Abeng* and *Moko*, and the more staid *Scope*. Even when social science staff, students or institutions were not the source from which a particular problem or issue arose directly, members of that faculty were always to be found in the vanguard of the battles. As Dean I found myself caught in an unenviable position, attempting to strike a balance between my roles as representative of the faculty and as a member of the 'administration': Council, Senate and other committees.

An incident occurred at this time which left an indelible imprint on my mind. Ken Post visited me at home on West Road one morning and told me of the decision by some members to hold a seminar that day on 'The Role of Social Scientists in the Contemporary Caribbean', and asked if I would serve as chairman and introduce the topic. According to the agenda, two well-known faculty members whom he named would make presentations following my introductory statement. The lecture theatre was packed. My opening gambit was greeted with the beginnings of a rumble, later growing in volume and becoming more audible. 'What about C.Y.'s case? We came to hear about C.Y.' I responded by indicating what the subject of the seminar was, according to the invitation I had received, and emphasizing that two other colleagues were scheduled to make their presentations. Neither of the two said anything in confirmation or otherwise. The angry crowd vented their frustration and rage with attacks against Lloyd Braithwaite, then a pro-vice-chancellor, and me as Dean. Realising that I had been set up by colleagues, brought there under false pretences to provide an imprimatur for the proceedings, I debated silently whether or not to get up and leave them to it. Eventually, I decided to remain; but the experience seriously shook my confidence in colleagues.

This event, together with the siege of the campus by the army a few months before, and the physical attack in Harvard Square 25 years ago, were the most traumatic experiences of my life.

The next episode which involved me directly was the government's decision to deport Ken Post, on the pretext that he was an active participant in the demonstrations. Since such action could only be carried out through a hearing before a judge, the cabinet proposed to have the law amended to dispense with this requirement. The vice-chancellor of Manchester University immediately sent Bill Tordoff to negotiate with the UWI authorities and the government. The government was persuaded to allow Post to complete his tenure. Imagine my consternation when Ken asked me whether he could have a year's extension!

This period marked the beginning of the age of publicly and militantly expressed dissent, of the demand for participation by, and representation of, students and junior staff members on decision-making bodies. This was partly influenced by a universal unrest, especially in the USA and Europe. Accompanying this were the Trinidad 'revolutions' of 1970, themselves, partly influenced by Black Power ideas and movement, being reflected in responses on the campuses.

It was a time of intolerance marked by the censoring and subsequent banning of books and of the withdrawal of passports. One of the most famous and highly publicised victims of the latter was economist George Beckford, for the 'sin' of visiting Cuba. However, manifestations of intolerance were by no means one sided. Many of those who were in the vanguard of the struggle for the right of dissent tended to defend their establishment by behaviour and expressions of intolerance no less excessive than they themselves suffered.

Within the academic community a very restrictive approach to appointments was adopted by some members of the faculty of social sciences, who expressed vociferous and vehement hostility to the appointment of 'expatriate' West Indians. This issue was no more significantly illustrated than during the university's attempt to appoint professors of Economics at Mona and Cave Hill in 1971. Prominent among the applicants were George Beckford and Al Francis, both on the Mona staff, Havelock Brewster and Bertie Hines. Francis had the department's support for the post. Coming from a poor background in Jamaica, Hines, as a young boy had emigrated to England with his parents and without secondary education, had succeeded in gaining university admission by dint of hard work and night studies. Performing well in his undergraduate degree examinations, he had produced an important postgraduate thesis on the significance of trade union pressure on the inflation rate in the UK.

During the interviewing sessions Beckford arrived, armed with a tape recorder, but the chairman refused permission for it to be used. Hines entered late due to flight delay from London and was the last to be interviewed. Following this, I took him to the senior common room for a drink to find the bar, crowded with social scientists, humming with chatter in anticipation of the interview results. With the exception of Randolph Williams, our colleagues, their backs turned, totally ignored Hines' presence. Hines was offered the position at Mona. After considering the offer for some time, he decided that there was no point in accepting, in the face of such great hostility. After all, he held a comfortable professorial position at Birkbeck College, London and was also considering an invitation from the Massachusetts Institute of Technology (M.I.T). Before the interviewing stage, Brewster had decided to withdraw, apparently on similar grounds, though he had been on the Economics staff at Mona for five years until 1968. He was eventually persuaded to accept the Cave Hill professorial post, but resigned after a year.

At that time also, the radical image of the UWI and in particular, of the social sciences staff and students began to emerge. Five years before these crises and troubles began, a set of faculty members together with a few from outside had formed the New World Group as a forum for study of West Indian society and economy, and dissemination via its *Quarterly* and other avenues, of ideas about restructuring these facets of life of the region. Amongst the group's leaders were two who have since died, Elsa Goveia and George Beckford, some who have moved to other universities, such as Clive Thomas and Orlando Patterson, some to other areas of activity including Lloyd Best, Owen Jefferson and Vaughan Lewis and others, Alister McIntyre and Norman Girvan who are still with us, after periods of sojourn elsewhere.

During the closing years of the 1960s the UWI developed a reputation as a repository of radicals, nurtured in the seedbed of the social sciences. Social sciences bashing was a popular sport and many of the barbs were based on anti-intellectualism, ignorance, irrationality or ill-informed foundations. This was reflected in the opposition and hostility, expressed by private sector representatives towards proposals in the late 1960s, to locate the new department of management studies in this faculty. Unfortunately, attacks were also levelled from quarters within the university and by graduates of the social sciences faculty.

Indeed, one of them, Reuben Harris of Antigua, a longtime minister of Education and Member of the University Council, commented, 'We are having too many radical elements on the staff, polluting our students when they go to the university.' The task of perpetually defending colleagues like Trevor Munroe and of promoting their cases for tenure and promotion in the face of persistent opposition from almost all colleagues on the Assessment and Promotions Committee, took a tremendous toll.

The 1970 upheavals in Trinidad affected the university directly, especially at the St. Augustine campus where a number of students were involved, notably Geddes Granger. Patrick Emmanuel, then a staff member on that campus, was incarcerated and Trevor Munroe, who had left Mona as the forerunner of members of a team to conduct a research study on the situation, was prohibited from entering Trinidad and sent back home on the next available flight. *En route* home from a seminar in Nairobi, I heard of the 'revolution' on the BBC news and discovered the next day in Kingston that Alister McIntyre, director of the Institute of Social and Economic Research had made a small grant for the project. Though absent when the decision was taken, I supported the project as one which would yield valuable results. However, from the perspective of the vice-chancellor and the non-social scientists, a visit to Trinidad for such a purpose was untimely in the context of the declaration of a state of emergency. Vice-chancellor Marshall made his views and sentiments clear to McIntyre and me. At the May 1970 meeting of senate, he made a long statement which included a strong condemnation of Trevor's behaviour during the episode. A statement which the senate received 'with approbation.'

During this period several significant incidents occurred. These included among others, the Creative Arts Centre sit-in, the siege of the senate building and confinement of the vice-chancellor and other top administrative officers. In addition a regime of industrial action was instigated by the three unions representing academic and senior administrative staff, junior administrative and clerical, and ancillary personnel. The series of go-slows and strikes occasioned by industrial action resulted in regular disruptions particularly in October, at the commencement of each academic year, which were almost predictable.

Among the significant issues which emerged was the propriety of members of the academic staff, aimed primarily at Trevor Munroe, actively engaging in union affairs. On this point, Sir Allen Lewis, soon after to become Chancellor, who was appointed sole commissioner to enquire into the disruptions of academic and administrative work caused by the UAWU strike of October 9 to 30, 1972 stated in his report dated March 23, 1974:

> 'In my view there is no impropriety in academic members of staff participating actively in the affairs of trade unions consisting of non-academic employees of the university (but) the line must be drawn somewhere to demarcate those persons who hold a managerial position in the university from the rest of the academic staff.'

However, as a consequence of these disruptive activities, Trevor was considered by some of the decision-makers of the institution to have been making a 'negative contribution' to the university. As I stated in a review of Sherlock's and Nettleford's history of the UWI, (*A Caribbean Response to the Challenge of Change*),

> 'No matter how one views his political orientation and activities, Munroe has without doubt, played a prominent part in UWI's history, and it is incredible that his name is mentioned nowhere.'

Another interesting and significant event which occurred during that period was the intense competition for succession to Roy Marshall as vice-chancellor in 1974. This was a saga which left a bitter and nasty taste with Aston Preston. He was described disparagingly and dismissively by one of his rivals as a mere accountant and not an intellectual. Yet, this longest serving vice-chancellor by far, appropriately assumed the mantle at a time when expertise in financial management was critically needed by the institution.

For me, as head of department and dean, it was a continuous challenge to hold together a department of diverse personalities and one which reflected in its composition, such diverse ideological orientations: Edwin Jones, Rupert Lewis, Trevor Munroe, Archie Singham, Carl Stone, Bertram Collins, Locksley Edmondson, Ann Spackman, Rosina Wiltshire, Sam Aymer and Ina Barrett and those strange earlier colleagues mentioned earlier. Within this atmosphere, there was many a heated debate, with Stone, Munroe Lindsay and Edmondson as prominent participants.

The department's staff has become more stable since the early 1970s and the times more quiescent within the faculty and the university. Trevor, graduating to respectability both within and outside of the walls, has become in the 1990s, a much sought after public speaker by significant private sector enterprises and organizations. Moreover, the private sector seems to have become reconciled to the fact that business management studies essentially rest on social science foundations. Not only do important sections of the sector provide employment for graduates of these programmes but they strongly support the new Executive Master's of Business Administration programme introduced in 1989. Significantly also, the Grace, Kennedy Company has funded a chair in management studies, in memory of its late Chairman, Carlton Alexander. I am chairman of the company's associated foundation which administers matters concerning that chair and a chair in environmental management, among other subjects.

In 1980, I gave up the headship after a 17 year spell and was again elected dean during the transition period leading to restructuring of the university, and I was re-elected to preside over the faculty's involvement in this decentralization exercise. While welcoming decentralization and greater autonomy in decision-making to campuses, I am unhappy about the consequences of some aspects. It was logical and inevitable for the less expensive programmes to be duplicated, some even triplicated. This has had negative effects on achievement of the ideal of a regional university and on the process of regionalism generally. The student bodies of the Mona and St Augustine campuses currently comprise 88% and 91% of nationals of their host countries respectively. After more than two decades of dialogue with student groups of public officials from around the Caribbean, who brought a variety of backgrounds and experience to our public administration courses, I now find it a disappointing experience to teach classes consisting almost exclusively of fellow Jamaicans.

In 1989 CARICOM heads of government appointed a regional team to undertake a comprehensive review of the Community's programmes, institutions and organizations. The team consisted of Sir Carlisle Burton, former head of the Barbados civil service, Dr. J. O'Neil Lewis, former ambassador of Trinidad and Tobago to the United States, Hon. Crispin Sorhaindo, speaker of the Dominican house of assembly, with me as chairman. Visiting all the member states, we consulted widely with heads of government, relevant ministers, senior officials, private sector leaders, representatives of trade unions, non-governmental organizations, the media, and ordinary citizens.

Among our comments on the UWI, was the suggestion that a contribution be made towards preserving its regional character by the introduction of a special scholarship scheme. This would ensure that a certain minimum percentage of students on each campus were nationals of CARICOM member states other than the host country. We suggested also, that a portion of the funding for postgraduate scholarships should be allocated to enable a few students to undertake thesis research outside of their home country.

As a long-time member of the management board of the International Association of Schools and Institutes of Administration (IASIA) and of the editorial board of their journal, the *International Review of Administrative Sciences (IRAS)*, I enjoyed countless opportunities to travel to all the continents. In Morocco and Tunisia I explored the mysterious casbahs, the meandering maze of enclosed souks, buzzing with sellers and prospective purchasers of food, fruit, clothing, brass and clay ware. In Tangier I learned firsthand about the art of haggling from a Nigerian friend, Dr Adebayo Adediji, then director of the school of administration at Ife University. He accompanied me to a shop, where I was attracted to some colourful cushion covers. In response to my enquiry about the price, the shopkeeper replied, say $X each, and when I immediately reached for my wallet to pay for four, Adediji reacted: 'Mills, don't be a fool! Leave it to me and keep quiet.' He began by offering $X for a dozen and emerging from the bargaining exercise, I obtained my four covers for a total sum of $X instead of $4X!

On a visit to Tunis for a meeting in 1986, I encountered a problem when on arrival at the airport, the immigration official seemed confused on looking at my passport; evidently he had never heard of Jamaica. Resorting to my schoolboy French, I ventured: 'Jamaique, une petite isle près de Miami.' His reaction was a blank look and a plea for assistance from his colleague in the adjoining booth who looked equally blank. Within a few minutes, with a flash of inspiration, I exclaimed, 'Bob Marley!' The reaction was immediate, his face lit up and he responded, *'Ah, oui! Mais il est mort. Quel dommage!'*

During the 1970 meeting at Kenya's Institute of Administration (K.I.A.) in Lower Kabete, I discovered that the Swahili word *nyama*, meant meat. I told my East African fellow participants of our Jamaican expression *Nyam and go wey* (to eat and leave immediately) One Ugandan was so intrigued by this, that whenever he saw me, even walking on the other side of the street, he would smile broadly and shout, 'Hello, nyam and go wey!'

An experience of an entirely different nature came in 1983, when I was invited to serve as a United Nations consultant to the government of Aruba in recommending the new administrative machinery which might appropriately be put in place to meet the island's new *status aparte*. One of my recommendations was the creation of a central, independent body of non-partisan persons to which authority would be assigned for recruitment, appointment and promotion of civil servants, instead of the system then obtaining, based mainly on political appointment etc. On reflection, I concluded that this recommendation stemmed from my own 'culture bound' perspective, having been socialized by, and steeped in the Westminster-Whitehall system.

My sojourn at the university has been replete with other interesting experiences. Among my initial observations was the extent to which priority was given to administrative rather than academic staff in the provision of office facilities such as carpeting, paintings and air conditioning. Staff at assistant registrar level enjoyed better amenities than academic heads. Indeed, it appeared that the primary purpose was the pursuit of administrative ends, rather than the achievement of academic objectives. Fortunately, it seems that the balance has improved in recent years.

Clothed with wisdom *ex post*, it appears to have been a mistake to link salaries of administrative with those of academic staff, for example, designating assistant registrars as equivalent to lecturers. The nature of their respective functions differs fundamentally, and the latter are subject to much more rigorous assessment and promotion criteria and procedures. Off-campus criticisms of the salary increases given to Mona staff flow primarily from the more obvious and easy comparison between the functions of administrative personnel at Mona and in the civil service and the private sector.

On the academic side, there has been a serious deterioration in the standards of English grammar, spelling and of the presentation of papers. The course in the Use of English does not really address the problem which stems essentially from appalling weaknesses in teaching at the primary and secondary levels where these problems should be addressed. The university is tackling the situation via a remedial English course which was introduced in 1988. As someone nurtured in the elementary school system of more than 60 years ago, I make it clear to students that the use of poor grammar will cost them marks. I value the virtues of analysis and parsing, elements which are seemingly missing from modern educational methods. Unfortunately, some of the worst offenders are teachers reading for the Bachelor of education degree. The vision of the vicious circular effect and the perpetuation of these appalling standards is mind-boggling.

Over the past five years I have collected a number of gems culled from essays and examination scripts. Here are a few examples from final year students: *'Little are no sanctions are imposed'*. *'An arcake notion.'* *'Is presently been.'* *'..... is froth with problems'*. *'Past approaches were simply hadoc.'* (Not a fish story!) As we speak, so we write. And among spelling variations of a term used frequently in our discipline, *'burrocracy'*. Presumably, government by asses.

My service at the UWI has provided other opportunities, including service on interesting and fruitful committees. These have included chairmanship of the committee which formulated proposals leading to the introduction of the hotel and tourism management programme, and of the group which made recommendations regarding the involvement of staff in consultancy activities external to the university. Among all of these engagements two have been particularly rewarding in their impact on student life and relations; As the first and long-serving chairman of the sports advisory committee during a period when we brought the touring cricket teams of New Zealand, India and Australia to play against the UWI at the Mona Bowl. The other came in 1991 when a system of awards was introduced to benefit students who contribute significantly to extra-curricular activities, in implementation of recommendations of a committee under my chairmanship.

One of my greatest sources of pleasure and pride is the recognition and the warm welcome extended to me by numerous graduates of our degree, diploma and certificate programmes in my travels around the region. I have appreciated the many invitations received from groups and individuals who are now to be found in a wide variety of areas. Perhaps the most touching and memorable experience for me occurred in Georgetown, Guyana. While I was at a conference there a blind gentleman entered our room, accompanied by a lady who asked whether that was the room in which a particular meeting was being held. When I suggested that she should enquire at the reception desk, the gentleman exclaimed, 'Professor Mills, what are you doing in Guyana?' He was Wilbert Williams, who had been one of our students and had become president of the Caribbean Council for the Blind.

On another occasion while participating in an inter-regional workshop held in Ghana in 1991, I discovered that one of our public administration graduates, Michael Morgan, then with the United Nations there, was responsible for administering housekeeping arrangements for participants, including payment of *per diem* allowances. On my return journey home via Lagos where I spent a day with high commissioner Dudley Thompson and his wife, the young staff member who was assigned to meeting me at the airport, reminded me that I had taught him in the certificate course. In addition, Dudley's deputy, Raymond Wolfe had completed the Bachelor's degree in international relations in the department.

The crowning point of my career at the university were the special functions and the symposium held in my honour by the vice-chancellor and the faculty of social sciences during April 1991, and the treatment accorded by media organizations in respect of my public service activities. I shall long remember my deeply-felt appreciation of those few days which evoked an intense and overwhelming emotion in me. Tributes were expressed by individuals representing several areas of my public activities and by former students and current colleagues who presented papers or participated in discussing them. I have been deeply touched too, by the enquiries made constantly about my wife's condition during the past five years, by UWI's academic, administrative, clerical and ancillary staff. I was pleased that on my retirement there was an obvious successor in Dr Edwin Jones — such ease in succession being one of the yardsticks of a successful administration.

When I joined the university staff more than 30 years ago, Sir Hugh Springer, the then registrar remarked to me, 'Charles, don't expect too much. Always bear in mind that the institution never remembers.' Never has someone been more wrong. In fact, the institution does remember.

In light of the opportunities which I have enjoyed at UWI, the farewell functions for me as a full-time staff member, and the encomiums showered on me by this very special faculty, it would not only be churlish, but also untrue in my case, if I were to endorse such sentiments.

8

IN THE SERVICE OF THE NATION

Reflecting on these 55 years in public service and also on the other lives spent beyond the walls of my two formal careers, I recognize how fortunate I have been in the many and varied opportunities afforded to me. A great debt is of course due to the fact that I was 'careful in the choice of my parents' (as Professor Laski enjoined us to do, in order to ensure success in life); partly attributable too, to a small coterie of close relatives, especially Uncle J.J. Supporting the influence from these sources were the educational opportunities enjoyed at J.C., L.S.E., and Harvard; opportunities denied to so many of my generation.

In a life spanning a period covering the final stages of the colonial system, and running through the beginnings of party and cabinet government, internal self-government to independence, there has been a double bonus. This has accrued from spending a significant part of the period during the decolonization process, in Great Britain, living and/or associating with future West Indian and African leaders, and working in the Colonial Office.

Uncle J.J. served on over 40 boards and committees (and was chairman of about 20 of these) on a variety of subjects which, excluding education, ranged across a gamut, from hurricane relief, industrial relations and sugar, to music and poetry. And his service was voluntary. In the words of a former student, Professor R.N. Murray, he was the 'Non-Established Civil Servant'. I seem to have inherited some of these genes. Although my service on committees and commissions has not been nearly as extensive, it has been more wide-ranging geographically, assuming regional and international dimensions; this derives from the wider opportunities open to someone of a later generation.

These committee activities began during my civil service career when, early in the '50s, I was assigned as secretary to two bodies, the Economic Committee of Executive Council and the Local Industries (Tariff Protection) Board, both under the chairmanship of Sir Robert Barker, a nominated member to the Council and Legislature, and substantively, Managing Director of M. M. Alexander Ltd. It was to his office at this store on Harbour Street, that I usually took my draft minutes for his perusal. This assignment was followed by the Match Industry Commission. At UWI there was of course involvement in numerous committees — in several, as chairman — but this was expected of a senior staff member.

Service on some 'extra-mural' committees and boards has been rewarding in enhancing and broadening my education through close contact with distinguished representatives from the business world. This is true particularly of the Grace, Kennedy Foundation (now in its eleventh year), of whose Board I am a foundation member and at Honourable Carlton Alexander's invitation, succeeded Sir Herbert Duffus as Chairman in 1989. I am also Chairman of the Scholarship Committee.

In 1938, long before it became the practice for private sector firms and families to endow tertiary education scholarships in such profusion, the House of Issa, led by Mr Elias Issa pioneered such a path of opportunity for young men and women who might otherwise not have been able to benefit from a university education. This initiative was taken when the only such scholarships available were the Rhodes, Jamaica and Agricultural. (The Centenary was added in the same year to commemorate that anniversary of Emancipation). To celebrate the Issa's 50th anniversary in 1988, a special, additional scholarship was awarded for study in UWI's Executive M.B.A. programme. A member of the family usually sits on the selection committee; in recent years Christopher Issa and Mrs Marjorie McCormack have been representing the firm. In 1962 I was appointed a member, and at the death in 1965 of Uncle J.J. who was Chairman, I 'inherited' the position.

My education was extended further, during the proceedings of the Sugar Commission of Enquiry (1987-'88), of which I was appointed Chairman, to recommend the proportions in which the net returns from cane and its approved by-products should be shared between canegrowers/farmers and sugar manufacturers, and on other matters. As Robert Humphries put it in a book reviewing the history of Price Waterhouse for the first 75 years:

> 'a member of that commission (which investigated the sugar industry in the 1950s) was Mr John James Mills, O.B.E., and almost thirty years later to the month his nephew Professor Gladstone Mills was appointed to head another Commission of Enquiry into the industry.'

In October 1992, I allowed my arm to be twisted serving as Chairman, with colleagues Nathan Richards and Peter John Thwaites, the Presidents of the National Development Bank and of Dyoll Insurance, respectively, of an arbitration panel to settle a dispute between the government and the Police Federation over the latter's claim for increased emoluments (including allowances) of its members. At the inception of proceedings, controversy centred on the participation of the Rt. Hon. Hugh Shearer and Dr Trevor Munroe, prominent trade union leaders, as leading advocates for the Federation. The government objected to their participation on constitutional grounds and on the basis of the provisions of the Constabulary Act, emphasizing the principle of the independence of the Federation from external influences. This issue was decided by the Supreme Court against the government, which has appealed.

Subsequently, during the hearings, another controversy surfaced concerning the appropriateness of the J.L.P. Chairman, Bruce Golding giving evidence as an expert witness for the Federation, in his capacity of Chairman of Parliament's Public Accounts Committee. In essence, the issues have focused on the role of the police — whether they provide a unique and indispensable service — on the erosion in the quality of life of their members, and constraints on attracting and retaining personnel; and on the likely consequential repercussions on claims from other public sector categories, on the public sector budget deficit, and the rate of inflation.

For most of my working life, like Uncle J.J., I undertook almost all committee and commission assignments on a voluntary basis. For example, the Committee on Local Government Reform (of which I was Chairman and which reported in 1974), held 33 meetings which entailed my travelling to Headquarters House on Duke Street — all without even the reimbursement of travelling expenses. I had a similar experience with the Advisory Committee on a National Registration System in 1982/1983 — an exercise which involved 21 meetings. Much later in my university career, I discovered from colleagues that I was being naive. The Act which established the Electoral Committee stipulates that the selected members should receive emoluments no less than those paid to a Puisne Judge. Notwithstanding this provision, we decided from the outset, that since the three of us were carrying out those functions on a part-time basis, we would accept only a portion of the emoluments. Yet, a newspaper published an item some years ago, in which a calculation was made of what the editor considered to be my gross income from various sources as a Professor at the UWI, as a member of the Electoral Committee, and from consultancies, without checking the facts; the calculation based on the full provision prescribed in the Electoral Reform Act and on the assumption that I received a fee for all the consultancies which I undertook. I have not yet come to terms with the tendency in the post-Independence period, for many of our fellow countrymen to denigrate, and attempt to tear down our home-grown national institutions or individuals prominent in public life, who have earned some success.

On the other hand, with the exception of action taken from time to time by revolutionaries, during the colonial period as a people, we were content to pay deference to the institutions of the time and to colonial officials. It seems to me that the contrast in attitudes stems partly from a sense of envy which appears to be ingrained in some of us, envy of the success of our own fellow citizens; and the behaviour of the detractors is no doubt an expression of the 'crabs in the barrel' syndrome.

Although I had left the civil service in 1960, I would continue to extend my skills and services to the public sector. This proved particularly gratifying after Independence in 1962 and I am especially proud of two such tenures of service.

In 1973 I was appointed a member of the Public Service Commission (PSC). The other members were Drs. Ludlow Moody and John Beckford with high court judge Ivan Eccleston as chairman. By the following year, when a new PSC was appointed I became chairman, with colleagues including former solicitor general Ewart Forrest, Dr. Phyllis McPherson-Russell, and business leaders Eric Abrahams and Oliver Jones. By that time, long-serving chief personnel officer and ex-officio secretary to the commission, A.B. Smith had retired and was succeeded by Pat Clerk, who not long after would be succeeded by Roy Forbes.

The commission of 1974-1977 attempted to introduce a number of initiatives in collaboration with the Ministry of the Public Service (MPS). Among these were career advancement on the basis of merit, selection and training of personnel officers, identification and development of management potential, and succession planning. The PSC and MPS perform complementary roles and a great deal also depends on the goodwill displayed by the leadership and general staff of both institutions. Real effectiveness will not be achieved if either one engages in ambitious empire building or in negative, foot-dragging exercises. This was the general experience in the relations between the two during the mid-1970s. Perhaps a contributing factor was the relationship between the first permanent secretary of the newly created ministry, Sir Egerton Richardson, and me, as PSC chairman since I had been a senior official in the ministry of finance when he was financial secretary.

On occasion I have been asked whether any attempt was ever made by a politician to influence me in making a decision during those four years. The answer is categorically and unequivocally 'No', except on one occasion. A minister, whom I had known since he was a student 40 years before, telephoned me at the university: 'Gladstone, we want to put up X's name for headship of Division Y.' I replied, also addressing him by first name, 'The proper procedure is for your permanent secretary to submit a recommendation to the C.P.O.; but since we are talking unofficially, let me say that although having a high regard for his intellectual capacity, I do not consider him suitable for that particular position because of his abrasive personality.' The reaction was immediate and he moved into a more formal approach: 'You and the commission are a set of obstacles. I am going to get the Prime Minister to abolish you!' I replied: 'Mr. minister, anytime you, the Prime Minister or the cabinet want to take such action, proceed; I do not depend on the PSC for my livelihood!' Thereupon, he banged down the telephone. To give him credit, about half an hour later, he telephoned to apologize.

In July 1975 I was invited by the British government through the high commissioner to Jamaica, in my capacities of PSC chairman and professor of public administration to visit the United Kingdom and meet appropriate officials such as the permanent secretary of the civil service department, the first civil service commissioner and the special adviser to Prime Minister Harold Wilson. The programme also included visits to educational and training institutions like Henley Staff College, the Civil Service College and the Management Centres of Oxford and Aston Universities. I was presented with a copy of the paper on 'Political Advisers' which had been presented by the Prime Minister to the Commonwealth heads of goverment meeting in Kingston a few weeks before. At the time, this was a highly controversial issue in Jamaica because of Prime Minister Michael Manley's emphasis on the recruitment of such advisers since the accession to power of the new People's National Party goverment three years before - and the anxiety expressed by the civil service association. The Wilson paper included the very significant assertion: 'For policies without politics are of no more use than politics without policies.'

One of the most interesting features of that visit was the experience of observing the selection process for the administrative class of the civil service and noting the emphasis placed on practical policy and problem-oriented tests. Significantly also, a psychologist is included in each interviewing team.

Following the general election of December 1976 which the People's National Party won by a large majority on its democratic socialism platform, members of the public service commission were asked by the Prime Minister through his permanent secretary, Gordon Wells, to hand in our resignations as was required of board members of statutory bodies. We declined, since we considered that the convention relating to statutory boards did not apply to the public service commission. This is so because of its establishment within the framework of the constitution which expressly constitutes the commission as a non-partisan, impartial and independent body. Further, if members were to resign automatically following general elections, inferences could be drawn which might detract from the integrity and the independent nature of the Commission.

When I expressed these views in a meeting with the Prime Minister, he indicated his awareness of the Commission's constitutional position; nevertheless, for the first time in Jamaica's history, fundamental policy issues and ideological positions had been clearly defined and the recent elections had unequivocally determined the outcome. In the circumstances, he felt strongly that all members of boards and commissions whose positions stemmed directly or indirectly from ministerial appointment or recommendation should offer their resignations as a matter of fundamental principle.

We reiterated and re-emphasized our disagreement with this view of the position so far as it related to the commission. Nevertheless, we did not wish to appear to have a vested interest in retaining our positions until expiration of our terms of office eight months later. Moreover, we preferred to avoid an impasse in light of the Prime Minister's strongly expressed views.

Accordingly, we submitted our resignations to the Governor-General, copying our letter to the Prime Minister. These resignations took immediate effect and we were not prepared when asked to do so, to hold on until a new commission was appointed. These events were taking place in a context in which the conventional concept of a depoliticized civil service was being questioned. Public controversy centred on the relative merits of commitment to the party's goals as against skills and competence as criteria for selection for appointments. It was a time when individuals were simplistically and often maliciously labelled politically and slotted into partisan pigeon-holes. Very soon after, the party's accreditation committee would be created.

Jamaica's electoral system which was controlled until 1979 by the incumbent government suffered for decades from a plague of ills both in the registration and polling processes. Among the most critical of these were the deliberate omission of qualified persons from the electoral list, padding of the list, bogus voting, that is impersonation, even of deceased persons, and multiple and over-voting. There were also glaring examples of gerrymandering of constituency boundaries.

The perception generally held was of a system weakened by loopholes and administered by officials under ministerial direction, some of whom were corrupt and biased in favour of the government in power. In this virtually tribal situation, the activities of fanatical party supporters have increased. An even more significant and alarming evil has appeared and begun to assume prominent proportions. This is the invasion of polling stations and the stuffing of ballot boxes, either by intimidation and force or with collusion on the part of some Presiding Officers and Poll Clerks.

Criticisms and strictures which became increasingly strident following the general election of December 1976 and threats of a boycott of future elections issued by the opposition Jamaica Labour Party led to the appointment by parliament of a special joint select committee on constitutional and electoral reform. Out of these discussions on reform and the recommendations of the bi-partisan committee was born the Electoral Advisory Committee (EAC), created by statute enacted in August 1979, and describd by Leader of the Opposition, Seaga, as 'this first giant step towards electoral reform'.

The committee was uniquely composed, and reflected the realities of the Jamaican political situation. There were two members nominated by the Prime Minister, two by the Leader of the Opposition, three independent members to be recommended by the other four and the director. The new committee assumed authority for appointment of all registration and election officials, and the preparations for, and the conduct of all elections. In addition, the committee assumed responsibility for determining the number of local government electoral divisions and delineating their boundaries. A fundamental change was made in the status of the institution to which this authority and these responsibilities were assigned. The electoral machinery was removed from its position as a department under the control and direction of a minister and re-located in a statutory body. Indeed, some years later during a visit to our organization, the chairman of the Barbados commission could not come to terms with the fact that the Prime Minister's nominees who were both at that time, ministers, would not as a matter of course, secure decisions in favour of the government.

In recognition of the deep distrust, wide polarization and cleavage which existed within the society, it was proposed that, in the event of the political nominees failing to complete their recommendations within a fortnight of their own appointments, the Governor-General would be empowered to appoint the required number of independent members. This could only be done after consultation with the Prime Minister and the Leader of the Opposition. Indeed, the governor-general was obliged initially to exercise his prerogative and appoint all three without the benefit of such recommendations. I learned subsequently, that whenever a name was proposed by one side, the other automatically rejected the individual on the assumption that he or she was likely to be a supporter of the proposer's party.

In October 1979, I received a summons to King's House from Sir Florizel Glasspole, then the Governor-General. He informed me of the decision to establish the Electoral Advisory Committee as the central component of the restructured electoral system and of his intention to propose me as a member. I expressed great appreciation for the compliment, indicated my interest, but requested a few days grace for discussion with my wife. Following this and further consideration, I decided that if I could make a national contribution by this means, I was willing to accept the position on the committee. I wondered whether as members it would be advisable to acquire bullet-proof vests. Indeed, we were offered special security protection but declined, taking the view that this would perhaps attract too much attention to us.

We were duly appointed and held our first meeting on October 9, 1979. Other foundation members were Dr. Paul Robertson, People's National Party deputy General Secretary and O.K. Melhado, group managing director of the State Trading Corporation, who were the Prime Minister's nominees, senator Bruce Golding, Jamaica Labour Party General Secretary and attorney-at-law Abe Dabdoub, who were nominees of the Leader of the Opposition; Mrs. Shirley Miller, director of legal reform and R.V. Irvine, who had recently retired as auditor general were independent members. Coincidentally, both Robertson and Golding were students in the department of government during my tenure as head. Our first tasks were to select and appoint a Director Elections who would also function as a non-voting eighth member, and to make preparations for a comprehensive enumeration, since the current voters list was three years old. Concurrently, we decided to terminate the appointment of all existing Returning Officers and their deputies, the Election Clerks and to advertise the posts, indicating that the previous incumbents could apply and would be considered.

Interviews were conducted in respect of all these positions, and an Assistant Attorney General, Carl Dundas appointed Director on secondment. He had served as adviser to the joint select committee of parliament — the parent of the new electoral system. His legal skills and special experience were to prove invaluable to the EAC's work. Meanwhile, Roy A. Forbes who had recently retired as chief personnel officer was recruited as the committee's administrative secretary, and during the next few months, Frank Weir and Noel Lee were appointed assistant directors of field operations and administration respectively. D.A. Dunkley was seconded from his post of senior executive engineer, ministry of construction, as manager of data processing. Mr Weir had long experience as a returning officer in the old system.

From the outset, the committee formulated objectives which we considered essential prerequisites for a democratic society. These objectives were that every citizen who is qualified to vote is allowed to exercise his or her right to do so and to express his/her preference for a political representative freely and without impediment; that no citizen who is not qualified to vote is allowed to do so; the preservation of the 'one person-one vote' principle; and that the outcome of all elections truly represents the will of the electorate.

We were deeply concerned with creating an electoral system which was characterized, both in its procedures and personnel, by fairness, integrity, impartiality and efficiency; one which would command general public confidence. Unless we succeeded in this effort, the consequent cynicism among the citizenry could be detrimental to the preservation of democracy.

Initially, we focused on the two major problems of impersonation and multiple voting. Elimination or a significant reduction of the first would require introduction of an effective means of voter identification. We decided that each elector would be required to bear a photograph as an integral element of an identification card. The photographing was to be carried out simultaneously with the house-to-house enumeration process. This would form the nucleus of a proposed national registration system agreed upon during the bi-partisan discussions of 1979. To avoid multiple voting, we introduced a lamp which emitted ultra-violet light, designed to detect within a 48-hour period, the presence of traces of electoral ink invisible to the naked eye. This, together with the special ink, comprised our 'integrity equipment.'

On February 3, 1980, the Prime Minister announced in a radio and television broadcast, that in the light of the economic situation and the failure to agree to the International Monetary Fund's terms for a new agreement, 'Jamaica needs to settle the economic strategy which is to be pursued in the immediate future...as soon as the electoral committee is able to advise me that an appropriate new electoral system is in place, I shall call a new election.' Near the end of March, Leader of the Opposition, Mr. Seaga wrote to me confirming the views he had expressed in a meeting with Mrs. Miller and me the day before, that following the government's withdrawal from the International Monetary Fund, in his party's opinion,

> 'the events of the past few days have so altered the course of the nation that in the interest of national stability and ultimately survival, mid-year general elections must now become the most urgent national priority.'

This view was supported immediately by Mr. Manley in a letter of the same date. Both leaders agreed that a modified system should be introduced which could be implemented at an earlier date than the proposed photograph identification requirement. They hoped the modified system would nevertheless contain adequate safeguards and ensure production of a fair voters list. The EAC had to be convinced that it was feasible to design a system which though 'second best', would provide reasonable safeguards against irregularities, especially impersonation. Concluding after serious consideration that we could do so, we informed them that in the national interest, we would proceed. And so we held the identification component in temporary abeyance.

The next seven months was a hectic period of preparing proposals for amendments to the representation of the people law, conducting a house-to-house enumeration and a valiant struggle to complete the voters list. We struggled to achieve this in an atmosphere of an unprecedentedly long campaign period, a record number of politically motivated murders and general violence. Indeed, on more than one occasion, electoral office staff were holed up through the night at their Duke Street headquarters because of gunfire outside. Incredibly, in spite of these considerable constraints, the field operations were completed in a record six weeks! Remarkably, both nomination and polling days were relatively free of violence.

Major problems were being experienced by the committee in proceeding with preparations for the elections in a particular area of East Rural St. Andrew and it was decided to invite the candidates, Roy McGann and Joan Gordon to meet the selected members. In view of the intense feelings of animosity between these two, who were perhaps the most aggressive pair of contestants, the committee agreed that Dr. Robertson and Abe Dabdoub should be present to assist in keeping the peace. After the discussions which took place on the eve of nomination day, October 13, I shook hands with one of them and looked around for the other who had disappeared. Hurrying downstairs, and finding him almost at the gate of the EAC's office, I shook hands and also expressed the wish for a clean contest as I had already done with his rival. Shortly after midnight, I was awakened by a telephone call informing me that McGann had been shot dead! For several years following the inception of the committee, I had consciously sought to ensure, even on social occasions, if I stopped to speak with anyone from one party, that I searched around for a representative of the other side. Such was the climate of paranoia and irrational suspicion which prevailed.

After a highly creditable performance in the enumeration exercise, the system encountered serious delays in the processing of the data from which the voters list would be produced. This was due primarily to the lack of adequate key-punching facilities within the electoral office and the need to depend on external sources. Following our representations to the Prime Minister about the need for additional data-processing equipment and his instructions to ministries and departments, a few machines were provided. One was loaned to us by the University of the West Indies. A very reluctant head of department had to be persuaded to comply after our appeal to the Prime Minister.

In the meantime, allegations were made that some elements in the People's National Party were seeking to have the election delayed until February 1981. In response to the *Gleaner's* editorial of September 10, 1980 that the Prime Minister should keep his commitment made in the broadcast on February 3 and 'set the date of the elections now', Mr. Manley, in a statement published the next day, re-iterated that he would honour his commitment when the electoral machinery was in place and the list ready.

A P.N.P rally had been planned for Sunday, October 5 at Sam Sharp Square, Montego Bay, and expectations were rife that the Prime Minister would announce the election date there. On the preceding Thursday, he asked Carl Dundas and myself to see him at Jamaica House to brief him on the state of preparations and of the readiness of the system. We informed him of the difficulties being encountered in printing the list, mainly resulting from frequent power outages. Immediately, he rose from his seat, telephoned the chief of staff of the Jamaica Defence Force and asked him to scan the length and breadth of Jamaica and locate a stand-by plant for the electoral office. Within a few days one was installed!

He also asked me to telephone him at his Montego Bay hotel on October 4, to inform him of progress in printing of the list. My niece, Denise Mills was married on that day, and during the reception, amid the sounds of music and revelry, I reached the Prime Minister. In response to my statement that the goverment printing office was not making satisfactory progress, he exclaimed: 'Offer them triple time, if necessary!' In our view, there was no evidence that Mr. Manley was stalling.

Late on the night before polling day, that memorable 30th day of October, when we were satisfied that all preparations were in place, it was discovered that the returning officer for north western St. Andrew had failed to prepare the constituency adequately. As a result, on the morning of the election he had to be replaced, a temporary appointment made, and presiding officers and poll clerks recruited. In any event, the election proceeded in that constituency only because of the invaluable support given to the electoral office by the two candidates, Carlyle Dunkley and Karl Samuda, and citizens of the community. As a final act crowning the relations between these contestants in that context of polarization and intense partisan feelings, Mr. Samuda drove his rival home.

A rumour had circulated in the immediate election aftermath, that the voting pencil possessed a mysterious feature which enabled the 'X' marking a vote for the People's National Party to move and be transformed into one for the Jamaica Labour Party! On the night of October 30, when the results emerged, the People's National Party General Secretary, D.K. Duncan, speaking on radio and television asked that the EAC's chairman and the director of elections should search their conscience and indicate whether they could sincerely say that there had been a fair election. As newspaper columnist Jennifer French stated in the *Gleaner* of November 3, 'These are the same men and the system which former Prime Minister Michael Manley had hailed at mid-day Thursday (Election Day) as an "independent body" and an electoral machinery that no-one could manipulate.'

Director Dundas thought that these comments could have triggered physical attacks against him and he had been advised not to visit certain areas. Consequently, the commissioner of police was asked to retain the security precautions at the electoral office and at Dundas' home. However, Paul Robertson interpreted D.K. Duncan's remarks as those of someone 'hitting out' after an election loss and in this case, raising questions concerning the conduct of the election in relation to irregularities experienced, rather than as an imputation against the integrity of the chairman and director. When Duncan was appointed a nominated member of the EAC, replacing O.K. Melhado, I was concerned about his possible behaviour at our meetings; but he behaved impeccably and made a real contribution to proceedings.

In 1981 the committee received a special *Gleaner* award for 'yeoman service in the establishment of a fair electoral system in

Jamaica.' Since that historic election progress has been made in a number of areas, which include introduction of the photograph identification, implementation of an updating system of registration, the acquisition of in-house ballot printing equipment, a radio communication network, and additional computer facilities. Between periods of comprehensive enumeration, persons are able to have their names placed on the voters list if they have attained the age of 18 since the last enumeration, or were unable to be enumerated then.

Unfortunately, the photographing operation has produced disappointing results, because of the relatively low quality of the personnel available, and the varying conditions of light in which the operation has to be conducted. A more satisfactory product could be obtained by the designation of centres distributed across the country, instead of using the present house-to-house system. This suggestion has so far been resisted on the grounds that the onus is on the electoral officials to go to the people. Considerable advantages have accrued from the installation of ballot printing equipment in the electoral office. This has provided the electoral organization with control over security in the printing and cut the previous dependency on outside printers. The benefits of the communication system can hardly be overstated. It is incredible that the system performed with a fair degree of success without radio contact with and between field personnel.

Undoubtedly, one of the most significant events in the history of the EAC centred on the general election of December 15, 1983, which produced the one-party parliament. The traumatic happenings of the period, following Prime Minister Seaga's decision to announce a snap election threatened the committee's future. Shortly after news reached Jamaica about the tragic events in Grenada of October 19, 1983 and the ensuing 'invasion/rescue mission', I mentioned in a meeting with selected members, that I would not be surprised if an election were called.

The committee was sharply divided about the Prime Minister's decision, which was fraught with fundamental issues. On one hand, it was argued that the electoral system was not in a state of readiness, primarily in respect of the state of the electoral list and the implementation of the photograph identification system. The list was three years old and did not include persons who had become 18 years old since the 1980 enumeration. Moreover, a new enumeration exercise from which such individuals would be placed on the list, had reached an advanced stage. As for the second point, the EAC had agreed, on the request made by both the former Prime Minister and the Leader of the Opposition in 1980, to postpone implementation of the identification system, although the committee adhered to its original conclusion concerning the need to include this as an element in future elections.

On the other hand, there was disagreement as to whether a 'solemn and binding agreement' had been made; and it was emphasized that a legally valid list was in place. Furthermore, the nature of the charges levelled by the opposition against the minister of finance in the call for his resignation, namely that he had 'misled' the nation involved the person who was also Prime Minister and the resignation of the latter would automatically trigger off an election. I shared that view. However, I also understand the point of view of People's National Party representatives who argued that the two ministerial positions should be viewed separately. In addition, the committee had no option, as the body charged with responsibility for the conduct of elections, but to carry out those statutory functions; to have done otherwise would have been tantamount to arrogating to itself a prerogative which it did not have. Presumably, circumstances can arise which could lead selected independent members to consider resignation. In coming to a decision, they would also, presumably, consider the likely consequences of such an action; for instance, that a crisis might ensue. For a brief period of a fortnight in December 1983, the absence of nominated members from committee meetings frustrated its work.

The selected members were strongly criticized by Mr. Manley and other high-ranking PNP officials for proceeding with the December 15 election, but they took the view, expressed above, about their statutory responsibilities. Strong feelings and resentment about our decision have rankled in the minds of some of these high-ranking People's National Party personnel, who have continued to hold this against us ten years after.

The one-party parliament which followed the PNP's decision not to contest, was not entirely without a spin-off. Paradoxically, it provided an opportunity for a demonstration of the spirit of Westminster-Whitehall democracy when, in the absence of a Leader of the Opposition and of PNP members in the House of Representatives, the government took legislative action which accorded with the realities of that party's position in the country's political life. Thus, the relevant Representation of the People Acts were amended to provide first, that in such an event, the Governor-General may consult with 'such person as he in his discretion thinks appropriate' and appoint two additional nominated members to the EAC to complete its complement of four. He proceeded to consult the President of the PNP. Secondly, where only one party is entitled to provide scrutineers for the enumeration registration process by having a minimum of five members in the House of Representatives, this requirement may be satisfied by reference to the composition of the preceding parliament before its dissolution.

The selected independent members, like the nominated bring skills and experience to the committee's deliberations, initiating ideas and proposals and participating fully in discussions. But more conspicuous is their role as referees, holding the balance between the contending parties. Performance of this latter function has, at times, entailed a delicate, sensitive tight-rope walk and on occasions, these members have had to draw deeply on their resources — especially during the period of wide polarization. An important convention has evolved out of the EAC's experience. Incidentally, it is a fallacy to assume that conventions can emerge only after centuries of an institution's life, as one critic insists.

In cases where there is continuing disagreement between the two sides on a fundamental issue, and this seems unlikely to be resolved, both agree to leave the issue to be determined by the selected members; agreeing also, in advance, to accept their decision even where it might seem to be against the interest of one side. This has become customary practice for example, in the siting of polling stations, the recruitment and review of the performance of election officials, firing or retaining, the delineation of local government electoral divisions and of constituency boundaries.

As for the last of these, the determination of parliamentary constituency boundaries lies within the constitutional authority of a Standing Committee of the Houses of Parliament, while the EAC is statutorily responsible for determining the number and boundaries of the electoral divisions which fall within these constituencies. However, the scope of the EAC's role and responsibility was extended by the decision taken as part of the bi-partisan agreements of 1979, that it would serve in an advisory capacity to the Parliamentary Boundaries Committee; and more recently, when that body decided that it would accept without amendment, recommendations from the EAC on this subject. These are critical decisions, given the perennial controversies which obtained pre-EAC, about gerrymandering.

The role of the selected members has never seemed more critical than in 1985 following Prime Minister Seaga's dramatic announcement via the electronic media, that the number of local government councillors, and hence, electoral divisions, were to be reduced by 57%. In response to questions asked next day, by a radio station representative, I had to admit publicly that the EAC was the body clothed with authority to decide on the number of divisions, that we had not been consulted on the issue, and I had heard of the decision in the same way and at the same time as he had. The government had apparently overlooked the piece of legislation whereby this authority had been transferred from the minister of local government to the EAC. Colleague Carl Stone expressed a highly complimentary sentiment in his column, when he stated:

> The country is indebted to Professor Mills for publicly setting the record straight on the powers of the Electoral Advisory Committee. So many persons in our society have failed to show similar courage in publicly disagreeing with Mr. Seaga out of fear. (*Gleaner*, April 17, 1985).

A long period of controversy ensued, after the Prime Minister eventually agreed that the issue should be settled by the EAC; to pursue his original intention by fiat would have necessitated an amendment to the Act which bestowed these powers on the committee.

In the long debate which followed, the political nominees of the Opposition expressed strongly, the view that the number of divisions, should remain intact; while the Prime Minister's nominees pressed his view that in light of the decision to introduce the payment of salaries to councillors, and the fact that their functions had been reduced considerably, the total should be whittled down to 120. For several weeks a stalemate existed with the positions polarized; then, following further discussions, aided by persuasion by the selected members, the gap narrowed. Eventually, both sides were persuaded to leave the resolution of the issue in the hands of the selected members, and the latter decided, on the basis of certain objective criteria, that the number should be reduced to 189.

I understand that one journalist took me to task for not recognizing that the selected members outnumber each side, and that the chairman has a casting vote. Thus, a decision could have been imposed. This opinion assumes evidently, that in that eventuality, both parties would then blithely proceed to engage in the exercise of re-defining the boundaries of the re-structured divisions. I adhere to my view that in such circumstances, this would have been, and would be if a similar situation should again arise, a simplistic solution. To have adopted the critic's 'advice' would in my opinion, have led to a deterioration in the working relations among members, thereby handicapping the committee's effectiveness. As a *Gleaner* editorial of October 19, 1985 observed: 'The role of the Independent members in breaking the political deadlock is an important precedent.'

Incidentally, this episode in the EAC's life seems to have set the stage for the beginnings of a significant change in the relations between nominated members and in the atmosphere in which we have been functioning. As selected members, we observed with considerable pleasure, these beginnings which seemed to coincide with the operation of re-drawing the local government divisional boundaries during October and November 1985. A sub-committee consisting of representatives from both political sides, with the Director of Elections as chairman was set up to make recommendations to the full EAC. Cases in which there was disagreement, were referred to the selected members for resolution. Along the way, sub-committee members arranged to meet alternately, at each other's homes. The developing goodwill and camaraderie were reflected in the front page photograph appearing in the *Gleaner* during November '85, of then minister Bruce Golding kissing Ms. Portia Simpson, with Dr. Paul Robertson standing by, all EAC members at the time, taken during a party at my home. This evoked expressions of surprise by a number of persons, but, as I remarked, 'it was no big thing!' Unfortunately, the relations deteriorated during the last year of my chairmanship, divisiveness returned, the pursuit of partisan interest appearing to predominate.

In my concluding remarks in an address to Police recruits at the beginning of September 1988, I deplored the fact that no member of the EAC had been invited to the bi-partisan 'Peace Accord' ceremony held at King's House the week before; pointing out that the committee had made a considerable contribution in bringing together representatives of the major parties. Columnist Dawn Ritch, in an incredibly intemperate, offensive, snide and sarcastic attack accused me in comments which misrepresented my remarks, of 'taking credit for the success of the peace effort' and of claiming that 'it was the nine years of "considerable contribution" of his committee which had brought together the major political parties.' (*Sunday Gleaner*, September 11, 1988.) All this, despite the full text of my address published in the *Gleaner* of September 6. Even more reprehensible was her comment. 'I think... the failure to invite gang leaders was deliberate, and a serious omission in the way that Professor Mills was not.'

These more than 13 years as chairman of the EAC provided many opportunities to observe electoral systems and elections in other countries. In some significant respects, Costa Rica is the most impressive society I have observed at first hand in Latin America, including in the south, Brazil, Colombia, Peru, and Venezuela. Apart from the absence of an army, and in most Latin American states, the military seems all-pervasive, beginning at the point of entry to the country, the distribution of income is less skewed in Costa Rica. According to the United Nations Development Programme's calculation, it is the only developing state which merits a place in the index of 'high freedom' ranking countries. (UNDP, *Human Development Report*, 1991) Its national registration system, a *sine qua non* for efficient identification to meet electoral purposes, has served as a model in Central America. From the Jamaican perspective, one observes, almost with disbelief, children assisting electors in directing them to the polling booths.

Perhaps even more interesting and significant is the arrangement for security; authority for control over and deployment of the security force becomes vested in the Electoral Tribunal for a period commencing some weeks before polling day. I understand that in the Dominican Republic, a special electoral security corps of approximately 20,000 personnel is recruited from the regular services and mobilized as soon as the election campaign commences, about two months before polling day. In our own EAC we have been considering whether a similar, though modified system should be introduced in Jamaica, since deficiencies in security arrangements represent one of the major weaknesses in the electoral system and the EAC has no control over this vital area. But introduction of such an arrangement would require us to have on the committee or staff, personnel with experience in managing a security force of this nature.

As I reflect on Costa Rica, it seems to me no coincidence that institutions which include the Centre for Electoral Assistance and Promotion CAPEL; its parent, the Inter-American Human Rights Institute, with Barbadian Oliver Jackman as one of its vice-presidents, and Board members, Dr. Lloyd Barnett and the *Gleaner's* Oliver Clarke, both of Jamaica; and the University of Peace are all located in San José.

In El Salvador I observed a violence-free election in the midst of a civil war; and was fortunate to observe unofficially the election which brought Corazon Aquino to power in the Philippines (1986) by the coincidence of a conference on electoral systems scheduled before the election was called.

During the mid-1960s to early 1970s, I visited Haiti on several occasions and was impressed by the people's vibrant art and dance in the midst of grinding poverty, extreme income disparities and the *Ton Ton Macoutes*. I usually stayed at the quaint, charming Oloffsson Hotel with its imposing gingerbread architecture and rooms named after some famous artists and writers who had been guests, and which would be the location for much of Graham Greene's *The Comedians*. Here too, one became accustomed, yet with concern, to the regular evening visits by small, dapper, Auberon Jolie-Coeur, bedecked immaculately in white and twirling cane. We wondered whether he was spying on new guests for the government. I recall the occasion when, sightseeing, I stepped on to the pavement surrounding the white Presidential palace, to observe at closer range, the resplendent red blooms of a poinciana in full flowering. In the next moment, a guard was pointing his rifle at me, with an order: '*Va t'en !*' At times, while walking on the street, I felt insecure, as if I was being followed. Yet, the incidence of crime was minimal; a reflection, no doubt, of fear of the consequences.

There was the time when, returning from a trip to Petionville and from tasting some of the variety of Barbancourt liqueurs produced from flowers, I asked the cab driver whether he knew the Brandts. Both Clifford and Franz were my contemporaries at JC and the former played on the Manning team captained by me. He did not reply to the specific enquiry, but some indefinable change in the atmosphere persuaded me not to pursue the subject. A few days following my return home, I noticed a news item in the *Gleaner* emanating from Port-au-Prince, indicating that one of the brothers had been arrested on suspicion of involvement in a conspiracy to overthrow the government. The Brandt family was wealthy and it was said that from time to time, when the public coffers were depleted, President 'Papa Doc' Duvalier would have a member of one of the more affluent families thrown into prison, to be released on payment of a ransom; an interesting innovation in public finance. One of the two brothers served as Honorary Consul for Jamaica.

I had not, however, revisited the country for some 15 years, and welcomed the opportunity of doing so in the company of Messrs Donald Buchanan, Anthony Johnson and Ryan Peralto, politically nominated members of our EAC, as part of a joint group of OAS/CARICOM observers of the December 1990 elections. Jamaica's contingent on this joint group numbered 23; representatives from a variety of organizations and including Rev. Raymond Coke, Dr. Mary Sievright and two former members of parliament, Mrs. Hyacinth Knight and Dr. Horace Chang. CARICOM observers were also included in former President Carter's high level delegation, in the persons of Prime Ministers George Price and John Compton and minister Ben Clare; while the University of the West Indies' Dr. Michael Dash, head of the french department was a member of the Caribbean Conference of Churches delegation.

Director of Elections Noel Lee who had been serving for some time as chairman of a CARICOM working group of senior electoral officials engaged in giving technical advice and assistance greeted us; while a fairly large batch of workers mobilized from various CARICOM states, including a group of French creole-speaking St. Lucians had been engaged in the registration process throughout the country for several months. Fifteen parties and 340 independents contested the elections for Senators and Deputies, eleven of these for President; and at the last two stations among 40 which fell within my observation responsibility, Aristide obtained the maximum 120 votes in one and 161 out of 174 in the other! When early news of his victory emerged next morning, we encountered jubilant crowds dancing on the streets, happy, without rancour and bearing bits of bush. We were told that the bush symbolizes an uprooting and was also displayed in great profusion following the ouster of the younger Duvalier almost five years before.

On every count that election was historic; a landmark which confounded and proved the skeptics wrong: those who doubted that the election would be held at all or felt that it would be seriously sabotaged, and those who thought that it would be aborted if Aristide appeared to be winning the presidential race. The Haitian people deserve high praise for their courage, patience and determination not to be deterred, in light of their recent history and especially the tragic events of November 1987 and of 5th December 1990, a few days before the elections. As a tribute to the contribution made by the CARICOM technical group, OAS Secretary-General Soares commented, 'CARICOM has made OAS better and stronger by its performance.' This is true, particularly of the creole-speaking St. Lucians who pioneered a path during the registration exercise, establishing close contact and rapport with the native community, especially in remote rural areas. Their contribution cannot be too highly praised. Indeed, on numerous occasions, Haitians, recognizing our T-shirt uniform carrying the CARICOM insignia, welcomed us, expressing gratitude: 'You enabled us to have an election.'

As we flew out of Port-au-Prince and crossed the complex of mountains, I reflected on the miraculous recovery of the notorious Artibonite, once entirely denuded of vegetation. The election results had brought a glimmer of light to these long-suffering people — the apparent precursor of the dawn of a new day. But this was dimmed ten months later, and perhaps, turned off totally, by the coup which aborted the budding democracy.

When I revisited Guyana in 1985, after a long hiatus, I recalled the wonder of seeing Georgetown for the first time, in 1960: of a well-laid out city of canals, tree-lined avenues and magnificent timber buildings. In my view, it was the most beautiful West Indian capital and the hospitality above and beyond all of the others. In the context of my contacts from student days, my life as the W.I. Students Liaison Officer, and new acquaintances made on that first visit, I had to hide from hospitality at times.

From the distant past of Nutford House, there were Forbes Burnham, Ivor Robinson, Richard Allsopp, O.A. Johnson, 'Sweetie' Hart; Frank Williams, an even earlier friendship, forged during the Atlantic crossing in 1944; Hutton Griffith; cricket colleague, Fred Wills; the Pollard sisters, whose Father an old Miconian I was meeting for the first time at Uncle J.J.'s request as well as Commissioner of Lands, Adrian Thompson, renowned for his generosity to visitors. By the time of that 1985 visit, the condition of the economy had already escalated to new depths, the dollar devalued, later, hitting a black market low of 150 to the United States dollar, the beautiful buildings in need of paint, and essential commodities in scarce supply. Yet, the generous hospitality of the people continued, intact.

Among CARICOM states, Guyana has had the worst record for the rigging of registration and generally, for corrupt electoral practices. The rape of democracy perpetrated and perpetuated by the People's

National Congress (P.N.C.) government started with seed sown during the regime of the late President and former Prime Minister Forbes Burnham in the mid-1960s, and reached full flowering by the time of his death two decades later. Thus, Guyana was an aberration within CARICOM, with its statutory provision for overseas and postal voting; while other features of the electoral systems of fellow member states, designed to minimize the opportunities for tampering, such as preliminary counting of the ballots at each voting location were absent from Guyana's system. Some Guyanese considered CARICOM a club whose member states closed ranks in protecting the Guyana government from criticism.

Although the intense internecine racial violence of the 1960s had simmered down, the political divisiveness along ethnic lines persisted; and the long experience of authoritarianism, taken together with the history of manipulation of the electoral system created an atmosphere of cynicism and distrust which pervaded the political climate. This feeling of lack of confidence continued, and was intensified by strong suspicions about the integrity and impartiality of some electoral personnel, especially one or two very senior officials, and by the seriously flawed preliminary voters lists prepared by the national registration department and the election commission respectively, in 1990 and 1991. In fact, both in predominantly afro-Guyanese as well as indo-Guyanese areas, significant numbers of qualified voters were omitted from the 1991 List.

It is to the credit of former President Desmond Hoyte, Burnham's successor, that he abolished some of the most conspicuous and significant sources of abuses and introduced a number of reforms, including restructuring of the elections commission, albeit under pressure, particularly from external sources. My own impression of him is that he was genuinely committed to a policy objective of transparently fair elections despite resistance from, and actions of some hawks among his fellow comrades who were strongly opposed to the concessions the former President made to facilitate improvement of the system.

In the pre-election period between October 1991 and September 1992, I visited Guyana on four occasions, first, on a team sponsored by the Carter Centre in Atlanta, Georgia, led by former President Carazo of Costa Rica, and which included senator Ben Clare, minister of state for foreign affairs in Jamaica and professor Robert Pastor, executive secretary of the Council of Freely Elected Heads of Government. It was as a result of our observations and investigations during this visit, that we declared the list too seriously flawed to be 'cleansed' satisfactorily so as to form the basis of a fair election by December 1991. Despite our advice, strongly expressed, President Hoyte proceeded to call the elections for December 16.

In response to a request from the Carter Centre for my comments on the question of the President's power to reconvene parliament in order to provide an opportunity for postponement of elections, I emphasized that I could do so only as a layman with an educational background and long experience in political science and public administration; but that I was not a legal or constitutional expert. However, my advice centred on the issue of the existence of a state of emergency and the circumstances and grounds on the basis of which the President could justifiably conclude that such a state existed. I concluded with a question and 'a word of caution: Is there a danger that declaration of such a state could open up a "can of worms"?' Incidentally, a Jamaican radio station reported in the news that I had advised against declaration of a state of emergency since dire consequences would result! Mr. Carter sent me a gracious and generously expressed letter of appreciation stating, *inter alia*:

> 'As a recognized expert on Caribbean and constitutional questions, your advice is held in high regard. I am therefore very grateful that you agreed to submit an opinion regarding the constitutional question of reconvening the dissolved Guyanese parliament for the purpose of allowing additional time to prepare a clean voters list.'

My next two visits were made in May and June 1992 with Mr. Frank Solomon, a distinguished lawyer from Trinidad, on a Caribbean Rights Mission to examine the arrangements and preparations being made for the forthcoming postponed elections, and to assess the prospects of such elections being free and fair. During the second of these visits, we discussed with representatives from the political parties, the state of the fresh Preliminary List which had been published a week before, and visited a number of registration centres where we spoke with officials and potential electors. On these three assignments I was able to hold several long discussions with Mr. Rudy Collins, chairman of the Elections Commission, individuals such as distinguished lawyer and member of the Commission, Miles Fitzpatrick, Claremont Lye and other members of the civic organization, the Electoral Assistance Bureau (E.A.B.).

We were all impressed by the work done by this last organization, in assisting telephone callers at the Bureau's office in getting their names on the list. As Solomon and I reported, 'the E.A.B. has earned a sterling reputation for impartial commitment ... and for high professional competence.' Rudy Collins too, is to be commended for the integrity, dignity, tact and considerable courage which he displayed in the face of pressures from internal and external sources. I was therefore, shocked to hear former Prime Minister Hamilton Green in a Jamaica Broadcasting Corporation television interview, accuse the commission of bias against the PNC, and the EAB of acting as part of the opposition during the elections. He seemed to be speaking about institutions which were fundamentally different from those I knew.

Along with other members of the Carter team, I had met representatives of all the parties and also with President Hoyte and some of his ministers. However, Solomon and I were most surprised when we were told that neither the P.N.C. nor any high government officials were willing to see us during our May or June visit, since Caribbean Rights had been very critical of the government. They would talk with me, but only in my personal capacity. When I replied, 'No! I cannot do that. I am here as a representative of an organization,' the tack was modified slightly: 'Come and let us talk informally over a drink.' So, that was the end of that effort!

Apart from this, we experienced one other, but more serious disappointment, stemming from the government's adamant refusal to permit accreditation for the elections, of a separate CARICOM observer team — including representatives from organizations such as the Caribbean Conference of Churches and Caribbean Rights — and of local Guyanese organizations. We ended our Report as follows:

> It would be most unfortunate if the people of Guyana and the Caribbean were to be denied the opportunity of having Guyana's return to political legitimacy witnessed and confirmed by as many reputable organizations of the region as are willing and able to attend. Transparency of a public event, after all, will be of little significance if only a selected few are allowed to look.

My last assignment in this respect came as an invitation from Major-General Robert Neish, Executive chairman of the Bustamante Institute of Public and International Affairs to take part in a week-end symposium on the role of the media in elections, to be held in Georgetown, mid-September, three weeks before the elections. In our group were the chairman, Carl Wint of the *Gleaner*, Leslie Pierre, editor of the *Grenadian Voice*, and Clive Williams, the Institute's Project Director. It proved to be a stimulating event, with sympathizers of several parties getting hot under the collar in discussions and Pierre expressing some home-truths in frank and trenchant terms. One fervently hopes that, with the new dispensation ushered in by the elections of October 5, 1992, Guyana will move to a long period of healing of the schisms within the society, focusing also, on developing its considerable resources, and on reviving an economy which has recently shown signs of recovery.

In Jamaica, the E.A.C has been very concerned for a long time, about the incidence of over-voting in particular constituencies and moreso, by the escalating incidence of violence-based invasion of polling stations and the stuffing of ballot boxes. This latter ill has been spreading recently, and was most pronounced during the Local government Elections of 1986 and 1990. It has now extended beyond the Corporate Area and the Duffus Commission, appointed to investigate the problems of the 1986 Elections made a number of salient recommendations, some of which echoed observations made by the EAC. There is a danger that these conditions may expand to plague-like proportions; and ultimately, destroy one of the essential foundations of our democracy. Associated with this evil of polling station invasion and ballot stuffing is the existence of so-called 'garrison areas', dominated by one major party or the other, where barriers, though invisible, but sustained by intimidation, stand in the way of scrutineers and electors for the opposing party and sometimes, enumerators attempting to enter.

In the Local government elections of 1986 an unusual incident occurred in the Washington Gardens Division of St. Andrew Western on the eve of Polling Day, when 43 ballot boxes were destroyed and the ballot papers removed. Incidentally, some of the culprits of this atrocious act were themselves election officials! They had decided that no election should take place in that division.

The EAC held an emergency meeting late that night until the early hours of Polling Day and decided that as a matter of principle, the committee should not yield to the action of those who seemed determined to thwart the democratic process. The decision to proceed was taken with the full knowledge that the stations would open late, since among other emergency requirements, thousands of substitute ballots would need to be printed on Polling Day. In the event, however, some of the Presiding Officers succeeded in their objective; they sat on boxes and refused to take them to the stations.

Traditionally, the route towards dealing with the problem of over-voting and stuffing of boxes is of course, by way of a petition by the aggrieved candidate. However, this tends to be a long drawn out process, beset with delays. Following discussion in February 1993 with the Chief Justice, the President of the Court of Appeal and a few other High Court judges and experienced attorneys, the EAC has recommended amendments to expedite and improve the process.

As to the question of an election being declared null and void because of such irregularities, this outcome would not necessarily follow, unless the irregularities are deemed to have affected the majority by which a candidate was elected. The Prime Minister has asked the EAC to give priority to consideration of the desirability of amending the Representation of the People Act to provide for declaration of an election null and void where there is clear evidence of such irregularities, without proceeding via the route of an election petition. One of the issues which arises concerns the possibility of a candidate who seems to be losing, interfering with the process, with the objective of having the election in his constituency declared void.

It seems clear that a fundamental constraint to ensuring the integrity and effectiveness of the electoral system lies in our political culture. This influences significantly the behaviour of voters and a number of our electoral officials, such as some enumerators, presiding officers and poll clerks. Efforts to change this culture, though a long range objective, should nevertheless, be made — as a responsibility of a wide range of citizens. In the short run, the problem focuses on reducing to a minimum, the involvement of the human element in the system. With this in mind, the E.A.C has been examining for some time, the feasibility of introducing a system which would be based on electronic registration, identification and voting by finger print. The high costs involved may prove to be a constraint; and consideration must also be given to the possibility of a polling station being invaded and the equipment damaged or removed.

Another critical and complementary element which could make an essential contribution towards reform would be the development of a national registration system designed to register, photograph, fingerprint on a continuous basis and provide an identification number for every person of a prescribed minimum age and above.

This number would also be used for other purposes, for example income tax, passports, drivers' licenses and social security. A committee, appointed by a minister, under my chairmanship and including fellow independent members of the EAC also recommended integration of the national registration and electoral systems under one umbrella organization. This arrangement would eliminate or at the least, reduce to a minimum, the incidence of multiple registration, impersonation and over-voting.

In addition to the problems indicated earlier, one of the most serious weaknesses is the difficulty experienced in recruiting competent, honest and impartial election officials, in particular enumerators, and presiding officers and their deputies who staff the polling stations. In the political context of Jamaica, and certainly until recently, one should not be surprised that most Jamaicans will sympathize with, or support a particular political party. However, the EAC attempts to eliminate known political activists in appointing its complement of personnel; the bottom line being the search for persons who have the integrity and courage to submerge any sympathy they feel for a particular party in taking and implementing decisions honestly in the wider national interest. The fact is, however, that many of the persons recruited have proved to be of a poor educational level, totally incompetent and/or strongly partisan in their behaviour.

The EAC is attempting to establish a permanent list of officials, built on the foundation of a cadre of civil servants, teachers, social workers and clergymen — the types of persons who used to offer their services until the 1960s, but who have been reluctant to do so since then, because of the context of violence and intimidation. Fortunately, at the level of Returning Officers and their deputies, there is a very high proportion of teacher trained personnel, most of them Mico College graduates — some trained by my uncle J.J.

At the committee level and in the senior ranks of the electoral office, there has been a number of personnel changes: as would be expected, the independent members tend to be more 'permanent' than the political nominees. The only changes here over these almost 14 years have been the early loss of R.V. Irvine to an assignment as a U.N. consultant in the Cayman and his replacement by Reg. N. Murray, a retired UWI Professor of Education, who was himself, succeeded on his death, by a former colleague Professor, Dr. Laurie Reid — both Mico graduates. While, considerable difficulty ensued in making the initial 1979 appointments, all subsequent appointments after each 18 month interval have been made on the unanimous recommendation of the political nominees — with the exception of the filling of this last vacancy, which required the G.G.'s intervention following a two-year stalemate. As for the nominated members, on the People's National Party side, Dr. D.K. Duncan was replaced by Ms. Portia Simpson and later, she and a foundation member, Dr. Robertson were succeeded by Donald Buchanan and the new General Secretary, Dr. Peter Phillips. For the Jamaica Labour Party, the original foundation members, Bruce Golding and Abe Dabdoub were succeeded by Dr. Mavis Gilmour and Errol Anderson, these subsequently replaced by Edmund Bartlett and Karl Samuda. Then, suddenly, without notice, at end-April 1990 these two 'Gang of Five' members were removed and the current members are senator Ryan Peralto and former M.P. Anthony Johnson.

Following Carl Dundas' departure after the 1980 Elections to a Commonwealth Secretariat assignment in London, and the promotion of Noel Lee to the Director's post, the electoral office's staff remained stable for a fairly long spell. However, with Frank Weir's retirement and the death of D.A. Dunkley, great difficulty was experienced in filling these positions of Assistant Directors of Field and Data, respectively, until the appointment of Newton Forbes and Albert Johnson.

Two other issues deserve to be mentioned. The first concerns the election system, the first past the post, which has at times, produced grossly distorted results. Hence, the call, especially by the now defunct minority Workers Party of Jamaica (W.P.J.), for the introduction, instead, of proportional representation. It has been suggested that this system would contribute towards narrowing the gap between the major parties and reducing the incidence of tribal warfare. Associated with this, is the criticism that the existing system has other built-in disadvantages for minority parties and perpetuates a 'duopoly', for example, in eligibility for representation on the Electoral Committee and to appoint party scrutineers.

The other concern relates to the status of the EAC as an interim institution whose life is statutorily restricted to a series of 18-month periods, with the appointment of all members, including the Director, expiring at the end of each such period. The intention, expressed in the parliamentary decisions on constitutional and electoral reform in 1979 and expressly reiterated in the statute, is that the committee would be entrenched in the constitution as a commission. Yet, after almost 14 years, the chief executive officer, the Director continues to function in a position devoid of security.

I conclude by returning full circle to the issue of democracy: from time to time I reflect on the considerable budgetary and foreign exchange costs involved in mounting and managing the electoral system. These include the employment of approximately 6000 teams, each consisting of three persons, for the house-to-house enumeration-registration process, equipping each team with a camera and film and the expenditure on data processing. To this should be added the cost of special printing equipment for the ID cards, the ballot printing machines and the radio net-work; for an election, again approximately 6000 teams, but each of two persons, for manning the polling stations, and the cost of providing 6000 integrity lamps. All these expenses do not include the normal administrative expenditure of running the electoral office and committee. I should emphasize that despite functioning in a situation of severe economic and financial resource scarcity and depleted foreign exchange reserves during the entire life of the EAC, governments of both parties have always acceded to requests for funding the importation of expensive equipment and consumable materials. So, I ask the question: In the light of budgetary and foreign exchange constraints and shortages of medicines, other health, housing, and educational facilities, is this considerable expenditure on the preservation of democracy justified? I have been assured on many sides that the answer is 'Yes'. And so we press on.

To close a conference, held in Guatemala, October 1992, the Tikal Protocol — signed in this same place, within sight of Mayan temples dating from 700 B.C., seven years before — was reconfirmed by representatives of the participating states. In its preamble, the Protocol asserts the conviction that:

.....the historic mission of democracy is to provide liberty and a favourable environment for fair, economic and social development; that free and fair elections and universal and secret suffrage are the most appropriate means to establish and consolidate representative democracy;...

However, we need to bear in mind that while the holding of free and fair elections is an essential criterion, this by itself, is certainly not a sufficient condition.

Interestingly, the EAC is being suggested increasingly as a model for restructuring of the governing boards of other organizations; for example, the composition of the new JBC board is based partly on the principles guiding the structure of the EAC, and similar proposals have recently been put forward for the creation of a management board for the police force.

9
CRICKET, CRICKET, CRICKET

It is inevitable that interspersed among these reflections would be references to cricket, since this sport which to me and many others represents more than a game, has been an essential part of my life, returning into the past as far as I can remember. So, when my playing days were drawing to a close, I turned, naturally to taking part in administration of the game, as a member of the Jamaica Cricket Board of Control (JCBC), first as assistant treasurer to Johnny Groves. Soon after this stint, I became an assistant secretary, to an old Chapelton friend, Sidney Abrahams and subsequently, to Pat Burke and Neville ('Fifi') Smith — both sets of assignments beginning under the presidency of JC alumnus V.C. McCormack. During the 1980s the basis of my position as a board member changed from cooption-appointment to election on the slate of corporate area representatives. For the past four or five years I have been serving as chairman of the board's umpires sub-committee and of a disciplinary committee. Membership of the board has extended so far, to 35 years continuously, as the longest serving member, serving during this period also with V.C.'s immediate successor, attorney R.C. Marley, another JC alumnus, and later, long-time president, Allan Rae and currently H.I. ('Rex') Fennell. Both Marley and Rae also became presidents of the West Indies Board.

For several years, one of my primary responsibilities as a member of the Cricket Board was as its press liaison officer. This function focused on making arrangements for press and electronic media representatives to facilitate their coverage of regional and international matches. Since the mid-1970s, very large media contingents have accompanied English and Australian touring parties, stimulated by the significant cricket success of the West Indies which continued for a decade and a half. However, this progressive succession of unprecedented successes provoked a barrage of unobjective media criticism, which, started during the West Indies 1973 tour of England under Rohan Kanhai, and escalated during the 1990s descended to depths of denigration, disparagement and dishonest, highly prejudiced reporting. Viewing the Edgbaston Test of that 1973 tour was a new experience for me. In their first innings West Indies began by losing three wickets for 39, then moved to 128 for 5, and the English weekend press berated the batsmen for eschewing the English conferred image of 'easy-going calypso cricketers' and instead, getting their heads down to stage a recovery.

While I agree fully with those who give credit to Frank Worrell for moulding the West Indies as a team and to Clive Lloyd for their phenomenal triumphs later, in my opinion, it was Kanhai who first instilled in the team a tough, professional approach. He has not received the credit he deserves. Indeed, at the end of that series, Kanhai was attacked by Michael Parkinson as being 'as lovable an opponent as Genghis Khan.' (*The Times*, September 7,1973) The *Daily Telegraph* in an editorial titled 'Not So Calypso', attempted to separate Sobers as the model of behaviour, for his 'demeanour and boyish relish for the game', from his team-mates. The editorial continued: 'the West Indians must pause to consider the example they are setting.' It seemed to me that the crux of the problem centered on a captain who inspired an approach which from the English perspective was alien to the 'calypsonians.' If they had played in the manner expected, and lost, they would have been hailed as 'splendid chaps', while England would have levelled the series. Of course, the attitudes of tough, professionally oriented, uncompromising England captains of the ilk of Jardine (of body-line bowling notoriety/fame), Close, May (who refused Kanhai a runner at Sabina in 1960), Illingworth, Kanhai's opponent in the 1973 series, were ignored or were not considered appropriate for the West Indies.

Among the media representatives, Robin Marlar of the *Sunday Times*, a former captain of Cambridge University and of Sussex has been the most notorious critic, the constant and most consistent detractor, moving from the snide and supercilious attitude typical of a certain type of Englishman, to virulence. Thus, he bemoaned the death of 'Calypso cricket', accused the West Indies of 'brutalizing the game' and of threatening to destroy it since 'most people on whose support English cricket depends believe monotonous fast bowling to be boring to watch.' These remarks were published on the eve of their 1984 tour in which West Indies 'blackwashed' England 5-0 for the first time. ('Killing Cricket the Fast Way'.) In the following year, in a farewell 'tribute' to retiring captain Clive Lloyd, Marlar commented on 'the cynical disregard Lloyd has shown for the spirit of cricket. He has made it into a coconut shy'. By the time of the return tour(1986), when England suffered a second, successive 5-0 'blackwash', he accused the West Indies and Malcolm Marshall in particular, of: 'First maim and then remove is now the basic West Indian tactic.' In fact, during the 1984 series, Marlar, paralleling Parkinson's earlier portrayal of Kanhai, depicted Marshall as 'cricket's equivalent of a cold-blooded assassin'.

The nadir was attained, following Lloyd's farewell appearance at Lord's in September 1986, which incidentally, I saw. Marlar, in a piece, purportedly a report of the match, scoffed at the standing ovation given by the spectators, though it was comparable to the celebrated Bradman farewell at the Oval in 1948:

> crowds can be somewhat soft-headed... I regard him as one of the most harmful influences on the game in my lifetime. It is a matter of some regret, in my opinion, that he has been granted British citizenship; spending the rest of his life in racially-divided Guyana might have been suitable penance.

West Indies cricket journalist and commentator, Tony Cozier referred to Marlar as the 'natural successor' to the notorious E.M. Wellings of the *Evening News* who wrote: 'West Indian supporters should be put in cages' and suggested that 'these are the thoughts of a mind warped by hate and vengeance.' ('More Malice from Marlar the Moaner', in *The Nation*, Barbados, September 1986.) An Englishman, in a letter to the *Sunday Times* mentioned the 'strong and intemperate' language used by Marlar and indicated that the suggestion of a suitable penance in Guyana for Lloyd seemed to him 'to be a piece of spite and nothing else.'

Not too far behind was the *Telegraph's* A.R. ('Tony') Lewis. Like Marlar, he was Cambridge educated, but an erstwhile England captain for a handful of Tests and a strong supporter of the South African rebels and advocate of the return of that country to the fold. Although a Welshman, Lewis seems to have been so socialized that his comments reflect a similar quality of snideness and superciliousness. For instance, on the eve of the 1984 series, he could bemoan having to face a summer of 'inevitable drudgery', the 'tediously glum professionalism of Clive Lloyd's weary bunch of mercenaries', and the 'dreary monotony' of seeing fast bowler after fast bowler. (*Sunday Telegraph*, April 28, 1984) Apart from other features of this spurious tale of woe, the fact that the quartet of bowlers at the time, Garner, Holding, Marshall and Baptiste represented different types (as did Croft) was conveniently ignored. Moreover, the West Indies would not have attracted the crowds they did wherever they played, had spectators considered their performance boring. But, his remarks descended to depths of nastiness when during discussions on the West Indies Cricket Board's (WICBC) proposal to the International Cricket Conference (ICC) that cricketers who work in South Africa should be barred from playing Test cricket, representatives of the Pakistan Board decided to lobby in support of the proposal. According to Lewis, members of that Board 'appear to have found some spare rupees under the mattress to get them air tickets to Australia.'

Among the charges levelled against the West Indies were excessive short-pitched bowling and slow over rates;these acquired the status of hoary and hardy perennials. For instance, take Terry Coleman's *Guardian* article headlined 'Fast, loose and without Grace' (August 15,1984). Even *The Economist* magazine got into the act with a short piece under the caption, 'Nasty, Brutish and Short', borrowed from Hobbes — not Jack, the cricketer, but Thomas, the 17th Century philosopher.

As I pointed out in correspondence with one of these critics, the West Indies did not invent short-pitched bowling nor the four-pronged pace attack. Learie Constantine emphasized the barrage of bouncers to which they were subjected in England during their first Test tour (1928), when the 'critics professed to see danger when we put them down and none when England's players bowled them' (from *Cricket in the Sun*) Four pace bowlers were of course, deployed by Jardine in the notorious body-line series of 1932-1933 (Larwood, Voce, Bowes, Allen); and again by England, (Trueman,

Statham, Moss, Bailey) on this occasion, in the West Indies, 1953-54. When Lillee, Thompson, Gilmour and Walker were on the rampage, battering the West Indies in 1975-1976, as Michael Manley has observed, 'neither Lloyd nor his men, nor the W.I.C.B.C. ever uttered a word of complaint. Even more glaring was the silence with which the world's cricketing press accepted the outcome without demur.' *(A History of West Indies Cricket)*

Matthew Engel (*The Guardian*), reporting on England's 1986 tour of the West Indies, opened with the sensational 'the primeval goring of England which went by the name of the First Test', (at Sabina Park) and continuing his lurid, purple prose referred to the 'blood red' features of the third day's play with the spectators 'baying for blood and behaving as though they were at the Coliseum.' Paradoxically, the only batsman who was seriously hurt during the match was West Indies opener Gordon Greenidge!

As I have emphasized, Marlar has accused the West Indies of destroying the spirit of the game. Earlier, during the 1984 series, the B.B.C. Evening News joined the orchestrated chorus of adverse commentary by media representatives on proceedings in the final Test with a statement: 'It was trench war out there at the Oval', coupled with a comment deploring the bowling of short-pitched balls at Pocock, 'who bats No.11 for Surrey.' In support, Sir Leonard Hutton was moved to remark: 'Pocock is a tail-ender. Cricket used to be a gentleman's game, but not any longer.' (*The Observer*)

While it is true that Pocock normally bats at No. 11, the fact is that he was sent in as night-watchman at No. 3. No commentator apparently noticed that when the West Indies No. 11 Davis was sent to bat as night watchman in the No. 7 position in the previous Test, bouncers were bowled at him, but he proceeded to make 77! Nor did they comment when short-pitched bowling was directed at the West Indies tail-enders during the Oval Test. Presumably, the really relevant issue is not whether bowlers indulge in such tactics, but how effective they actually are. Returning to the first Test of the 1986 series at Sabina, Engel referred to 'the ten years of this type of cricket which has dulled everyone's sensitivity.' Of course, this period coincided precisely with a decade of West Indian dominance.

In 1984, following the series against the West Indies, England played one Test against Sri Lanka at Lords. This provided *The Cricketer*, with an opportunity to disparage the West Indian bowling tactics. In an editorial, this monthly magazine contrasted the latter against those of Sri Lanka whose approach was consistent with the original intention and the 'true spirit of the game', which was to bowl to hit the stumps. According to the editorial, the West Indies had taken relatively few wickets by this route.

In a letter to the editor (which was published), I pointed out that the Laws of Cricket are totally silent about the suggestion that a wicket obtained by 'clean' bowling a batsman is assigned a greater weight than one earned by any of the seven or more other methods. In any event, in the 1984 series, of 96 England wickets which fell, more than 20% went via the bowled route (plus 23% l.b.w.); while West Indies lost 13% bowled (plus 17% l.b.w.) among 63 wickets which fell.

To be fair, there is a small set of objective and fair reporters and commentators, standing tall among whom was John Arlott, followed by Peter Smith and Henry Blofeld the first two unfortunately no longer with us. Arlott, former doyen of cricket broadcasters and writers expressed the following observations following England's devastating defeat at the hands of Lillee and Thompson in 1974-1975, and the squealing by English media critics:

> Whenever they are beaten at any sport there are complaints from those who believe in England's divine right to win.... The dominance of a series by fast bowlers is not new; neither is intimidation by short-pitched bowling. It has been used since cricket began. Neither England nor any other country is in a moral position to condemn it. Everyone of them has used the weapon when it has commanded it.
> (*The Guardian*, February 15,1975)

This search for alibis to explain defeat has nowhere been more graphically expressed than in the 20 excuses listed in relation to England's disastrous 1993 series against India, (David Hopps, 'England's Downfall', *The Guardian*,February 23, 1993.)

Also, in contrast to Marlar's malicious response to Clive Lloyd's retirement, Arlott expressed a typically gracious farewell in *The Guardian*:

> Some among his opponents have criticised him for the ruthless use of his mighty battery of fast bowlers....but his captaincy has been impressively marked by dignity; firm and unfussy discipline; and cool, realistic strategy. He retires a respected cricketer.. who played and conducted his matches in a fashion free from the acrimony which has infected the cricket of some of his opponents.

I concluded an article on the English media coverage of the 1984 series as follows:

> As a former colonial and one of a generation which was nurtured on the tenets of British sportsmanship, this writer is moved to reflect on Hutton's remarks about 'a gentleman's game' but from a different perspective, and to pose the question: Is this much vaunted tradition of sportsmanship a myth — a fantasy which loses form in the act of losing? (*Sunday Gleaner*, September 16,1986)

The dominance by the West Indies from the mid-1970s sparked a series of suggestions designed with the obvious objective of blunting the effectiveness of attacks focusing on fast bowling. Some of these ploys were conspicuously ludicrous. They included proposals for lengthening the pitch and drawing a line across it beyond which a 'good' ball must pitch, anything short of that line being called a 'no ball'; restricting the length of the bowler's run up; limiting the number of fast bowlers in a team; and of course, focusing on the over-stressed issue of over rates. But, perhaps the most ludicrous of all was the suggestion, seriously made, that in future, 'a batsman should only be out if the ball has touched the blade (or the back) of the bat; any ball caught off the handle or the gloves would not be out.' (*The Cricketer*) Sir Donald Bradman and Sunil Gavaskar responded with a summary dismissal of the suggestion. Persistence has however, paid off in the ICC's decisions limiting the number of bouncers per batsman in an over, and prescribing a minimum of 90 overs per day, subject to modification in certain circumstances. If the ICC accepts the recommendations from an international meeting of umpires in August 1993 that this new and much criticised rule should be rescinded after a very brief experience, the ball will be returned to the umpires' court, presumably with the expectation that they will exercise their authority more actively.

There have been other incidents or remarks, not as serious, but which have provided sources of laughter. For instance, during the triumphant West Indies tour of England in 1950 when we won our first Test in that country, one of the most distinguished cricket journalists of the day, and an Oxbridge graduate, R.C. Robertson-Glasgow wrote: 'Ramadhin is from India of the East, but plays for the West Indies.' (*Daily Telegraph*) I observed in a letter (which was published), that on this basis, Ramadhin's partner Valentine could similarly be considered an African playing for West Indies and Bradman, an Englishman representing Australia!

The third Test at Old Trafford (1976 series) provided a fascinating instance of a pitch suffering dramatic 'sea-changes' within a very short period. On the first day, the West Indies batting (with the exception of Greenidge), collapsed. No commentator implied by the slightest hint that the pitch might be at fault. Yet, next morning, with England's innings in ruins, Trueman was calling for an enquiry into the state of the pitch. Within two hours after this, the West Indies openers produced their best partnership of the series up to that time; Greenidge was able to make a second hundred in the match, and Richards, a second innings century — all presumably on the same strip. The real answer, shorn of excuses was provided by John Arlott:

> For more than three hours Greenidge provided unquestionable evidence that it was possible to bat splendidly on it...The pitch looked far more difficult when England batted...That invariably means that the true difference lies in the quality of the respective attacks. (*The Guardian*)

Similarly, when England's first innings was folding rapidly at Edgbaston (1991), radio commentator Trueman, repeatedly remarked on the unfitness of the pitch and called for an investigation. But, there was no repetition of similar comments or of his call, only euphoric gloating and commendations for Chris Lewis' bowling when West Indies lost six wickets for 39 runs.

There was also the occasion, though the West Indies were not involved, when a Sunday paper in a report on a county match played by Bradman's invincible 1948 touring team in England created the immortal headlines: 'Essex First County to Bowl out Australia in a Day.' Only on reading the fine print on the score card did we realise that Australia had compiled 721 runs in that one day!

Paradoxically perhaps, it was not the tabloids, the so-called 'gutter press', but the elite papers which were primarily engaged in the business of unfair reporting. Even *The Times*, that bastion of respectability, was guilty at times. There was the occasion when, in August 1987, a news item appeared under the caption 'Politics threatens talks', in which the vice-president of the South African Cricket Union who was visiting London was reported to have stated that the attempts being made to persuade the ICC to readmit his country to Test cricket 'were being thwarted by some politicians who doubled as cricket administrators'. According to him, 'Allan Rae, the president of the West Indies Cricket Board was intent on becoming the Prime Minister of Jamaica.'

I wrote to the Editor pointing out that Allan Rae had no such intention, nor was he involved in partisan politics. I went on to underline my main point that, whatever the views and sentiments of the paper's correspondent on the South African issue, (I knew from an association of 20 or more years, that their leading cricket correspondent, John Woodcock was a South African sympathiser), I would have expected an objective approach and balance to the news item. This could have been provided by seeking a response or reaction from Rae and/or his West Indies Board colleagues who, as the Times' correspondents were aware, were in London for the ICC meeting. My letter ended: 'That would have represented a fairer and more balanced item. But then, of course, times have changed, haven't they?'

The sports editor's reply emphasized that the vice-president's remark 'did not really call for reaction from Mr. Rae himself. The views from all sides (on the South African issue) will continue to be aired in *The Times*, and I think it unnecessary to seek comments from everybody on every single remark.' In response, I indicated that the question regarding Rae's political activities was a fact, not a view; that I thought incredible, the dismissal of the need to seek a comment from Rae in terms of comments from everybody; and I was sufficiently oldfashioned to retain a belief in a set of ethical standards and behaviour, even on the part of the press, though more cynical colleagues scoff at this as myth. In conclusion, I informed him of my hobby of collecting 'gems' illustrating the lack of objectivity of cricket commentary by the English media and that his response would occupy a hallowed place in this collection.

On a number of occasions my letters were published, in the Guardian, Sunday Times and frequently, *The Cricketer*. However, those letters which contained more trenchant comments more often became the subject of correspondence in which the Sports Editor, or Editor attempted to justify his or her correspondent's statements as in this case of *The Times* and: 'We quite understand your position on West Indies tactics. We also quite understand Marlar's' (*Sunday Times*, April 1986), in reply to my rebuttal of Marlar's 'maim first'). Sometimes, he/she would retreat to a position of hollow, hypocritical praise such as 'we have nothing but admiration for the present West Indies side' (*The Economist*, following their item headlined 'Nasty, Brutish and Short') and 'this is not an attack on West Indies cricket or an attempt to nullify the advantage they have enjoyed, but...' (*The Cricketer*, 1984.) One of the most amusing replies was addressed to me in a third person note on a card: 'The Editor of the Times presents his compliments and regrets that he is unable to avail himself of the communication kindly offered him.'

I am convinced, though English 'tact' or hypocrisy would not permit admission of this, that elements of racism entered the arena and some of the critics have been motivated by such attitudes. For instance, comments by David Frith (now Editor of *Wisden Cricket Monthly*), appear to reflect rankling resentment of the ruling of the cricket roost for such a long time, by a team of blacks:

'...Afro-West Indian stock has physical advantages over the Caucasian and Asian competition, but the field of fast bowling bears the mark of West Indian dominance based on force.' (My emphasis) (From 'Crescendo of Cricket's Steel Band', *The Times*, March 6, 1986)

The Australians tend to be less diplomatic, more directly frank, some would say crude. During the highly successful 1988-89 West Indies tour of that country, apart from the bleating and whingeing about short-pitched bowling, unexpected of Australian commentators who should remember Lillee and Thompson, there were undercurrents of racism, especially in remarks by one Jeff Wells about 'black brutality, brinkmanship and boorishness.' Moreover, in the night matches of the one day series, 'alibis' for Australian defeat also included, problems of batsmen seeing a red ball bowled by a black hand. Fortunately, more objective, balanced and honest views were expressed by former captains Benaud and Ian Chappell.

In recounting this saga of insensitivity and prejudice, it would be ungracious if I did not record the exceptional behaviour of an English press representative when, almost precisely 25 years ago as I write, the second Test at Sabina Park was interrupted by rioting, bottle throwing spectators in the bleachers, incensed at the dismissal of Butcher at a stage with the West Indies in serious trouble, having been bowled out for 143 in their first innings by John Snow and forced to follow-on. When play resumed, first Seymour Nurse (73), then Sobers (113 not out) provided superb displays on a pitch covered in cracks and crevices, but this still left West Indies only 158 runs ahead. The game was extended by 75 minutes into a sixth day to compensate for the time lost through the riot. Sobers then proceeded to remove Boycott and Cowdrey, each for a 'duck' and England were facing defeat, at 68 for 8 when the match ended. I was relieved, not wanting us to win in such circumstances, since when play was interrupted, England were well on top. Next day, I received a most generously expressed and sympathetic letter from a member of the English press, who, sitting close by in the old press box located between the bleachers and the south-western stand, had observed my distress during the proceedings commencing with the rioting and the tear gas response by the police. Interestingly, the tear gas propelled by the wind, by-passed those against whom it was launched, scored a direct hit on occupants of the members' pavilion, and floated across to the building overlooking the George VI Memorial Park (now National Heroes Circle) where the Cabinet was in session!

I must confess that the relics of the umbilical cord have produced in me what is perhaps a psychological effect in an ingrained desire to win against erstwhile 'Mother' above all other opponents. However, this sentiment has been intensified by the attitude and behaviour of the English media, especially since the tour of that country in 1973 and the developing supremacy of the West Indies in international cricket. During that latter series I would recall the Sabina incident, when, with West Indies very much on top at Lords, there was a bomb scare and all spectators were asked to vacate the stands. I responded reluctantly and slowly, concerned lest this would take England off the hook. This was the match in which Kanhai, followed by Sobers struck scintillating centuries, for both their final appearances in a Test at Lords, and Sobers proceeded to nurse Bernard Julien to the third century of the innings.

While membership on the Cricket Board has involved responsibilities and tasks which have at times, been demanding and unpleasant, it has also provided considerable opportunities for enjoying a number of Test matches as a guest of other cricketing authorities and seeing cricket played outside of the front-line Test playing countries. Thus, I have watched matches in Los Angeles (where Mike Brearley was playing while he was a post-graduate student); in The Hague, and in Singapore, across the road from the Raffles Club. While attending a Public Administration seminar in Brisbane during 'Expo' '88', I was taken by the Secretary, on a tour of the club and grounds of 'The Gabba', relatively small and charming, and was told of the exploits of West Indians (especially Wes Hall) who had played Sheffield Shield cricket for Queensland.

Almost without exception, the hospitality provided at Test and other matches, whether regionally or internationally, has been excellent, generally including complimentary tickets, and an invitation to lunch and tea. There is an unofficial understanding of reciprocity among cricketing authorities, and for some years I doubled up as both Media Liaison Officer and the member responsible for complimentary tickets, and passes for visiting Board members. I recall two occasions on which hospitality was less than warm: once in Trinidad, when a Board official whom I knew transported me to Queen's Park, took me to a seat and left me to fend for myself all day, including searching around to buy sandwiches.

The other incident occurred in St. Lucia, where a visiting (unofficial) English team, was playing while I was there on UWI business. Hollis Bristol, brother of Carol (a former fellow resident of Nutford House and cricket colleague in London), invited me to the game. Not long after, he telephoned and very embarrassed, explained that the chairman of the board, Julian Hunte, a long time member of the West Indies Board, who was also, Leader of the Opposition had said: 'No way! He was not concerned that Mills was a member of the Jamaica Board. He must pay to enter.' Hollis insisted on pressing the issue despite my assurance that it did not really matter, since I would not be too disappointed if I did not see the game. Eventually, the chairman appears to have relented and reluctantly, not to be discourteous, I went along. I found it most amusing that on entering the stand I heard someone calling out 'Charlie Mills!' Looking up I recognised Dr. Jim Clarke (who would become Governor-General), the father-in-law of both Prime Minister Compton and the Leader of the Opposition.

There were also incidents and events of another type. The most notable and memorable occurred at the England vs West Indies Test at Lords 30 years ago. This was exceptional in several ways. I have never experienced watching a match at this level in which the contending teams' fortunes see-sawed to such an extent, throughout the five days of the game. When the West Indies first innings ended about an hour before lunch on the second day, Charlie Griffith proceeded to dispose of the England openers, Stewart and Edrich for 27. At lunch seated under an attractive, multi-coloured marquee, I was the only West Indian in a group of six among whom were former England players Leslie Ames and Freddie Brown and former Glamorgan player (and Welsh rugby star), Wilf Wooller. Almost as soon as lunch began, ruddy-faced Brown opened. 'I would no ball him five times out of every six, both for stepping over the line and for throwing!' The conversation continued as though no one else but those five men were there. After some minutes had elapsed, of discussion in the same vein, I intervened: 'Excuse my interruption gentlemen. You are not talking to me, but I cannot avoid hearing the subject of your discussion. Ever since the tour began several weeks ago, Griffith's action has been the object of microscopic inspection and has evidently been cleared. He was not particularly successful in the first Test (only one wicket) and no comment was made on his action. Now that it seems he may run through the side, you are again raising questions on this issue. This could smack of gamesmanship.' His face flushing and becoming even more florid, Freddie Brown stuttered: 'No! No! I...,I...was not suggesting that...'; the conversation then ceased abruptly.

I was on study leave, and had arranged to see the first three days of the match, then to leave for Paris on Sunday, where I had appointments to discuss features of the French perspectives on the teaching of Public Administration; thence, to Brussels and The Hague, to visit the International Institute of Administrative Sciences and the Institute of Social Studies, respectively. However, the see-saw situation was so fascinating that I decided to postpone my departure from London until late Tuesday afternoon. I waited until the very last moment to leave Lords, with Hall bowling a marvellous, marathon spell, England needing less than ten runs with two wickets in hand including Cowdrey — to bat, with a broken arm. Rushing to reach West London terminal, almost late, I kept on looking back, but eventually missed the grand finale. I did not know the result until my return to London some three weeks later. Of course, it could have gone to either side or ended in a draw. It was drawn.

Almost four years later, while in India for a seminar, I saw the first three days of the West Indies Madras Test at a time when the newspapers were full of reports about Captain Sobers' engagement to an Indian beauty and I had visited David Holford, struck down by pleurisy — in a Delhi hospital. It was at this game that I discovered why it was relatively easy for spectators to burn down stands during riots at matches: some of these stands were constructed of coconut thatch. In the game, I had never seen the bowling of Hall and Griffith handled so disrespectfully as it was by Farokh Engineer, the wicket-keeper-opening batsman, who was Clive Lloyd's colleague at the Lancashire C.C.C. By lunch he had reached 98 (his partner Sardesai, 28) and a century shortly after. It was in Madras too, that I saw Frank Worrell for the last time, when at a dinner given by the local Board on the Saturday night (January 15,1967), he arrived from another city, just in time to speak. He was then on a tour of universities, sponsored by the Indian Universities Council and died before my return from a sabbatical.

This performance by Engineer, the innings of Sobers at Sabina on that terrible pitch in 1968, at Leeds in 1966 and his last hundred, made at Lords in 1973 are certainly among the best I have witnessed. But two performances stand out above all, and remain etched in the memory — both occurring within a period of two years. At the Oval in 1976, despite the magnificent batting of Richards (291) and the more staid and courageous Amis (203), for me the most memorable spectacle was the bowling of Michael Holding. There on that dead, placid pitch, on which five other fast bowlers on both sides captured only six wickets between them, he mowed down England almost single-handedly, capturing 14 wickets; even more remarkable was the fact that nine plus three of these fell clean bowled and by the l.b.w. route, respectively! No one who saw Holding in action during his heyday will forget that smooth, silky, silent, gliding and long run-up, which earned him the sobriquet 'Whispering Death'. As his career moved to a close, conservation compelled a reduction in its length, but after this respite, he returned to full length at the Oval in 1984, in his final spell, thrilling a crowd which responded with applause — 'even the ranks of Tuscany could scarce forbear to cheer.'

In March 1974, I decided to stop over in Barbados on my return journey home from UWI meetings at St. Augustine, to see a portion of play in the Test against England at Kensington. My hosts at Culloden Farm, were friends from the London days, Errol Barrow (by that time, Prime Minister) and his wife, Carolyn. Lawrence Rowe, the star in the Jamaican firmament had a dream Test debut with a double followed by a century vs New Zealand (1972) and another 100 vs England (1974); but these performances took place at home (Sabina), and some expressed doubt whether he could perform as well, in a Test away from that venue. After England were dismissed in late afternoon of the second day at Kensington, Rowe proceeded to outscore Fredericks, his opening partner — an unusual occurrence since the latter had always assumed a more aggressive role. Indeed, along the way that afternoon, receiving a bouncer, he moved inside it, looked at the ball with both eyes (unlike those who hook instinctively without any certainty of the direction in which the ball would go), and hit it over square leg for six. Certainly, until I left after two days, with Rowe just past 200, no further attempt was made to bowl a bouncer at him.

At the close on that first afternoon, his score was 48 (Fredericks only 28) and like J.K. Holt Jnr. with his 166 at the same venue in 1954, he had been adopted as a 'Barbadian' by this most percipient and knowledgeable of cricket aficionados and crowds in general. Next day, Barbadians turned up in droves, many without tickets, hoping to get into Kensington. The scenario was described in a newspaper almost in poetic language. As nearly as I can recall it, the piece read: 'They came from St. David, they came from St. Lucy, they came from St. Joseph, just to see.....'

Rowe did not disappoint his fans. Other features of this display of effortless artistry left indelible impressions, remaining rooted in the mind's eye these 20 years. Time and again, when he was about to stroke the ball to the off, as the appropriate fielder moved in, he would postpone playing the shot, frustrating first, extra-cover, then cover point, delaying and playing finer and finer, ultimately tickling the ball via late cuts through the gully or slips, all along the ground, with consummate wrist-work, reminiscent of Worrell. The quality of his timing was demonstrated too, when he played forward defensively, quietly to one of the fast bowlers, Willis, Old or Arnold, and the ball would incredibly travel slowly past the bowler to the boundary. In the same vein, on numerous occasions the ball would travel apparently slowly trickling a few inches ahead of the pursuing fielder who seemed sanguine that he would apprehend it, only to see it rolling across the boundary line, leaving him frustrated. In fact, the climax was reached when Greig, chasing one of these crashed into a section of the crowd, knocking down one or two spectators; deliberately, according to some English media representatives who knew him well. When I was leaving, one of the umpires, talking to a group of us enquired whether we observed that no delivery had hit Rowe's legs up to that stage.

I have often speculated about the reasons underlying the unfortunate, almost tragic vicissitudes of Rowe's career and wondered whether the causes of his illnesses were not to a great extent, psychosomatic. My analysis — and it is that of a layman — suggests that he was lionised too much and too early in his career: the adulation by some in high places, the cash and other material awards. The stage arrived where he feared failure and was afraid to go out to face the bowling.

Reference to Rowe reminds me of the sorry South African affair. I have for a long time felt very strongly about the period when there were strong advocates for the return of that benighted country to the international cricket arena; but more than this, when teams and individuals, including some from the West Indies were lured by the tainted lucre offered, to play there. I still feel strongly on the issue, and considered premature, the visit of a South African team to the West Indies to play a Test and a series of limited overs games in 1992. Two illustrations of the lack of integrity displayed by certain regional players are instructive. Colin Croft, the Guyanese pace bowler who was residing in Miami was suffering from a back problem, and then president of the West Indies Board, Allan Rae told him that provided some notice was given, Professor John Golding, UWI's noted orthopaedic surgeon would willingly see him. When Croft arrived in Kingston suddenly, Rae, experiencing difficulty in locating the surgeon asked me to try. When I eventually found him during the early evening, (Sir) John agreed at once to see Croft next morning. A few days later, Allan Rae, in addressing a Shell cricket luncheon at which Rowe and Croft were guests, referred to them in commendatory terms, since they had told him that they were not going to South Africa, despite rumours to that effect. In fact, they departed for that destination next morning — Rowe as captain of the touring party.

The other case involved Herbert Chang. During a Shell Shield game at Sabina Park, having heard a rumour that Chang was planning to leave soon for South Africa, president Rae invited him in the course of Jamaica's first innings, to an emergency meeting of the Cricket Board. The following conversation ensued:

Rae:
'Mr. Chang, there is a rumour that you are going to South Africa to play cricket. If this is not true, let us know, and we will assist you in scotching it.'

Chang:
'Mr. Rae, I have no contract to play in South Africa'.

Rae:
'I did not ask you if you have a contract. Are you going to South Africa?'

Chang:
'Me going to South Africa? No, Sir.'

I still recall after these many years, all of us standing around, while Chang facing Rae, looked at him with innocent seeming blue-grey eyes as he answered the questions. Immediately after the match, he was off with Rowe's group. We had decided, if we found clear evidence that he was going, to pull him out of the game at once, despite the disadvantage his absence would mean for Jamaica, since he was one of our more reliable batsmen.

In revisiting the South African issue, it should be recalled that some sympathizers and players continued to cling to the claptrap, the shibboleth 'politics should not be mixed with sport.' They behaved and acted as if in ignorance of the inevitable and inextricable nexus between international sport and politics; as if they were unaware also, of the fact that the purchase price, the pieces of South African rands proferred to the players were not randomly arranged but were the product of a political policy supported by the South African government and financed by a government-sponsored 'slush fund'. Or again, some expressed the naive notion that the two tours by Rowe's team of blacks would contribute towards breaking down the barriers of apartheid. One wonders whether these mercenaries really and sincerely believed that the price paid to purchase their services represented their true value as cricketers only. In 1983, a columnist in a local newspaper asked the question: 'And what is immoral about being paid for work done?' And Rowe, at about the same time, in South Africa: 'We are professionals. We play cricket anywhere we can.' He might have added, with an emphasis on 'business as usual',....'provided the money is good.'

The tours of South Africa took place in a period when non-material values had begun to assume a pre-eminent position, the non-material such as self-respect and dignity being sacrificed and subordinated, relegated to the position of the peripheral, regarded as luxuries. The craving for Mammon became even more pronounced during the '80s. I recall remarking to a UWI colleague, following a snub to local media representatives during president Reagan's visit to Jamaica, that we were in danger of selling our national self-respect for a mess of pottage. His response: 'Self-respect can't buy bread.' The condition has been succinctly summarised by former president Julius Nyerere:

> There are Third World countries which accept their neo-colonial status and even glory in it. They point to the statistics of their gross national product as an example of what can be gained from it — rather in the manner of a high class prostitute glorifying in her furs and jewels.

Consistent with the ban imposed by the WICBC on those regional cricketers who had played in South Africa, the Jamaica Board also precluded our national players who had committed the same offence, from participating in any competitions or matches played under the aegis of the JCBC. This was not uniformly followed throughout the region in Barbados, for example, no local ban was introduced. At an annual general meeting of the Jamaica Cricket Association (JCA) during the mid 1980s, a resolution was moved proposing lifting of this penalty, but the resolution was supported only by the members who moved and seconded it. However, when, following the removal of the ban at the international level, a similar resolution was introduced in 1990 by the same member, it was approved by a large majority, the only representatives voting against being Allan Rae, Courtney Orr and myself. As I have indicated before, I have not relented in my strong sentiments and views about the South African issue, particularly in relation to those who returned to play there after imposition of the ban and those like Kallicharan, who also repeatedly returned on contracts with provincial clubs. Nevertheless, I do feel a tinge of sympathy for one or two national representatives (who were also Test players), who, in my opinion, were not fully aware of the implications and consequences of their actions; and I consider at times, whether the ban could equitably and practically have been selectively determined.

From time to time, controversy has surfaced about the standard of umpiring in international matches and suggestions that the problem stems from the fact that particular home umpires are motivated by partisan considerations rather than from incompetent umpires. From the West Indian perspective, as far as I recall, the issue was first emphasized during that memorable tour of Australia under Worrell's captaincy in 1960 -1961. With the series tied at 1:1, following the historic tied first Test at Brisbane, West Indies were well on top in the fourth, but held up by a last wicket partnership between Mackay and Kline. Not long from the close, the West Indies players began their run from the field when Slasher Mackay appeared clearly to have been caught by Sobers at leg slip but the umpire decided otherwise. So the game was drawn. In the final and deciding Test, with Australia still short of their target with seven wickets down, Grout was given 'not out' when he was apparently bowled by Valentine. They eventually won by two wickets and the series 2:1.

I have always held the view that the unprecedented and wonderful ticker-tape farewell given by hundreds of thousands of Australians in Melbourne, apart from reflecting a sincere tribute to the fresh approach to Test cricket, infused by the West Indies and the mutual spirit of goodwill between the two teams, was attributable to a sense of guilt on the part of the public. At the end of the West Indies tour of 1975-1976, two U.W.I. colleagues, Drs. Hal Dyer and E.V. Ellington sent a cable to one of the Australian umpires who had stood in the series, which read: 'Congratulations on your performance. Only regret that rules of the game do not permit **you** to be named "Man of the Series".' As I write during the current series 1992-1993, on several occasions the television monitor has disclosed cases of Australian batsmen who should have been given out, including one l.b.w. against Steve Waugh, another run out against Border, early in their innings. Both made centuries in the same innings! These, in addition to West Indies batsmen, particularly Lara and Richardson given out when the monitor indicated that the decisions were erroneous. Certainly, errors were also made in favour of the West Indies, but it seems as though the balance, especially in terms of critical errors has been against the West Indies.

I am yet to be convinced that in the 'stumping' of Lara, which ended his innings in the first Test at 58, wicket-keeper Healy was not aware that the ball was not in his hand or glove. Consider, in contrast, Walsh's action in not running out that Pakistan batsman, out of his ground backing up, which would have won West Indies that game in the World Cup of 1987. Or consider Simmonds' act when in the tense, closing stages of the dramatic fourth Test against Australia on January 26,1993, with the umpires uncertain and seeming about to decide against the batsman, he intimated that he had not taken the catch cleanly. Would the Australians have acted similarly in similar circumstances? Some perhaps, but I doubt that these would have included Healy. A clear illustration of contrasts in sportmanship. Tony Cozier, writing perhaps with tongue-in-cheek suggests that the current experience reflects not partisanship, but incompetence. At the time of writing (January 26,1993), West Indies had just won the fourth Test at Adelaide, by one run,apparently despite the umpiring.

Problems have also been experienced in New Zealand and Pakistan. Indeed, Tony Cozier commenting in the *Barbados Nation*, on a New Zealand umpire during the West Indies 1987 tour, asserted:

> West Indians regard Umpire Goodall in the same way as Ronald Reagan does Colonel Gadhaffi (with deep suspicion.) New Zealand had not been beaten in a home Test for five seasons and it was clear in this Test match to understand why.

In Pakistan there was the notorious incident when, with the West Indies in a very strong position to win a Test which would almost certainly have given them victory instead of a drawn 1986 series, the umpires decided to call an end to play prematurely. Play had been suspended earlier because of poor light but when the light conditions improved before the scheduled close, despite protests from the West Indies, the umpires declined to resume.

Recounting of these experiences is not intended to deny that there have also been occasions when the shoe has been on the other foot, when West Indian umpires were suspected of acting in a partisan manner or at the least, were considered incompetent. The first incident of this kind, which has become part of West Indies cricket lore occurred more than 60 years ago, in the first home series versus England in 1929-1930. The visitors were making a desperate bid to save the third Test at Bourda when Voce was adjudged leg before wicket to Francis to the last ball of the match. Several knowledgeable West Indians who saw the match, recounting the tale long afterwards, have expressed serious doubt about the decision, and this is an understatement! More recently, in the Barbados Test of the 1990 home series, again against England, with West Indies striving to draw level following the defeat at Sabina, and England determined to deprive them, the dismissal of Bailey, given out caught on the on-side close to the wicket sparked considerable controversy. Umpire Barker was strongly criticised for succumbing to intimidation by West Indies fielders and Martin-Jenkins' accusation of cheating culminated in a law suit, eventually settled out of court.

There have also been conspicuous cases of courageous umpires in the context of excitable home crowds; perhaps the most significant illustration being the l.b.w. decision by Perry Burke (of the Jamaican firm of Ewart and Burke), against J.K. Holt Jnr. at Sabina Park in January 1954, with his score at 94 on his debut. Following threats against Burke, police protection was provided for him. Five years and a decade and a half later, respectively, decisions against home team batsmen Charran Singh and Basil Butcher by Lee Kow and Douglas Sang Hue, in circumstances which found the West Indies in deep trouble, incited riots and the intervention of tear gas-equipped police squads at Queen's and Sabina Parks. On his return from Australia in 1961, I questioned Worrell about the umpiring. His response, with a characteristic shrug, 'You expect to get the rough with the smooth.'

I support those who have called for a panel of the best umpires, recruited internationally, to be available for official international matches, provided funding is feasible. However, such a system could have the effect of retarding the development of those who have not reached this standard, and programmes should be designed to provide training and experience for the best of these, though this would not eliminate problems of partisan behaviour. As for the use of electronic devices such as the television camera, I confess to being a traditionalist who has long preferred to rely on human judgement, but I have recently moved to a less extreme position. Perhaps the monitor should be used in respect of run outs. However, one of my concerns centers on the effect on the umpire in perhaps rendering him uncertain and indecisive; moreover, I would suggest that some l.b.w. decisions based on a camera view could be dicey, depending on its position, perspective and angle and the height of the ball's movement. It should be noted too, that the U.S. football authorities (presumably the inventors of such devices) have recently decided to abandon the use of the electronic umpire.

Let me stress however, how much I support the introduction of the referee, in particular his role in terms of taking disciplinary decisions and implementing action; but referee Subba Row seems to have exceeded his authority during the 1993 West Indies vs Pakistan series. Interestingly, on hearing of my appointment as chairman of the newly created electoral committee in 1979, a former president of the Jamaica and West Indies Boards commented that the authorities had acted wisely in selecting a cricketer for this umpiring position. Coincidentally, I played cricket with the leaders of Jamaica's two major parties. I was a member of Michael Manley's informal team playing in a London park at the end of the 1940s and bowled on a Kingston C.C. team with Edward Seaga as wicket-keeper-batsman during the late 1950s.

During the last two years, unfortunately some negative manifestations have appeared in West Indies cricket. These include the booing of Captain Richie Richardson in Jamaica, the threat by the President of the Trinidad and Tobago Board to boycott the Pakistan Test at Queen's Park Oval, and the spectator boycott of the South African Test at Kensington, Barbados. The lowest point was reached in May 1994 when the Trinidad and Tobago Board, issued a public statement of condemnation of the W.I.C.B.C., alleging a conspiracy, an 'orchestrated plot to undermine Trinidad/Tobago's cricket and cricketers'. All of these incidents flowed from the omission of specific island players from the Test team and reflect a resurgence and re-surfacing of attitudes of parochialism and insularity which had remained dormant during the period of dominance. For those of us who have known Dr Baldwin Mootoo for many years, the resignation from the Trinidad Board of this Vice-President, and incidentally, Head of St. Augustine's Chemistry Department, was entirely consistent with his character. I fervently hope that this deplorable condition will be laid to rest.

POSTCRIPT

Since the establishment of the Electoral Advisory Committee , no general election has created so intense and extensive a degree of controversy as did that of March 30, 1993. Indeed, this comment applies also to all general elections held during the past two decades, including that of December 1976 when, in the aftermath, Jamaica Labour Party threats of boycotting future elections led to bi-partisan parliamentary discussions on electoral reform, culminating in the creation of the EAC.

The problems began with the enumeration exercise when many qualified individuals refused to be enumerated, apparently disillusioned by their experience of politicians and the political system. A few even set dogs on enumerators. The result of such reactions and of the low fee received per elector processed, was that many enumerators were demotivated and declined to undertake the work enthusiastically and energetically. Some of those who refused to be enumerated initially, scurried to have this done subsequently when an election was imminent, but it was then too late.

Fundamental errors committed during the field operations did not come to the attention of head office staff until months later; and suspicion of fraudulent attempts by a relatively large number of persons to be registered on the basis of spurious claims of residence in two constituencies, led to the suspension of enumeration in those areas for several weeks. Legal advice had to be sought and a screening process was used to sort out those who were eligible for enumeration.

As a consequence of these and other factors, the date originally scheduled for the completion of the field work was extended on several occasions. In fact, this was the worst experience we had encountered in conducting a full enumeration since the inception of the EAC.

Other problems surfaced during the processing of the data and in the preparation of the voters list. A significant and much publicized one arose from the discovery that the data for 47,000 electors in nine constituencies had been scrubbed from diskettes. Sabotage was never established.

Early in 1992, the EAC had yielded reluctantly to pleas made by the Commonwealth Secretariat and the U.K.'s Overseas Development Administration on behalf of the Government of Lesotho, for the release of Director of Elections Noel Lee to serve temporarily as Chief Electoral Officer of that country and assist the Government in putting an electoral system in place. The Committee expressed reluctance initially on the grounds that we were engaged in an enumeration process and the two Assistant Directors were inexperienced, having been in office for only a few months. In deciding eventually to release the Director, the committee took into consideration that at the time, the enumeration operation appeared to be proceeding fairly satisfactorily, apart from the attitude shown by those who refused to be enumerated; and that Jamaica would be rendering worthwhile technical assistance to a fellow Commonwealth country. A condition was imposed requiring his return to Jamaica immediately, should an election be called during his absence, that is, before December 31, 1992.

Noel Lee was granted leave from May to end-December. It was during the latter part of this period that the most serious problems in the enumeration and data processing emerged, and these had natural consequences in delaying production of the Voters List. In the meantime, the EAC had had to resist firmly pressures from the Lesotho government, for extension of the Director's period of secondment, primarily on grounds that his departure before the impending election was held, could lead to internal unrest and possible invasion from external sources. In fact, it was the Director who, on his return and when preparations were in train for publication of a preliminary list on January 25, 1993, discovered the problem of the missing 47,000 electors. It was he too, who proposed that the names of approximately 17,000 persons enumerated erroneously as old instead of new electors, should be placed on an addendum list.

The efforts being made to complete preparation of the voters list and the delays experienced in having this done were the cause of a serious debate and a basic division in the ranks of the EAC which continued until polling day. This problem became a fundamental cause for criticism and complaint on the part of the Opposition and some members of the public, well into the aftermath of the election. The Jamaica Labour Party representatives advanced the view strongly that insufficient time was being allowed for satisfactory preparation of the preliminary list, for its checking by the political parties and public, and for the Electoral Office to cope with the queries received about errors and omissions, and complete the preparation and publication of the final list. Hence, there was a serious risk that a credible electoral list would not be produced in the time available.

On the other hand, the government representatives expressed concern about the protracted enumeration exercise which was delaying production of the List and this reflected badly on the performance of the system. Local Government elections were due shortly and the government could be embarrassed if the list was not ready in time for these statutory obligations to be met. As Chairman, I emphasized to the Committee on January 20, that it had two obligations, namely, to give the government the opportunity to call Local Government Elections within the prescribed statutory period, but in doing so, to ensure that the electoral list was efficiently and accurately prepared.

Later, after much deliberation and following publication of the Preliminary List, the Electoral Office top management informed the EAC that they would be able to publish the final list on March 10. The Prime Minister was so advised at a meeting he held with the Director and me. However, the Jamaica Labour Party representatives persisted in expressing their opinion that the Electoral Office would not be able to complete examination of the queries on the Preliminary List by that date. On March 9, in response to an enquiry from the Prime Minister, and on the basis of a letter from the Director, I reiterated in a note the information conveyed to him orally a few days before.

A series of unprecedented incidents and events occurred during the two months preceding polling day. A new element represented by threats, verbal and physical attacks against election officials had entered the scene and moved on to the stage. In early February a man had entered the office of a Returning Officer and shot at him; and another Returning Officer was assaulted in his home by men who accused him of deliberately omitting from the voters list the names of some persons who supported a particular political party.

The drama took a new turn with verbal public attacks on the Director of Elections by Leader of the Opposition, Edward Seaga. In a speech from a party platform on March 10, he was reported as saying that some 55,000 persons had been removed from the list, and that he held the Director responsible. He cast aspersions on the Director's competence and stated that if these omissions were not rectified in time for the election, he would call for Lee's resignation. This and other allegations against the Director, including implications of partisanship continued and escalated during the run up to the election and the early post-election period.

I told the Committee that I considered it unfair for the Director to have been singled out for public attack and it seemed that the rules and conventions to which I had become accustomed, no longer applied. We were also concerned about the danger of physical attack on the Director by fanatical party supporters. He had reported that four members of the Electoral Office staff were threatened and abused in the precincts of a party office and threats were issued against him. On Nomination Day, a mob attacked a senior officer. Security protection was therefore extended to the Director. All these events had a negative effect on staff morale.

But the saga of errors and unfortunate incidents had not ended. On Friday March 26, the day scheduled for voting by the Security Forces, we received a telephone message that problems were being experienced in producing the list of police and military electors. Despite efforts by the Director who had been at the National Computer Centre throughout the previous night, the polling had to be postponed until the next day.

The discovery of significant errors on the addendum to the list was made a few days before the election. The documents supplied to several rural constituencies had to be withdrawn and corrected replacements provided.

The climax was reached with the news, conveyed to me by Noel Lee in the early hours of Sunday morning, March 28, of the murder of Returning Officer Dennis Brooks. An emergency meeting was called by Returning Officers later that day, at which many of them emphasized their determination to withdraw their services. Only the

Director's persuasive powers succeeded in preventing abortion of the election!

These incidents resulted in almost the total loss of the week-end preceding polling day: a period critical for preparations involving the despatch of equipment and materials throughout the Island. As a result of the murder, many presiding officers withdrew their services: some not turning up on polling day. Consequently, some polling stations opened late, while some did not open at all; and some were short of supplies.

The story of the events of March 30 has been told again and again, by the media organs, members of the public, election officials and by the Jamaica Labour Party. The independent members of the EAC listened in the Director's office to reports relayed by Returning Officers on our internal radio network and by the electronic media. Despite having heard similar reports of incidents on previous elections such as the 1986 Local Government contest, though not on the same scale, we were nevertheless shocked by the intensity of the violence and thuggery. Contrasting views have been expressed about the level and scale of violence, intimidation and fraud in terms of the invasion of polling stations, the stealing of ballot boxes, open voting. From one perspective, the extent and intensity were unprecedented; from another, they were not greater than in some previous elections since 1980, but appeared to be worse because of the proliferation of electronic media. My own impressions on polling day supported the former view.

There has been a strong and sustained clamour for urgent fundamental electoral reform by certain organizations, notably the Private Sector Organization of Jamaica and the New Beginning Movement, by press columnists, radio programme hosts and other individuals. Some of these organizations and individuals have observed and emphasized that though the electoral system itself is in need of significant improvement, the root of the problem lies in our political culture of tribalism, dependent patron-client relations and garrison constituencies. Even the most advanced system cannot perform efficiently and effectively in such a context. Until this cancer is rooted out and excised, fundamental problems will continue to appear and the electoral institution, its leaders and personnel will continue to serve as convenient scapegoats. More seriously, we are faced with the danger of allowing one of the essential foundations of our democracy to be destroyed.

Commenting on the 1993 Election, Professor Errol Miller in an address to a group of teachers, is reported to have said:

The two major political parties should seek to demonstrate greater control of their supporters, instead of seeking to replace the EAC....Those who were the villains or condoned them are now — having played foul — wanting to fire the referee... (*Gleaner*, June 26, 1993)

Nothing that I have said is intended as an excuse for the internal administrative and operational weaknesses which emerged during the preparations for the Election and on polling day itself. Indeed, by April 14 the EAC had begun a thorough investigation of the sources of these problems and had already interviewed thoroughly the system's two Assistant Directors and all the senior members of the data processing staff, before the independent members' term expired on May 14.

Mrs. Miller, Dr. Reid and I were taken totally by surprise when we learnt of Prime Minister Patterson's statement made in Parliament on May 4, that:

> When we first constituted the EAC, it was intended that the Independent Members should be full-time officers and, for this reason, their remuneration was set at the same level as Puisne Judges. In fact, they are being so paid. We are not getting the benefits of the full-time attention which is required not only for the electoral system, but for the National Registration System where they were intended to be Commissioners in the first instance.

According to the *Jamaica Herald*, 'Mr. Patterson scores independent members of the EAC.'

Writing on behalf of the three of us, I informed the Prime Minister of the fact that from the outset, in October 1979, we had decided to take only a portion of the statutorily prescribed emoluments, since we already had full-time positions elsewhere and that we had never been paid the full emoluments. Further, the issue of serving as Commissioners of the National Registration System did not arise at the time. (In fact, 14 years later, such a system is not yet in place). In reply, the Prime Minister indicated *inter alia* and without apology:

> As a creature of the Law, I was entitled to rely, and did so rely, on the clear provisions contained in the Act establishing the said Committee, for the Statement I made in Parliament on Tuesday.

Moreover, he reiterated the intention that the independent members are to serve on a full-time basis; and this intention was widely publicized.

Apart from the facts, two associated issues were of concern to us. We had expected that, since a statement which would include a criticism of us was to be made publicly in Parliament, as a matter of courtesy we would have been informed in advance. At the least, the Minister responsible for electoral matters, with whom we were in fairly close contact, could have been asked to warn us and avoid our learning of the Prime Minister's comments through the media. The other issue concerns the negative inferences relating to our integrity which could have been drawn from the content of such a public statement, though we did not think that this was intended, and the Prime Minister confirmed this in his reply to me. All of us guard jealously our reputation for integrity. In fact, several persons who have known me for a long time, expressed surprise to me or asked me directly: 'Charles how could you have been accepting money under false pretences?' All this was particularly galling to me in light of my long history of voluntary service. Unfortunately, the Prime Minister's statement will remain uncorrected in Hansard, the record of proceedings of Parliament.

Ironically eight months after my colleagues and I vacated office, an accolade was bestowed on us in the People's National Party's contribution to the Sunday Gleaner column, 'The Parties Speak', which stated:

> The integrity of this committee under the chairmanship of Professor Mills has been vindicated. They carried out their tasks in a period of the most intense party rivalry and hostility ever experienced in this country since Universal Adult Suffrage in 1944. These true Jamaican patriots served their country well.

Hansard remains uncorrected and EAC members continue to serve part-time.

It was, therefore, personally gratifying that I received a number of letters and oral expressions of sympathy, and concern that persons who had rendered such significant public service could be treated in this way.

On reflecting further on my experience as Chairman of the EAC these almost 14 years, I think of some of the lessons learnt. One is the position of risk involved in the role of independents. The views they express, the decisions they take and their actions will inevitably offend one side or another. Sometimes, but rarely, both sides will be unhappy. Another syndrome is manifested in 'scapegoatism' — the tendency for some of those in positions of authority and decision-making to cast the blame on others where projects have gone sour.

Since the inception of the EAC both major parties have always been represented by General Secretaries or their deputies and/or ministers in its membership. These political nominees have been intimately involved with the independent members in restructuring the electoral system over the past 14 years. Incredibly, some political nominees assume a 'holier than thou' attitude, conveying the impression that they are the only members genuinely concerned with reform. They condemn the system as if they are not at all responsible for its condition, as if it is someone else's fault, or the responsibility of others.

My own philosophy is 'let the chips fall where they may.' One of the problems which currently bedevil our civic and social lives is the notion that a person who is selected as neutral in the sense of being non-partisan should behave as a cipher. He or she should be bereft of views or should never express a view no matter how strongly held and objectively based, if this would indicate or imply a criticism of one side or another in a discussion. I consider this an erroneous position to adopt and an unfortunate attitude. If it persists, the country will eventually be deprived of the public services of independent and courageous citizens.

Despite my university education in political science and first career in the civil service working closely with ministers, my real education in politics did not begin until this intimate experience of the electoral system. I was naive, a neophyte in this world of the professionals. It is a world of dual and self-righteous personalities, in which it is unwise to judge on the basis of external appearance or verbal expressions of some individuals who seem to be highly civilized and cultured but are quite the opposite. It took me some time to come to terms with some of the methods employed to beat and pervert elements of the electoral system. Yet, there were also those who at times submerged party advantage in the wider national interest.

Nevertheless, I do not share the view that party representatives should be excluded from membership of the EAC or of a successor electoral commission. In my opinion, based on experience, they perform an essential role and function given their intimate knowledge and experience of activities in the field which independent members are unlikely to have. On the negative side, there is of course, the danger of a partisan approach and activity superseding concern for electoral reform. For most of the life of the EAC the broader view was generally taken, though the situation seems to have deteriorated during the past few years. Perhaps, however, the composition of the body should be changed to provide for a larger number of independent than political members.

Since the events of March 30, there has been much public expression and emphasis on the need to recruit for polling stations a higher calibre of presiding officers and poll clerks who would behave in a non-partisan manner. During the 1980s I drew attention to this problem in numerous speeches and newspaper articles in an effort to encourage the types of citizens who used to offer their services 30 years ago. But my pleas fell on deaf ears. Some of the strongest advocates of such recruitment practice have themselves been unwilling to volunteer.

Those who now so vocally deplore the quality of these officials continuously turned deaf ears to such appeals. They confined participation in the electoral processes to funding one or the other, or both of the major political parties and perhaps, to casting their vote.

It is also interesting to observe how often critics of national institutions behave as if history began with the particular individual. Some of the severest critics of the track record of the EAC are evidently ignorant of, or choose to ignore, the gross ills perpetrated before 1979 when the electoral system functioned under the direct control of the governing party. And during that period the social context was comparatively quiescent.

The political nominees having failed to agree on a new slate of independent members after May 14, 1993, the selection was placed in the hands of the Governor-General. He too experienced great difficulty in identifying suitable appointees. Despite the public clamour that electoral reform should be tackled as an issue of great urgency and the government's assurance of its support for reform, the electoral system remained without its policy board and no meeting of the EAC was held for more than ten weeks.

Two factors seemed to be responsible for the long delay in recruiting new independent personnel. In the first place, scarcely anyone of the required calibre would be prepared to give up a current assignment for a full-time position as a member of the Committee. Hence, the sources of recruitment are likely to be restricted primarily to retired persons. Secondly, I would expect individuals of stature and independent minds to hesitate about accepting positions in this system, in light of the treatment meted out to the previous long-serving incumbents. As early as April 1993, I intimated to a number of persons, including some members of the EAC, that having served for almost 14 years, it was time for me to withdraw from public service.

Appointment of the new set of independent members was eventually announced on July 22, 1993: the new Chairman, the busy President of an insurance company; the other two, practising attorneys-at-law: none serving full-time! The outcome seems to confirm the suspicion or conviction voiced initially by a few cynical friends and acquaintances that a 'hidden agenda' lurked behind the scene.

The treatment of Director Noel Lee was even more significant. Certainly, as manager of the organization he cannot avoid ultimate responsibility for some of the administrative and operational deficiences which appeared during the preparations for the Election and on polling day. But insufficient consideration has been given to his absence for almost eight months in Lesotho. Moreover, any charge of bias on his part or hint of such a charge is unfounded and grossly unfair.

The Committee proposed some years ago that since the decision to convert the body into an entrenched Commission seemed unlikely to be implemented within the near future, action should be taken early to provide a greater degree of security for the post of Director. Fortunately this has been done.

So long as the representatives of the Leader of the Opposition continued to express lack of confidence in Noel Lee, he could not remain as Director, even if an overwhelming majority, of say five to two, were in favour of retaining his services. Indeed, shortly before its term ended, the previous Committee discussed his performance and the question of his future, and the verdict was, without a vote being taken, five — two in his favour and two against. Mrs. Miller and Dr. Reid also spoke strongly in support.

Following the manner in which he has been treated, the EAC will have considerable difficulty in recruiting a replacement of appropriate calibre for a post which is also hazardous. It is perhaps paradoxical that in May 1993 Noel Lee received a letter of commendation from Baroness Chalker, Minister of Overseas Development of Lesotho. He was recently appointed a consultant to South Africa's Independent Electoral Commission for the historic

April 1994 elections and is currently serving in a similar capacity in Liberia.

In the long hiatus which ensued during the search for a new set of independents, Noel Lee remained in office at the request of minister Mullings but in an anomalous and uncomfortable situation, *sans* statutory status. During this period, placed in a 'no man's land', the Electoral Office staff were twiddling their thumbs, their morale at a very low point, a downward process begun with the physical and verbal attacks during the run up to the Election. The urgent exercise of electoral reform remains in abeyance.

I have been fascinated by the history of changes of policy towards national economic development which have occurred over the past four decades. During the 1950s, mid-way in my Civil Service career, government's economic policy emphasized a role for the State as catalyst, serving to create a climate conducive for private enterprise development. The 1970s witnessed a fundamental change, with the State becoming the engine of growth, a gospel given flesh with the burgeoning of state-owned enterprises. By the 1980s, the wheel had turned full circle and some of the most ardent preachers of this gospel during the 1970s have now become equally ardent evangelists for privatization, the market and private enterprise as the engine.

In conclusion, I reflect on a recent return to LSE in June 1993, for a reunion of those who graduated between 1946 and 1954. The principal speaker at the banquet was Hungarian-born alumnus George Soros, self-styled 'financial and philosophical speculator', who is reported 'to have set a Wall Street record by earning $650 million in 1992 and to have placed a $10 billion wager that the Major government would be forced to devalue sterling'. (Guardian Weekly, June 27, 1993). More recently, he has given considerable humanitarian aid in Bosnia-Herzegovina. Interesting too, was the following experience at a pre-banquet reception attended by approximately 400 persons, where at first I recognized only two of my contemporaries. After some time, I was confronted by a man with: 'Charlie, don't you recognize me?' Noting my embarrassment, he showed two twisted fingers and reminded me that he had kept wicket to my bowling, and that was one of the consequences. Then, he took me to a group who he said were waiting to see me. They turned out to be colleagues (including the Vice-captain) who had played cricket or football, or both, under my captaincy during the mid-1940s almost 50 years ago. I would not have recognized any of them on the street, if walking separately. They had all either put on a considerable amount of weight or lost a good deal of hair, or both.

C'est la vie!

INDEX

Abrahams, Allan R. **34,59,67,70**
Abrahams Clan **16**
 Busha Tom **17**
 George **16, 29**
Abrahams, Sidney **17,27,63**
Administration **99**
Africans **87**
Agriculture **1**
Ableton, Tony **10**
Alexander, Carlton **17, 33**
Alexander, Franz 'Gerry' **91**
Alexander, Maisie O'Reggio **111**
Alexander murder case **18**
Alexander, Wesley **65**
Allan, Lady Edris **67**
Allan, Sir Harold **6, 66**
Ally, Asgar **117**
Anderson, Dale **112**
Anderson, Errol **112**
Angola **14**
Armstrong, Edith **10**
Arnett, Vernon **73**
Arscott
 Ivan
 Ken **44**

Ashenheim
 Richard
 Edward **44**
Ashenheim, Leslie **31,32**
Ashenheim, N.N. **31, 71**
Ashley, Paul **118**
Atkinson, Cyril **17**
Atkinson, Dr. Monica **27**
Atwell, Winnifred **90**
August Town **13, 14**
Auxiliary Territorial Service (ATS) **81**
Awon, Max **108**
Bag-an-pan **4**
Bailey, Amy **4**
Bailey, MacDonald **106**
Baker **38**
Banks, Don **4**
Bank of Jamaica **73**
Baptist Church **13**
Baptiste, Fitz **118**
Barber, Bunny **33**
Barber, Horace **69**
Barker, Sir Robert **67**
Barnett, Lloyd **117**
Barongo, Paul **115**

Barrow, Errol **83, 96**
Batchelor, Denzil **7**
Batchelor, Owen **75**
Bauxite **2**
 royalties re-negotiation
 G.Arthur Brown
 Sam Moment **75**
BATCO **34**
Bean Jr., D.D. **71**
Beckford Snr., D.P. **65**
Beckwith, Percy **59, 70, 73**
Bedward, Alexander **13**
Bedwardism **13**
Bedwardites **13**
Belle, George **118**
Benewick, Bob **116**
Bertram, Arnold **31**
BITU **53, 71**
Black Bradman **7**
Black Power **122**
Blackman, Kenneth **100**
Blake, Hazel **60**
Blake, Joyce **60**
Blake, Viv **62, 88**
Bolton, Warner **44**
Bond, Frederick **55**

INDEX

Bonnick, Gladstone **117**
Bottom Chapel **15**
Bourne, Kathleen **26**
Bowen, Dr.Francis **108**
Boys Athletic Championships **32**
Braham, H.A. Charlie **71**
Brandon, Ken **16**
Brandt
  Franz
  Clifford **44, 150**
Brash, Rosa **27**
Bretton Woods **85**
Bridge, R.C. **69**
Briggs, George **112**
Bristol, Carol **86**
British Army (Infantry)
  Kebble Munn
  M.G. Smith
  Douglas Hall **80**
  Leo March **76**
  Arundel Moody **81**
British Council **94, 97**
British Further Education and Training Programme
  see FEVT
Broadcasting
  David Dunton
  Jamaica Broadcasting Corp. **74**
Broderick, Mrs. Percy **28**
Brown, A.F. **9**
Brown, Canon Walter **87**
Brown, G.Arthur **68, 73, 75, 83, 88, 108, 117**
Brown, Geoff **75**
Brown, L.K. **33**
Brown, Leroy **113**
Brown, Sam W. **32**
Browne, Ivan **104**
Bryan, Colin **94**
Buchan, Og **110**
Bullying **40**
Burgess, Chester **33**
Burke, Eddie **24**
Burke, Morris **33**
Burke, Pat **90**
Burke, Pat W.C. **35, 36, 68**
Burke, R.M. Sam **35**

Burke, Rudolph **32**
Burke, Samuel Constantine **35**
Burnham, Forbes **88**
Burrough, Elsie **10, 44**
Burrowes, Earl **34**
Burrowes, J.T. **8**
Burrowes, Keith **34**
Bush tea
  fever grass
  John Charles
  leaf of life
  cerasee **20**
  ramgoat dashalong **20**
Bustamante, Alexander **3, 53, 66, 105**
Bustamante Industrial Trade Union
  see BITU
Butler, Mario **112**
Byrne-Massiah, Joycelin **112**
Cadbury, George **72, 73, 75**
Cafe de Paris **90**
Cameron, F.Jimmy **36, 37**
Campbells **18**
Campbell, Ethelred Erasmus Adolphus **4**
Campbell, Granville **10, 21**
Campbell, Selvin **28**
Cappe, Icy **60**
Captain Cipriani **10**
Carberry, Dossie **47, 108, 117**
Carberry, J.E.D. **56**
Cargill, Morris **62**
Caribbean Conference of Churches
  Haiti **151**
  Guyana **155**
Carmichael, David **109**
Carnegie Corporation **113**
Carnegie, Viv **60**
Carpenter, Gloria **84**
Carter, Sam **60**
Cash, Gerald **88**
Cattouse, Nadia **90**
Cawley, C.Lynden **33**
Cawley, T.J. **6**
CD & W **10, 58ff**

Sir Frank Stockdale
  Professor Simey
  Dora Ibberson **58**
Central Planning Unit (CPU) **72, 73, 74**
Chambers, Daisy **55**
Chambers, Hugo C.W. **32, 38, 45**
Chambers, Sidney **8, 34**
Chapel of Ease **15**
Chapelton **15ff, 24**
Chapel Town **15**
Chapman, Brian **110**
Charles, Eugenia **88**
Chen-Young, Dr. Paul **17**
Civil Service **54ff, 132ff**
  public service selection commitee
  married woman **55**
  Jews
  Roman Catholics **55**
  War restrictions **61**
  Treasury **68**
  Dept. of Commerce and Indusries **69**
  Ministry of Finance **69**
  Central Planning Unit **72, 73**
  Clare McFarlane, J.E. **59, 67, 68**
Clarendon College **16**
Clark, B.M. **8, 32**
Clarke, Belfield **95**
Clarke, Bertie **95**
Clarke, D.R 'Jack' **72**
Clarke, Edith **55**
Clarke, Oliver **83, 150**
Clegg, J.B. **68**
Clerk, John **68**
Clerk, Pat **68**
Collins, Lloyd **59**
Colonel Ward **9**
Colonial Development and Welfare **9**
Colonial Development and Welfare Organization
  see C.D.&W.
  Colonial Office liaison officer **95ff**
Compton, John **96**
Connor, Edric **90**

Constantine, Learie **107**
Constitution
　ministerial system **66, 68**
　Executive Council
　Universal Adult Suffrage **66**
　MacGillivray proposals **68**
Cooke, Howard **109**
Coore, David **71**
Coore, Lawson **60, 66, 79**
Corporal punishment **26, 39**
Costa Rica **11**
Cousins, Rudolph **84, 90**
Cowper, William **38ff**
Cover, Barbara **10**
Cricket **7, 22**
　throwing of the cricket ball **37**
　Kensington Cricket Club **57**
　Wembly Cricket Club **63**
　Emmet Park **64**
　Boys Town
　Lucas **65**
Cricket **12ff, 162ff**
Jamaica Cricket Board of Control **162**
　South Africa **165, 176**
　ICC **165, 168, 169**
　WICBC **165, 169, 178, 182**
　West Indies Madras Test Indian Universities Council **174**
　Jamaica Cricket Association **178**
　umpiring **179**
　referee
　parochialism and insularity **182**
Cripps, Sir Stafford **53**
Crookes, Joe **76**
Crooks, R.B. **33**
Cross, Ulric **94**
Crosswell, A. Noel **33**
Cuba **11**
Cummings, Ivor **101**
Cunningham, O.J. **64**
Cupidon, Ernest **10**
DaCosta, Eric **33, 44**
DaCosta, Harvey **9**

DaCosta, Huntley **33, 44**
DaCosta, Trevor **72**
Dahl, Roald **40**
Daily Telegraph **163**
　R.C. Robertson-Glasgow **168**
Dalhouse **34**
Dark Blues **33**
Davy, Rev. Lester **16**
Dawes, Laura **87**
Dawes, Neville **13, 47, 69**
Dayes, Harry O.A. **33**
D'Costa, Alfred **2**
Dear, Jack **84**
DeJong, Jan Jelle **115ff**
DeLeon **8**
Delgado, Ruby **10**
Denham, Sir Edward **53**
Development Finance Corporation **72**
Development Plan 1957 - 1967 **74**
Dickson, Roy **72**
Dickenson, W.N. **31**
Dignum, Faith **60**
Discrimination
　racial **101ff**
　BOAC **106**
　Harvard Square **102**
Dolly-Besson, June **111**
Donaldson, Trevor **33**
Douglas, Enid **20**
Douglas, Rhona **87**
Douglas, Sir Randolph **83, 91**
Downer, Henderson **112**
Duffus, Herbert **16**
Dujon, L.V. **36, 65**
Duncan, Neville **118**
Dundas, Carl **139, 142, 167**
Durant, Orville **111**
Earle, A.F. **71**
Edelweise Park **9**
Edwards, Horace **34, 39**
Eccleston, Ivan **16**
Effat **37**
Ehrenstein, R.H. **6**

Electoral Advisory Committee **139ff, 185ff**
　Paul Robertson **139, 141**
　O.K. Melhado **139**
　Bruce Golding **139, 141**
　Abe Dabdoub **139, 141, 159**
　Shirley Miller **139**
　R.V. Irvine **139, 158**
　Reg. N. Murray
　Laurie Reid **158**
　Donald Buchanan
　Anthony Johnson
　Ryan Peralto **151, 159**
　electronic registration **158**
　national registration system **158, 188**
　remuneration **188**
　Hansard
　PNP
　The Parties Speak **189**
Electoral systems
Ellington, Alton 'Duke' **35**
Emmanuel, Patrick **112, 118**
Empire Windrush invasion **102ff**
Escoffery
　W.H. 'Billy'
　Michael **44**
Evans, Dr. E.R. **67**
E.M. Wellings **164**
Facey
　Maurice
　Lloyd **44**
Farley, Rawle **108**
Farquharson, Jean **17**
Farquharson, Jimmy **35**
Father Coombs **53**
Feanny
　Ralston
　Philip
　Lloyd **44**
FEVT
　Accounting **99**
　Administration **99**
　Architecture **100**
　Construction **99**
　Economics **99**
　Electronics **99**
　History **99**
　Humanities **100**
　Law **99**
　Medicine **99**
　Quantity Surveying **99**
　Social Work **99**

Veterinary medicine **100**
Fifi Smith **64, 68**
Fighting Barrister **4**
Fleming, Odel **84**
Fletcher, R.H. **56**
Fletcher, Richard **112**
Folkes, Douglas **4, 113**
Fonseca, Donald **35**
Foot, Sir Hugh **67, 68**
Forbes, Urias **113**
Ford Foundation **113**
Forrest, Ewart **93**
Foster, G.C. **36**
Foster-Davis, Sybil **10**
Fowler, Greta Bourke **63**
Fowler, Henry **46, 63**
Fox, H.L. Tubbin **33, 35, 44**
Francis, Amadeo **116**
Francis, Frank **69**
Francis, Sybil **83, 86**
Fraser, Aubrey **94**
Fraser, Rev. **87**
Frasers **17**
Fraser-Scott, Gloria **60, 73, 85**
Free Villages **13**
Gairy, Eric **9**
Garifunas **11**
Garvey, Marcus **6**
Garvey Jnr., Marcus **69**
General Elections (1944) universal adult suffrage **66**
General election December 15, 1983 **144ff**
General election March 30, 1993 **183ff**
    voters list **185**
    Edward Seaga **186**
    Dennis Brooks
    Jamaica Labour Party
    PSOJ
    New Beginning Movement **187**
George, Emil **94, 117**
Gibraltar Camp **58**
Gibson **38**
Gilchrist, Roy **64**

Girvan, D.Thom **19, 58**
Girvan, Gaston **19**
Girvan, Norman **112**
Glasspole, Florizel **74**
Glegg, Ronald "Billy" **35, 44**
    Neville **44**
Glossop-Harris, Florence **9**
Golding, Bruce **16**
Goldson, Paul **71**
Gonsalves, Ralph **115, 118**
Gordon House **68**
Gordon, R.A. **24**
Gore, James **33**
Goveia, Elsa **88, 108**
Government
    representative **5**
    colonial rule
    legislative council **6**
Grace Kennedy Company
    management studies **125**
Grace Kennedy Foundation **132**
Grant
    Gerald
    Vivian
    Kenny **44**
Grant, Cy **90**
Grant, H.A. **35**
Grant, Louis **33**
Grant, Rolph **91**
Grant, St. William **53**
Great Exhibition **13**
Groves, Johnny **8**
Guardian
    Terry Coleman **165**
    Matthew Engel **166**
    John Arlott **167, 168**
    David Hopps **167**
Guilbride, Mary Winch **73**
Gyles, John P. **38**
Haiti **150ff**
    OAS/CARICOM observers
    Caribbean Conference of Churches
    President Carter's delegation **151**
Hall, Dennis
    Jimmy **44**
Hall, Douglas **35**

Hall, Dr. Joe St. Elmo **60**
Hall, J.M. 'Fire' **32**
Hamilton, Harold
Hamilton, Lena **60**
Hammersmith Palais **90**
Hammond, Oscar **111**
Hanna's **3**
Harding, Oswald **83**
Harewood, Jack
Harney, Lenore **88**
Harrison, Hon. A.B. 'Wagga' **38**
Hart, Richard **58, 62**
Hart, Sam **87**
Harvey, Lena **17**
Harvard Square **121**
Headley, George **7, 65**
Hearne, John **47**
Heath, Ivo **96**
Hendricks, Mickey **47**
Henriques Bros. **70**
Henriques, O.K. **67, 72**
Henriques, R.D.C. 'Dossie' **16**
Henriques, Roald **117**
Henry, Arthur **58**
Henry, Mervyn **88**
Hill, Frank **58**
Hill, Ken **58**
Hill, K.G. Anthony **112**
Hodges, A.H. **60**
Hodges, Bill **76**
Holt Snr, J.K. **64**
Holding, Ralph **33**
Holding, Michael **175**
Hollar, Anna **45**
Hollar, Constance **46**
Holtz, Noel **59**
Horseshoe Curve **24**
Hosang, Lloyd **61**
Huggins, Lady Molly **67**
Huggins, Sir John **67**
Huie Albert **47**
Humphries, R.C. 'Bob' **34**
Hutchinson, Leslie 'Hutch' **90**

Hylton, Leslie 65
IMF 84
Ingram, Ken 47
Initiation rites 40
Inniss, Probyn 112
Institute of International Relations 114
Institute of Jamaica 62
Inter-American Human Rights Institute 149
International Association of Schools and Institutes of Administration 126
Irvine, Mrs. Rudolph 17
Isaacs, Kendall 96
Issa Scholarship 66
Jackman, Oliver 96
Jacobs, H.P. "Jiggy" 46
JAGS 7, 11
Jamaica Banana producers Association Ltd. 3
Jamaica Cricket Association 178
Jamaica College 30 ff
Jamaica Defence Force 120
Jamaica Federation of Women 67
Jamaica Free School 30
Jamaica High School 30
Jamaica Library Service 61
Jamaica Schools Commission 30
Jamaica Vegetables Limited 19
Jamaica Youth Corps 75
James, Dalton 49
James, Seymour 36
Jelf, Arthur 5
J.J Mills 13
   See also Mills, John James
Johns, David 10
Johnson, Charlie 3
Johnson, Hines 65
Johnson, Irving 35
Jones, Creech 84
Jones, Edwin 115, 118
Jones, F.E. 87

Jones, Gresford 33
Jones, Roy 72
Kelly, Lloyd 36
Kelsick, Fred 84
Kensington Cricket Club 57, 64
King, E.H.J. 46
Kingston Athenaeum 62
Kingston College 32
King Street 3, 4
Kingston 3, 61
   banks 4
   Institute of Jamaica 62
   Kingston Athenaeum
   Phoenix Library 62
   Sangsters Bookroom
   Kinkead R.F. Dickie 34
Kipling, Rudyard 9
Kirton, Allan 111
Knibb, William 12
Knight, Marcel 111
KSAC 1
Kyle Twins 44
La Guerre, John 118
L.A. Henriques 3
Lampart, Lawrie 24
Lamparts 18
Laski 82
Laubach, Dr
Lawrence, Lennie 64
Lawrence, Vin 75
Lawson, Alvin 22
Lawson, Gifford 22
Law Students 97
Leahong Donald 8, 9
Lee, G.K. 111
Lennon, Archdeacon 19, 87
Leon, Gerardo 10, 21
Levitt, Kari Polanyi 83
Levy, Roy 45
Lewin, Olive 29, 98
Lewin, R.J.M. 27
Lewin R.N. 34
Lewis, Arthur 82
Lewis, Dr. Heloise 19
Lewis, Gordon 58
Lewis, Harcourt 111

Lewis, Jackie 60
Lewis, Vaughan 118, 119
Light Blues 33
Lightbourne Robert C. 33
Lindo, Cedric 38
Lindo, Fay 10, 98
Lindo, Laurence 9, 31, 39, 68
Lindo, Vernon 91
Lindsay, Delroy 4
Lindsay, Hyacinth 12
Lindsay, Louis 118
Little Theatre Movement see LTM
Llewellyn, Rev. R.A. 87
Lloyd, Jimmy 8, 76
Lloyd, Ken 69
Lloyds 25
Logan, David 117
London School of Economics 82ff
Lopez, Brenton 17
Lopez, Charlotte Lulu 17
Lopez, Manley 16
Lopez, Melba 17
Lowe, A.B. 7
Lowi, Walter 63
LTM 63
Lumsden, Del 57
Lumsden, Dottie Hogg 24
Lutchman, Harold 112, 118
MacDonald, Malcolm 60
MacDonald, Sir Herbert 8, 17
MacGillivray, Donald C. 68
MacPherson-Russell, Phyllis 88
Mailer, Nora Sifleet 83
Mair, Lucille 62, 88
Mais, Roger *Now we Know* 47, 59
Major Moxsy 17, 19
Makerere University
   Mazrui, Ali 115
Maloney, Judith 112
Manchester University 121
Manderson-Jones, James 87

INDEX

Mandeville
    horticultural society **24**
Manhertz, Huntley **117**
Manktelow Commission **113**
Manley, Douglas **88,111**
Manley, Michael **40,83,88,108**
Manley Michael *A History of W.I. Cricket* **166**
Manley, Norman **2, 18, 31, 32, 40, 47, 49, 73**
Manning Cup **8,32**
Mark, Francis Xavier **110**
Marley, R.C. **33**
Marryshow, Albert **10**
Marsh
    Leslie **44**
    Delroy **44**
Marsh, Norma **60**
Marsh, O.D. **60,83,88**
Marshall, Vice-Chancellor **124**
Marson, Una **90**
Martin, Sydney O. **8**
Matalon, Mayer **73**
Matalons **44**
Match Industry
    Commission of enquiry
    Jamaica Match Industry Ltd.
    Henriques Bros **70**
Maxwell, Rev. E.L. **8,12**
Mayers, T. Henry **67**
Maynard, Charles **111**
Maynier, Earle **69,70**
McCaulay, W Hyde **18**
McFarlane, Basil **47**
McFarlane, J.E. Clare **59, 68**
McFarlane, Vincent **68**
Mckay, U.Theo "UT" **18**
McKell, W.H. **112**
McKenley, Herb **106**
Mckenzie, Arthur **8**
McKenzie, Joe **8**
McMorrises **17**
McMorris, Herman **9,26,39**
McMorris, Norman **24**

McNeil, E.A. **6**
McPherson, J.A. **67**
McWhinnies **19**
Media
    A.E.T. Henry
    Calvin Bowen
    A.F. Raymond **97**
Medical and Health Care Students **96**
Meikle, H. Ivan **65**
Melbourne, Park **8**
Mellad, Dr. E.V. **17**
Melrose hill **24**
Miller, Hugh **33**
Miller, Shirley **83**
Mills, Ada **12**
Mills, Charles Wade **109**
Mills, David **12**
Mills, Don **31,60,62,88,108**
Mills, Eric **67**
Mills, John James **20, 133**
    See also J.J. Mills
    Mills, Papa Gilbert
    Maxwell **12**
Mills, Sybil **32**
Mills, Violet **10**
Moment, Sam **75**
Mona estate **13**
Moody, Arundel **81**
League of Coloured Peoples **81**
Moody, Locksley **33**
Moo Young, Noel **69**
Morales, C.M. **31**
Mordecai, John **59,67,68**
Morgans Pass **19**
Moses, Robert **74**
Moss, Winnified McKay **48, 93**
Moving pictures
    Gaiety
    Palace **63**
movies
    Carib
    Tivoli **63**
Moyne Commission **3,7, 57ff**
Mudie, George **64**
Munroe, Huntley **8, 16**

Munroe, Muriel **17**
Munroe, Trevor **83, 112, 118**
Munro
    Lennox
    Owen **44**
Murray
    Ossie **44, 69, 70, 73**
    George **44**
Murray, Reginald M. **31, 36, 45, 47**
Murray, R.N. **63**
Nam, Wallace **24**
Narcisse, Audley **34**
Nathans **3, 62**
Nethersole, N.N. "Crab" **9,31,55,71,72,76,89**
New World Group
    Elsa Goveia
    George Beckford
    Clive Thomas
    Orlando Patterson
    Lloyd Best
    Owen Jefferson
    Vaughan Lewis
    Alister McIntyre **123**
    Norman Girvan **123**
Newman, A.J. **61**
Newton, Robert **68**
Nicaragua
    Garifunas **10**
Nightclubs
    Glass Bucket
    Silver Slipper
    Colony Club
    Morgan's Cove
    Sugar Hill
    Springfield
    Bournemouth **63**
Nutford House **85-86**
Obi, Chike **108**
Olivier Shield **9,32**
Ollman, Bertell **116**
One-party Parliament **144ff**
O'Reilly, Gwyneth **88**
Ormsby Memorial Hall **9**
Oswins **17**
Owen, Glen **75**
Paisley's **16**
Palisadoes Peninsula **4, 74**
Palmer, Rhoda **13**

PANAM 4
Panama Canal 10
Panniers 27
Participation 37
Passailaigue, Clarence 8
Patterson, Eric 68
Patterson, Orlando 112
Patterson, P.J. 118
Payton, Joseph 134
Payton, Josephine Isilda 134
Payton, Rose 14
Payton, Thomas Alexander 134
Peat, A.A. 'Gussie' 335
People's National Party
see PNP
People's Progressive Party 6
Pershadsingh, Dr 178
Philippo, James 123
Phillips, George 59,68,70
Phillips, Reg 90
Phillips, Rev. R.E. 19
Phillips, Sydney 33
Phoenix Library
Doris Duperly 62
Pindling, Linden 96
Pitt, David 95
Pixley, Frank 67
PNP 53,139,149
Accreditation committee 136, 145
Polack, Eric 'Rico' 69
Police Federation 133
Police force 14
Police service
Nathan Houston
Ken Maynes
A.C. Foulkes
Sidney Anderson
Orville Bernard
Fred MacIntosh
Basil Robinson 99
Political Advisors 136
Powell, Wesley 75
Price, Rev 38
Pringle, K. 'Soapy' 38, 47
Pross 38ff
Providence Church, Liguanea 13

Public Service Commission
see PSC 134,136
Racca and Sandy 9
Racism 171ff
Jeff Wells
Ian Chappell
Benaud 171
Rae, Allan 36, 107
Railway 4
Rainford, Roderick 112
Ramsay, Ian 96
Rennie, Alfred B 16, 155
Rhodes Scholars 31, 45, 68
Roy Levy 47
Henry Fowler 45
Roy Dickson 71
Ron Sturdy 80
Trevor Munroe 83
Richards, Sir Arthur 59, 67
Richards Reservoir 59
Richardson, Sir Egerton 9,59,68,72
Richardson, Willie 94
Ricketts, Angelita 28
Riley, Reuben 65
Ripley, R.J. 13
Risden, O.St. C 17
Rob, Dr. Vincent 17
Robertson Paul 118
Robinson, A.N.R. 95
Robinson, Joyce 61
Robinson, Leacroft 62,88
Robinson. Leslie 88,91,104
Robinson, Pansy 62
Robinson, Philip 15
Robinson, R.A. 37
Robotham, Felix 17
Robotham, Upton 17
Rockefeller Foundation 114
Rodney crisis 120
Rose, Andrew 77
Rose, Muriel 'Cissy' 24
Ross, Bertram 91
Ross, K.H. 31
Rowe, Lawrence 175
Royal Air Force (RAF) 80-81

Royal Naval Reserve
Ron Sturdy 80
Sabina Park 7, 171
Safeguarding of Industry Law 70
Sandham, Andy 7
Sangster, Donald 9,16,70
Sangster's Bookroom
Ferdie Sangster
Miss Cunningham 62
Sanguinetti, Elsie 60
Sarkar, Nobel 95
Scotland Yard 95
Scott, O.C. Tommy 7
Sealy, Ken 89
Seemungal, Lionel 84
Sevens Estate 33
Seymour-Seymour, George 6
Sex Disqualification (Removal) 55
Shaw, Henry 79, 91
Shawbury 12
Shearer, Hugh 71
Shelton, Winston 34
Sherlock, Hugh 75
Sherlock, Sir Philip 47, 58, 66
Sherwood, Marika *Many Struggles* 81
Silvera , Noel 64
Simms, Canon 31
Simon fellows 119
Simpson, H.A.L. 6
Sinclair, John 'Bull' 8
Singh, Dalip 94
Singham, Archie 117
Sir Donald Bradman
Sunil Gavaskar 168
Skinner, Marion 16
Sleggs, J.C. 'Poogy' 38,45
Slyfield, Marie 12, 112
Smallman, Barry 95
Smith
Max
Michael 44
Smith, Carmen 60
Smith, Michael 47
Smith, Douglas 101

Smith, Frank **17**
Smith J.A.G. **6,18**
Smith, Joe **16**
Smith, Madge **60**
Smythe, Johnny **94,102**
Snaiths **17**
Snake-Lips Johnson **91**
Solomon, Wilton **111**
Sorhaindo Crispin **113**
Soursop Turn **15**
Soutar
    Donald
    Farren **44**
Southgate, John **105**
Southwell, Paul **76**
Spackman, Ann **117**
Spanish Honduras
    Garifunas **11**
Sponer, William **9,21**
Stark, D. Kelvin **66**
St. Cyprians **84**
St. Dunstan's Chapel **37**
Stewart, John **68**
St. Georges College **33**
St. Hill, C.A.P. **112, 113**
St. Paul's Anglican Parish Church **15**
Stone, Archdeacon Alvin **28**
Stone, Carl **118, 147**
Strathie, Sir Norman **66**
Stuart, C.L. **16**
Stuart, Winston **34, 44**
    A.H. 'Bunny' **44**
Stubbs, Edward **5**
Sturge Town **13**
Sugar Commission of Enquiry (1987- 88)
    Brian Young
    John James Mills **133**
Sugar industry **2**
Sullivans **16**
Sutherland, Victor **35**
Swaby, Raphael 'Raph' **73, 75**
Swaby, William **56**
Tame, Horace **60**
Tavanore property **17**
Taylor, Gladstone **18**

Taylor, R.W. **67**
Taylor, Sir Robert **60, 66**
Telegraph
    A.R. 'Tony' Lewis **165**
Tennis **8**
Jimmy Farquharson **36**
Terrelonge, L. **73**
The Ark **18**
The Economist **165,170**
The Nation
    Tony Cozier **164**
The Observer
    Sir Leonard Hutton **166**
The Role of Small Countries in a Big World **114**
The Role of Social Scientists in the Contemporary Caribbean **121**
Thomas Arnold's Rugby **31**
Thompson, Dudley **94**
Throwing of the cricket ball **38**
Tomlinson, Ivan **16**
Tourism **2**
Town and Country Planning **74**
Townsend, George **57**
Trafalgar Hill
    Tavanore property
    Manley Lopez **16**
Triumph property **12**
UAWU **112**
UCWI **58**
    Dept of Government **110, 119**
    Diploma in Public Administration
    Certificate in Social Work
    Certificate in Public Administration **111**
    Carnegie Corporation
    Ford Foundation **113**
    Rockefeller Foundation
    Institute of International Relations **114**
    Diploma in Health Management
    USAID
    University of Pittsburgh's Graduate School of Public Health

    American Public Health Association APHA **114**
    Trade Union Education Institute
    Extra Mural Centre, Kingston
    Faculty of Social Sciences **119**
    Rodney crisis **120**
    appointments **123ff**
    New World Group **123**
Umpiring **179**
    Martin-Jenkins' accusation **181**
Unifruitco **65**
United Fruit Company Ltd. **3**
United Nations **84**
University and Allied Workers Union (UAWU) **112**
University of Peace **150**
USAID **115**
UWI
    Creative Arts Centre sit-in
    siege of the Senate building **125**
    Dept of Government **126**
    Masters of Business Administration **126, 133**
    Management studies environmental management
    decentralization **126**
    salaries
    English grammar
    hotel and tourism management **129**
    Sports Advisory Committee
    extra-curricular activities awards **129**
Valentine, C.H. **33**
Valentine, V.A. **33, 69**
Vassell, Dick **22**
Vaz, Harold **57**
V.E. Day **84**
Vere Trust Scholarship **29**
Virtue, Vivian **47**
Waddell, Martin **22**
Walker, Mayor **4**
Ward, Henry **87**
Waterhouse, James **38, 45**

Weekes, Ken "Bam Bam" **65**
Welds, Ruby **109**
Weller, Dorothy (Williams) **73**
West Indian Students Union (WISU) **89ff**
West Indies Home Contractors **73**
White Headley **7**
White, Hector **59, 67, 70**
Whites **17**
Whittaker, Iris **24**
Whyte, J.C. **16**
Whyte, Monica **16**
Williams, Dr. Eric **77, 114**
Williams, Frank D.C. **70**
Williams, Leslie "Bunny" **91**
Wilson, W. Jeffrey **33, 34, 44**
Wiltshire, Rosina **118**
Wint, Adele **111**

Wint, Arthur **37, 106, 108, 109**
Wint, Norma Marsh **94**
    see Marsh, Norma **60**
Wint, D.J. **13**
Wisden Cricket Monthly
David Frith **170**
    see **89ff**
WISU **108**
Workers Party of Jamaica (WPJ) **112**
Workmen's Compensation Act **60**
World Bank **84**
World Students Union **89**
Wright, Ashton **60**
Wright, Owen **61**
Wynne, J.P. **71**
Wynter, Hector **62, 88**
Yallahs Valley Land Authority **68**

Young, H.B. **64**
Youth movement **62, 91**
World Federation of Democratic Youth **108**
ZQI
    Gick Denis **60**